Living Wisdom
Vedanta in the West

Edited by
Pravrajika Vrajaprana

Vedanta Press
Hollywood, California

Vedanta Press
1946 Vedanta Place
Hollywood, California 90068-3996

First printing 1994
Second printing 1998

If you wish to learn in greater detail about the teachings
contained in this book, write to the
Secretary, Vedanta Society
1946 Vedanta Place
Hollywood, CA 90068-3996
e-mail: info@vedanta.org

Printed in the United States of America.

Library of Congress Cataloging-in-Publication Data

Living Wisdom: Vedanta in the West / Edited by Pravrajika Vrajaprana
    p. cm.
    Includes bibliographical references and index.
    ISBN 0-87481-055-8
    1. Eastern Philosophy / Personal Growth
          I. Vrajaprana, Pravrajika, 1952-
    B132.V3L58   1994
      181' .48—dc20   93-43745
                        CIP

Cover Photograph Copyright ©1998 James T. Aeby

Living Wisdom

Preface

VEDANTA IS NOW in its second century in the West. Since the Vedanta movement has always had a strong literary basis, it seems fitting to mark this passage with a successor to the spiritual classic, *Vedanta for the Western World*.

Does a spiritual classic *need* updating? Vedanta philosophy is, by definition, timeless. But while spiritual truths are eternal, the society which interprets them changes from generation to generation. Each generation looks at the world through its own prism of experience. For that reason *Living Wisdom: Vedanta in the West* has been born—offering fresh insight into a timeless philosophy.

The most outstanding articles from the 1945 *Vedanta for the Western World* have been included in this book. They were chosen because they withstood the test of time and integrated seamlessly with material written a half century later. Also included in this volume are articles from the book *Vedanta for Modern Man* as well as from various Vedanta journals, each article having passed the same criteria. In addition, a great deal of new material is published for the first time here.

A word on language: Some of the articles written in earlier days use the terms "man," "men," and the impersonal "he" to refer to humanity in general or to a nonspecific individual. The authors were writing according to the style of the times; the terms are not meant to be gender-specific.

An attempt has been made in this volume to represent the widest possible spectrum of thought. The reader will find in these pages authors from America and India, women and men, monastics and nonmonastics, younger people and older people. The reader will find various spiritual approaches from people of all races, cultures, and creeds. East, West, North, and South are all represented here.

The articles have been arranged solely by order of subject matter, going from the general to the particular. Yet while the material has been arranged for sequential reading, it certainly need not be read that way. The reader can pick and choose as he or she feels inclined.

This book has come into being through the help, support, and freely given time of many, many people. I would first like to thank Swami Swahananda for his consistent help, expert advice, and wise direction. While all my sisters at Sarada Convent contributed in many untold ways in bringing this book to fruition, special gratitude is owed to Pravrajika Anandaprana for her painstaking and unflaggingly cheerful work.

To Anne Lowenkopf and to Shelly Lowenkopf many, many thanks. Nothing can take the place of professionalism, and both these professionals were *always* available, *always* enthusiastic, and *always* eager to give their time and expertise. To Shelly, who created this book's masterly index, again heartfelt thanks.

Special mention also needs to be given to Swami Adiswarananda of the Ramakrishna-Vivekananda Society of New York, and to Ann Myren of the Vivekananda Foundation. Their encouragement and help far exceeded the call of duty; much gratitude is owed to both of them.

Thanks are also due to the Advaita Ashrama in Calcutta, the Ramakrishna Math in Madras, the Ramakrishna Mission in New Delhi, the Ramakrishna Mission Institute of Culture in Calcutta, the Ramakrishna-Vivekananda Center of New York, and the Vedanta Society of St. Louis for their permission to reprint various articles. Specific information on these articles can be read in the "Notes on the Contributors" section of this book.

Finally, no expression of thanks could be complete without acknowledging our unpayable debt to those pioneer swamis who came to the West, following in the footsteps of Swami Vivekananda. These swamis— Ashokananda, Nikhilananda, Prabhavananda, Satprakashananda, among others—endured many hardships and made many sacrifices. That the Vedanta movement in the West is what it is today, is the result of their quiet heroism. We are all standing on the foundation they built.

—*Vrajaprana*

Contents

Contents

Part 2
Perspectives

Part 3
Practice

Contents

Part 4
Paradigms

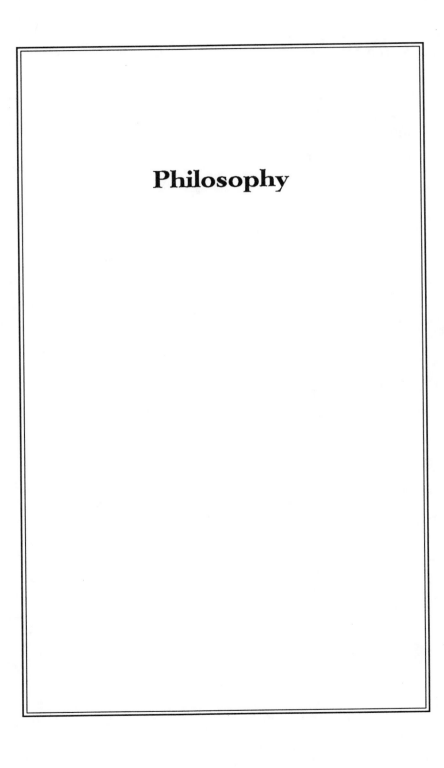

Philosophy

What Is Vedanta?
An Introduction

by Christopher Isherwood

VEDANTA IS THE philosophy of the Vedas, those Indian scriptures which are the most ancient religious writings now known to the world. More generally speaking, the term "Vedanta" covers not only the Vedas themselves but the whole body of literature which explains, elaborates, and comments upon their teaching, right down to the present day. The Bhagavad Gita and the works of Shankara belong to Vedanta: so do many of the articles in this volume.

Vedanta is often, but less correctly, called "Hinduism"; a foreign word. The inhabitants of India were described by the Persians as Hindus, because they lived on the other side of the river Sindhu (the Indus). The Persians, apparently, could not manage the sound of the letter S.

In India today, as elsewhere, there are hundreds of sects. Vedanta philosophy is the basis of them all. Indeed, in its simplest form, it may be regarded as a statement of the Philosophia Perennis, the least common denominator of all religious belief.

Reduced to its elements, Vedanta philosophy consists of three propositions. First, that man's real nature is divine. Second, that the aim of human life is to realize this divine nature. Third, that all religions are essentially in agreement. We shall examine each of these in turn.

Man's real nature is divine: what does this actually mean? Vedanta asserts that the universe which is perceived by our senses is only an appearance. It is not what it seems. Here, the modern scientist will, of course, agree. Who would ever suppose, in looking at a flower, a rock, and a waterfall, that each was merely a different arrangement of identical units? The universe is other than its outward aspect. Moreover, this outward aspect is subject to perpetual change. The hills, said Tennyson, are shadows.

Vedanta goes on to assert that, beneath this appearance, this flux, there is an essential, unchanging Reality, which it calls Brahman, the Godhead. Brahman is existence itself, consciousness itself. Brahman is also said to be that almost indefinable quality which is called in the Sanskrit language "ananda," and in the Christian Bible "the peace of God, which passeth all understanding." "Ananda" may be translated not only as "peace" but also as "bliss"; since this absolute peace, when it is known beneath all flux, appearance, and unrest, must give the only permanent kind of happiness.

At the mention of Brahman, the scientist will become skeptical. And rightly so; for none of his apparatus is capable of detecting the existence of this fundamental Reality. Vedanta will reply that this proves nothing, either way. The scientist cannot possibly detect Brahman, because scientific analysis depends, necessarily, upon the evidence of the five senses, and Brahman is beyond all sense perception. Why, it will be asked, should we believe with Vedanta instead of doubting with the scientist? But the answer to this question must be delayed for a moment, until we begin to consider the nature of the mystical experience.

Let us assume, in the meanwhile, that Brahman does exist. If there is indeed an essential Reality, a Godhead, in the universe, then it follows that this Reality must be omnipresent. It must be within each one of us; within every creature and object. It does not matter exactly what we mean by "within": that is a point for theologians to argue. Let us say simply, at the risk of offending the exponents of semantics, that Brahman is our real, essential nature. When speaking of Brahman-within-the-creature, Vedanta uses, for convenience, another term, "the Atman." The Atman, in Christian terminology, is God immanent; Brahman is God transcendent. Atman and Brahman are one.

And now, with the second of the Vedanta propositions, we come to most of our difficulties. The aim of human life, we are told, is to realize the Atman, our essential nature, and hence our identity with the one, underlying Reality.

Why? How? Who says so? How does he know?

In the first place, why? The answer to this question is by no means evident to the majority of people alive on earth today. Human life has many apparent aims: we can find them stated in the headlines and advertisements of any newspaper. Win the war. Win the peace. Get your man. Get a home. Get a better job. Become beautiful. Become strong. Become educated. Such are our objectives. And millions strive for them, with the greatest courage and devotion, year after year.

To seek to realize my essential nature is to admit that I am dissatisfied with my nature as it is at present. It is to admit that I am dissatisfied with the kind of life I am leading now. But am I, honestly? Oh yes, we admit our faults. We admit that the political and economic condition of the world leaves much to be desired. But we are optimistic. We believe in patching up and muddling through. We are prepared to take the rough with the smooth. We have our moments of triumph, we enjoy periods of vivid happiness; and for these we are ready to pay, if we must, with spells of disappointment, boredom, regret. On the whole, the majority of us are content. The great mass of normally healthy, well-adjusted men and women, absorbed in their families and their jobs, will protest: "Leave us alone. We are well enough off as we are."

"Are you? We doubt it," say Buddha, Jesus, Shankara, Shakespeare, and Tolstoy. And they proceed to point out, in their different languages and figures of speech, that death brings an end to all desire, that worldly wealth is a house built upon the sand, that the beautiful body is a decaying bag of filth, that ambition will be pricked like an inflated bladder, that our bustling activity resembles the antics of patients in a madhouse. Their words depress us: for the truth is obvious, if we consider it. But we do not wish to consider it. There is no time, we say. We are in the midst of whatever we are doing. Action is begetting action. To pause, to philosophize, seems feeble, cowardly, and even downright wicked. So we dismiss our prophets as pessimists, and their teaching as otherworldly defeatism. We hurry away with a sigh, resolved to have our fun while we can, or, at any rate, to get on with the next job.

But suppose I really am dissatisfied with my life and myself. Suppose I have actually attained some of the world's advertised objectives, and found beyond them an emptiness, a teasing question which I cannot answer. I am confronted with life's subtlest riddle: the riddle of human boredom. In my desperation, I am ready to assume, provisionally, that this Atman, this essential nature, does exist within me, and does offer me a lasting strength, wisdom, peace, and happiness. How am I to realize this nature? How am I to enjoy it?

The answer is given, unanimously, by all the teachers and prophets. It is very disconcerting:

"By ceasing to be yourself."

"What do you mean? That's nonsense. How can I stop being myself? I'm Christopher Isherwood, or I'm nothing."

"You are the Atman."

"Then why do I think I'm myself?"

"Because of your ignorance. Christopher Isherwood is only an appearance, a part of the apparent universe. He is a constellation of desires and impulses. He reflects his environment. He repeats what he has been taught. He mimics the social behavior of his community. He copies gestures like a monkey and intonations like a parrot. All his actions are conditioned by those around him, however eccentric and individual he may seem to be. He is subject to suggestion, climate, disease, and the influence of drugs. He is changing all the time. He has no essential reality."

"How did this ignorance start? What caused it?"

Here, the prophets will give slightly different answers. Buddha will refuse to discuss the question at all, saying that it is not important. When the house is burning, does it matter if the man who fired it had red hair? It is only necessary that we should realize that the house *is* burning. Or, to put it more mildly, that we should be dissatisfied with our present condition and ready to do something about it.

Christian theology will speak of Original Sin, and postulate a Fall of Man from consciousness of his divine nature. Vedanta does not accept this idea. It conceives of a universe coexistent with Brahman, equally beginningless and endless. Even if this universe should apparently be destroyed, it will only have gone back into a kind of seed state, a phase of potentiality, from which, in due time, it will reemerge. Vedanta teaches that the stuff of this universe is an effect or power of Brahman. It stands to Brahman in the same relation as heat to fire. They are inseparable. Yet Brahman does not intervene in the world's affairs. The question, Why does God permit evil? is, to a Vedantist, as meaningless as, Why does God permit good? The fire burns one man and warms another, and is neither kind nor cruel.

An inhuman philosophy? Certainly. Brahman is not human. We must beware of thinking about the Reality in relative terms. It is not simply a giant person. It has nothing to do with our shifting standards of good and evil, pleasure, unhappiness, right and wrong.

"Very well: we'll forget about the cause of my ignorance. Now how do I stop being Christopher Isherwood?"

"By ceasing to believe that you are. What is this belief? Egotism, nothing else: an egotism which is asserted and reinforced by hundreds of your daily actions. Every time you desire, or fear, or hate; every time you boast or indulge your vanity; every time you struggle to get something for yourself, you are really asserting: I am a separate, unique individual. I stand apart from everything else in this universe. But you don't, you know. The scientist will agree with me that you don't. Every living creature and every object are interrelated, biologically, psychologically, physically, politically, economically. They are all of a piece."

"So I merely have to stop believing I'm an individual?"

"It isn't so easy. First, you must start acting as though you had ceased to believe it. Try to overcome this possessive attitude toward your actions. Stop taking credit for your successes. Stop bemoaning your failures, and making excuses for them. Stop worrying so much about results. Just do the best you can. Work for the work's sake. Think of your body, if you like, as an instrument."

"Whose instrument?"

"The instrument of the Atman."

"Why should I work for the Atman? It doesn't need my help."

"There is no question of helping the Atman. All work done in this spirit is symbolic, like ritual. It becomes a form of worship."

"How dull that sounds! Where's the inducement? What's the motive?"

"Love."

"You mean, I should love the Atman? How can I?"

"You love Christopher Isherwood, don't you?"

"Yes, I suppose so. Most of the time. When I don't hate him."

"Then you ought to love your real Self much more. The Atman is perfect. Christopher Isherwood isn't."

"But I know him. I've never seen the Atman. I'm not even sure it exists."

"Try to feel that it exists. Think about it. Pray to it. Meditate on it. Know that you are it."

"You mean, hypnotize myself?"

"If it's nothing but autohypnosis, you'll soon find out. Hypnosis wouldn't give you any lasting results. It wouldn't give you the peace and understanding you are looking for. It wouldn't transform your character. Neither would alcohol, for that matter, or any other drug. I'm only asking you to try it. This is a matter for personal experiment."

"All right. What else am I to do?"

"Judge every thought and every action from this standpoint: Does it make me freer, less egotistic, more aware of the Reality; or does it attach me more tightly to the illusion of individual separateness? You'll find, in practice, that certain thoughts and actions obstruct your progress. Give them up. Other thoughts and actions will assist your progress. Cultivate them."

"Tell me some."

"Chastity, truthfulness, charity toward others."

"Chastity? I'm to give up sex?"

"You'll find you have to, sooner or later."

"Why? It's not wrong."

"I never said it was. But what does it lead to? Attachment to this world of appearance. An added conviction that you are Christopher Isherwood, not the Atman."

"Oh, you just hate the world, that's all!"

"It's you who hate the world, in your heart of hearts. You are bound to hate it, because you know only its appearance, and its appearance seems to end in death. But I see the Reality within the appearance. I see the world within Reality. And I love it as I love the Reality itself."

"I must say, all this sounds very selfish. I'm to spend the rest of my life trying to know my real nature. Thinking about myself, in fact. What about my neighbors? Am I to forget them altogether? What about social service? What about my duty to the community?"

"As soon as you start thinking and acting in the way I have shown you, your life will be nothing but social service. You will be more available to your neighbors than ever before, because you will be less egotistic. You will do your duty to the community far better, because your motives will be less mixed with vanity and the desire for power and self-advertisement. You think you love some of your neighbors now. You cannot dream how you will love them all, when you begin to see the Reality within each human being, and to understand his absolute identity with yourself. What is it that your neighbor needs most? Isn't it just that reassurance, that knowledge and peace which are the objects of your search? How can you transmit them to others until you have won them for yourself? By helping yourself, you are helping mankind. By helping mankind, you are helping yourself. That's the law of spiritual progress."

"Provided, of course, that the Reality exists."

"The Reality does exist."

"How do you know?"

"Because I have experienced it."

"Why should I believe you?"

"Because you can experience it for yourself."

There we have it, our greatest difficulty. There the scientist cannot help us. He only shrugs his shoulders and says, perhaps. The prophet tells us that he has seen God, and we have each of us to make up our minds whether to believe him or not.

In order to be able to decide if the prophet is telling the truth or lying, we shall have to investigate the mystical experience for ourselves. This can be done in two ways: from the outside, by studying the biographies and writings of the saints; and from the inside, by following the instructions they have given us. To follow these instructions is to lead what Christians call "the unitive life." In Sanskrit, the word for this unitive life is "yoga," from which is derived our English word "yoke," i.e., union. Yoga is the technique of union with the Atman.

However we may choose to explain it, the historical fact remains that thousands of men and women, belonging to every century, country, and social class, have attempted, with apparent success, to follow this unitive way of life. According to the evidence of their contemporaries, they have undergone that slow, strange transformation, that inner process of readjustment, which ends in what is called sainthood. Hundreds of them, Christian, Vedantist, Buddhist, Taoist, Sufi, and Jew, have left records of their experience; and these records show remarkable similarity. Remarkable, because the saints themselves are so very different. Some are devotional in the extreme: they worship the Reality in human form, a Krishna, a Rama, a Christ, with ecstasies of love. Some meditate on the impersonal Brahman, with the seeming coldness of pure discrimination, bowing before no altar or image. Some have visions. Some have powers over material nature and can heal the sick. Some live in caves or cells; some in crowded cities. Some are great orators; some refuse to utter a word. Some are laughed at and believed to be mad; some are respected for their qualities of clear judgment and sanity. Some are martyred.

It is upon the nature of the final mystical experience that all agree. What is this experience? It seems that when the ego-sense has, through constant self-discipline, grown very weak, there comes a moment (it may be the moment of death) at which the presence of the essential nature is no longer concealed. The saint becomes aware that the Atman actually does exist. Further, he experiences the nature of the Atman as his own nature. He knows he is nothing but Reality. This is what Christian writers call "the mystic union" and Vedantists "samadhi."

We have been told that the Reality is beyond sense perception. How, then, can it be experienced? This is a very difficult question. Perhaps it cannot be answered in words. Samadhi is said to be a fourth kind of consciousness: it is beyond the states of waking, dreaming, and dreamless sleep. Those who have witnessed it as an external phenomenon report that the experiencer appeared to have fallen into a kind of trance. The hair of the head and body stood erect. The half-closed eyes became fixed. Sometimes there was an astonishing loss of weight, or even levitation of the body from the ground. But these are mere symptoms, and tell us nothing. There is only one way to find out what samadhi is like: you must have it yourself.

Vedanta's third proposition, that all religions are essentially in agreement, needs less discussion. But it is psychologically very important. Being a philosophy rather than a creed, Vedanta is not sectarian and therefore not exclusive. It appeals, as it were, over the heads of the sectarians and dogmatists, to the practicing mystics of all religions. Also, by classifying the sects themselves as different paths of yoga leading to the same goal, it seeks to establish a sort of religious synthesis. Tolerance is, in any case, natural to the Indian temperament. But, unfortunately, it cannot be claimed that this unifying effort has, so far, been very successful. Vedanta may accept Christ as the Son of God; it may acknowledge Allah. But Christians and Muslims persist in regarding their respective religions as the only true faith. Christian and Sufi mystics have been compelled, by the very nature of their mystical experience, to take a more liberal attitude. In consequence, they have often been suspected of heresy and sometimes actually condemned by their coreligionists.

Nor does the Vedantist, in expressing his reverence for Allah and Christ, mean quite what orthodox Muslims and Christians would like him to mean. Vedanta, as I have said already, offers a philosophical basis to all sects. It can do this precisely because it is fundamentally monistic; because it teaches that there is one Reality and nothing else. "Thou art That." The creature is the Atman; the Atman is Brahman. The creature, in his ignorance, may think that he worships the creator. Very well: let him think that. It is a necessary stage in spiritual progress. The ultimate truth cannot be apprehended all at once. The Atman must be personified at first, if it is to be loved and realized; otherwise it will remain a mere intellectual abstraction. The true monist never disdains dualism. But it is very hard for the rigid dualist to accept monism. St. Ignatius Loyola was dismayed when the vision of his beloved Jesus faded into the impersonal, all-embracing Reality.

The Indian mind, because it is fundamentally monistic, has no difficulty in believing that the one impersonal Brahman may have an infinite number of personal aspects. As many, indeed, as there are worshipers; since an aspect is literally a view, and each traveler may see a different angle of a mountain. These aspects are represented in Indian art, sculpture, and literature with such a wealth of form and attribute that the Western foreigner, whose religious mentality is dualistic, is apt to mistake them for gods and goddesses in the pagan sense, and to exclaim indignantly that this is polytheism. Hence, much misunderstanding arises.

According to Vedanta, the Reality may also take human form and enter the world, from time to time. Why it should do this is a mystery which no amount of philosophical analysis can solve. It is the paradox which we call grace, expressed in its most startling terms. The Reality is manifested, occasionally, amidst the temporal phenomena. Brahman *does*, after all, sometimes intervene. As Sri Krishna says in the Gita:

> In every age I come back
> To deliver the holy,
> To destroy the sin of the sinner,
> To establish righteousness.

The Vedantist calls such incarnations of the Reality "avatars." He recognizes Rama, Krishna, Buddha, and Christ as avatars, along with several others, and believes that there will be many more. But the Christian, convinced of the uniqueness of Christ as a spiritual phenomenon, can hardly be expected to subscribe to this belief.

What follows samadhi? What happens to the few who attain it, and to the hundreds of millions who don't?

This brings us to the hypothesis of karma and reincarnation. I use the word "hypothesis" deliberately, because I am writing for Western and, I hope, intelligently skeptical readers. It is my business to describe, not to dogmatize. Here is one explanation of the known facts of our human experience. You can accept or reject it. But, unless you understand its main propositions, the literature of Vedanta will scarcely be intelligible to you.

Philosophically, karma and reincarnation are inseparable. Nevertheless, they have been separated by the leaders of the many esoteric cults in Europe and America, which have brought Indian thought into such discredit, and made the word "yoga" synonymous with dishonest mystery-mongering and the exploitation of the superstitious. We have all met people who like to believe that they have lived through previous births as Marie Antoinette, Cleopatra, or a priestess in an Egyptian temple. The character chosen is invariably glamorous, beautiful, distinguished, tragic. No cultist would ever admit to a former existence as an ordinary housewife, a small tradesman, or a cook. Here, the idea of reincarnation, unconditioned by karma, floats in a romantic, meaningless void. It is a convenient daydream for the escapist.

"Karma" means action, work, a deed. Not only physical action, conscious or reflex, but also mental action, conscious or subconscious. Karma is everything that we think or do. Philosophically speaking, karma also means the law of causation: a law which is said to operate in the physical, mental, and moral spheres of our lives.

I do an action; I think a thought. The Vedantist tells me that this action and this thought, even though they be apparently over and done with, will inevitably, sooner or later, produce some effect. This effect may be pleasant, unpleasant, or a mixture of both. It may be long delayed. I may never notice it. I may have altogether forgotten the action or the thought which caused it. Nevertheless, it will be produced.

Furthermore, every action and every thought makes an impression upon the mind. This impression may be slight at first; but, if the same action or thought is repeated, it will deepen into a kind of groove, down which our future behavior will easily tend to run. These mental grooves we call our tendencies. Their existence makes it possible to predict fairly accurately just how each of us will behave in any given situation. In other words, the sum of our karmas represents our character. As fresh karmas are added and previous karmas exhausted or neutralized, our character changes.

So much is self-evident. But now comes the question: where does karma begin? Are we all born equal? Do we all start life with the same chances of failure or success? Why Shakespeare? Why the mongolian idiot? Why the ordinary man in the street? Is there any justice at all?

There seem to be three possible answers to this problem. The first is the simplest: "No, there is no justice. Heredity and the accident of environment account entirely for your condition at birth. No doubt, you can improve your situation to some extent, along the lines of your inherited capacities and with the help of a good education. But there is a limit. Shakespeare was very lucky. The idiot is extremely unfortunate."

The second answer is more or less as follows: "Certainly, there is inequality, but there is justice, also. Life is a handicap race. To whom much was given, from him much will be expected. Shakespeare had better make good use of his talent. As for the idiot, the handicapped, and the poor, let them be patient. After this life, there will be another, in which each will be judged, punished, and rewarded according to his deserts."

This answer rightly infuriates the socialist, who exclaims: "What hypocrisy! What religious opium! Clean up your slums, establish prenatal clinics, provide free education, share the profits of industry. Never mind your promise of justice in heaven. Let's have justice here on earth."

The third answer is the one given by Vedanta. It is more complex, but also more logical than the second, more optimistic than the first. "I quite agree," says the Vedantist, "that existence continues after death. I agree that our actions in this life will condition the circumstances of that existence, since the law of karma will not cease to operate. I don't know why you limit yourselves to two lives. I foresee thousands. Lives on this earth, and lives elsewhere. I believe that an accumulation of very good karma will cause the individual to be reborn in what may be described as 'heaven,' and that very bad karma will place him in a sort of 'hell.' Only, my heaven and my hell have a time limit, like life in the world. When the good or bad karma is exhausted, the individual will be reborn here on earth. I say this because I believe that human life has a peculiarity: it is the only condition in which one can create fresh karma. Elsewhere one merely enjoys or suffers the karmic effects of one's earthly actions. The socialist may disapprove of my attitude, but I thoroughly approve of his activity. I do not believe that it can produce any permanent material improvement in this world; but it is spiritually constructive, and that is all that finally matters. Right action is the language of spiritual progress.

"You claim that this particular birth was your beginning. I don't see why. Philosophically, your position is awkward, because it compels you to believe that the condition of the idiot and the genius of Shakespeare are due to the justice or injustice of some external power. God is supposed to bind one man and free another, and then tell them both to make the best of it. Why blame God? Why not say that the idiot is an idiot because of his past actions in previous lives? It may sound brutal, but it is much more consistent. Don't misunderstand me: I am not denying heredity. I believe that heredity operates. But I also believe that the sum of our karmas compels us to be born into a certain kind of family, under certain physical and economic conditions. You may ask: Who would choose to be an idiot?

I reply: Who would choose to be a cocaine addict? Our thoughts and actions, apparently so harmless, create these appalling tendencies; and the tendencies are finally too strong for us."

The Vedantist has finished, and we can begin to heckle him.

"If we had past lives, why can't we remember them?"

"Can you remember exactly what you did this time yesterday? Can you remember what it felt like to be sitting on your mother's lap at the age of eighteen months? As a matter of fact, there is a yoga technique of concentration which is supposed to enable you to recall your previous existences. I'm not asking you to believe this. You would have to try it for yourself, and it would be a stupid waste of time. If you want a working hypothesis which sounds scientific, can't you simply assume that we suffer a kind of amnesia? After all, birth is a terrible shock."

"How do you account for the fact that karma ever started at all?"

"I can't. I only say, as I have said already, that the phenomenal universe is beginningless and endless, coexistent with the Reality. The law of karma was always in operation. It always will be."

"Then we just go up and down, getting better, getting worse, forever?"

"Certainly not. The individual can escape from karma at any given moment, as soon as he realizes that he is the Atman. The Atman is not subject to reincarnation. It stands beyond karma. It is only the individual ego which passes from life to life. Every individual will realize this, sooner or later. He must. The Atman within him will draw him to itself."

"And then?"

"When samadhi has been attained, the law of karma ceases to operate. No new karmas can be created. The liberated saint may live on in his human body for a while, just as a wheel goes on revolving after its motive power has stopped. But he will never be reborn, either in this world, or in any other karmic sphere. He will remain in the Atman. As an individual, he will have ceased to exist."

"What happens when everybody has attained samadhi? Won't the supply of individuals run out? Won't the universe disappear?"

"No. The ego-sense, which is the basis of individuality, will continue to work its way upward, through inanimate matter, through plant life, through the lower animals, into human form and consciousness. . . . But how can we discuss these things? We stumble over our own words. The universe is an illusion. Our essential nature is Reality. We are never separated from it for an instant. The concept of karma is only valuable insofar as it reminds us of the extraordinary importance of our every thought and action, and of our immense responsibility toward each other. . . . We have talked enough. Now do something. Start to practice yoga. Try to realize the Atman. All your questions will ultimately be answered. All your doubts will gradually disappear."

DURING THE LATE middle years of the nineteenth century, there lived, in a temple garden at Dakshineswar, a few miles outside Calcutta, the man who is, perhaps, Vedanta's greatest human exemplar. His name was Sri Ramakrishna.

He had come to the city as a sixteen-year-old boy, to join his elder brother, who was a priest. When the two of them moved out to Dakshineswar, Ramakrishna himself took up priestly duties in the Kali temple. Kali symbolizes Reality as the Mother of the universe, giver of life and death. Because of her dual aspect, she is the most misunderstood figure in Indian mythology. "How can you ask us," exclaims the foreigner, "to accept a Mother who is also a destroyer? What a horrible parody of motherhood! Look at her; distributing boons with one hand while the other holds a sword!" Yet Kali embodies a profound spiritual truth. She teaches us to look beneath the appearances of life. We must not cling to what seems beautiful and pleasant; we must not shrink from what seems ugly and horrible. The same Brahman underlies all experience. When we have learned to regard death and disaster as our Mother, we shall have conquered every fear.

Ramakrishna understood this. His intense devotion soon began to attract the attention of those who met him. The formidable stone image of the goddess was to him a living presence. He talked and joked with her, adored and reproached her with the freedom of perfect innocence and the candid faith which makes blasphemy a meaningless word. Kali was his own Mother, he was her son. Why would she not reveal herself to him? "O Mother," he wept, "another day has passed and I have not seen you!"

His ardor was rewarded by a vision. But he was not satisfied. Desiring perpetual awareness of Kali's presence, he entered upon a period of severe austerities, passing weeks and months in almost unbroken meditation. Religious fervor is not considered unhealthy or abnormal in India, even by the layman, but Ramakrishna's ecstasies were so extreme that fears were expressed for his sanity. He particularly scandalized the temple attendants by giving some consecrated food to a cat. Why not? Mother was in everything. After a while, he ceased to officiate as a priest. But he remained at Dakshineswar until the last year of his life.

Gradually, his fame spread. Two celebrated pundits visited him, discussed his visions, and subjected them to elaborate theological analysis. At length, both the great scholars solemnly declared that, in their opinion, the young man was an avatar, an incarnation of the ultimate Reality. Ramakrishna received this staggering announcement with childlike indifference and a certain sly humor. "Just fancy," he remarked: "Well, I'm glad it's not a disease. . . . But, believe me, I know nothing about it."

The dualist's approach to God may correspond, in type, to any one of our earthly relationships: it may be that of the servant, the child, the parent, the husband, the lover, or the friend. As the years passed, Ramakrishna explored them all. It is easy enough to write these words, but almost impossible to imagine, even faintly, what such an undertaking would involve. Here is a complete sublimation of life, in every aspect: a transposition, as it were, of the entire human experience into another key. Perhaps the nature of Ramakrishna's achievement can best be hinted at if we compare it with that of Shakespeare or Tolstoy in the sphere of art. Beside these masters, the intuition of lesser writers seems partial and restricted; it can only function along certain narrow lines. The essence of spiritual, as of artistic greatness is in its universality. The minor saint knows one way of worship only. Ramakrishna's genius embraced the whole of mystical realization.

Nothing now remained but the supreme monistic experience, the union with impersonal Reality. In 1864, a monk named Totapuri came to Dakshineswar to instruct Ramakrishna in this highest truth, the Brahman which is beyond all forms and aspects. The lesson was a hard one, even for such a pupil. Again and again, as he tried to meditate, the figure of his adored Kali rose before him, creating the illusion of duality. At last, Totapuri picked up a piece of glass from the ground, stuck it between Ramakrishna's eyebrows, and told him to fix his mind on that point. "When Mother appeared," Ramakrishna said later, "I drew the sword of discrimination and cut her in half." For three days, he remained absorbed in samadhi.

To most mystics, samadhi comes as the crowning attainment of a lifetime: for Ramakrishna, it was only the beginning of a new phase of experience. Established in the knowledge of Reality, he was now able to regard the entire phenomenal universe *sub specie aeternitatis*, seeing in all matter and circumstance the play of the divine Power. He loved the world, as only the illumined saint can love it. Kali, Shiva, Rama, and Krishna, the personal aspects and incarnations of the impersonal Brahman, were still his constant companions. He did not deny duality; but now he knew it in its true relation to the unity of the Absolute. He lived always on the threshold of transcendental consciousness, and the least word or hint was sufficient to raise his mind into oneness with the Eternal. An English boy watching a balloon happened to cross his legs in the attitude of the young Krishna; a lecturer with a telescope talked of the heavenly bodies; the sight of a lion at the zoo suggested the traditional mount of the Divine Mother—and Ramakrishna was in samadhi at once. It was necessary to accompany him everywhere, or he might have fallen to the ground and been injured. Once, in an unguarded moment of ecstasy, he did fall and dislocated a bone in his arm.

His appetite for spiritual experience in all its forms was insatiable. "Cake tastes nice," he used to say, "whichever way you eat it." In 1866, we find him practicing the disciplines of Islam, dressing as a Muslim, and repeating the name of Allah, under the direction of a Muslim teacher. Eight years later, he became fascinated by the personality of Jesus. The Bible was read aloud to him. He went into ecstasy before a painting of the Madonna and child. One day, while he was walking in the temple garden, the figure of Christ approached him, embraced him, and was merged into his own body.

At the age of twenty-three, Ramakrishna had been betrothed, to please his mother and in conformity with ancient Indian custom, to Saradamani, a little girl of five. In 1872, Saradamani, now eighteen years old, came to join her husband at Dakshineswar. The idea of a sexual union was utterly repugnant to Ramakrishna's nature; and Sarada, herself a saint in the making, gladly agreed to their monastic relationship. When the day came round for the worship of Kali, Ramakrishna did homage to his wife as an embodiment of the Divine Mother. Sarada outlived her husband by many years. She became the spiritual mother of the Ramakrishna Order.

During the last ten years of Ramakrishna's life, a number of disciples began to gather round him. Some of these were famous men, such as Girish Ghosh, Bengal's most distinguished dramatist, and Keshab Sen, the religious leader and social reformer. Others were schoolboys in their teens: the future monks who were to preach his message throughout India, and to carry it overseas. There were also many women.

In 1882, the circle of visitors to Dakshineswar was joined by Mahendranath Gupta, headmaster of a Calcutta high school. To Mahendranath's devotion and unusually retentive memory we owe a record which is almost unique in the literature of religious biography. From the day of his first visit, Mahendranath (or "M," as he modestly signed himself) began to write down everything which was said and done in his presence by Ramakrishna and his disciples. The result is a very large volume, known in English as *The Gospel of Sri Ramakrishna.* Its most recent, and only complete, translation is by Swami Nikhilananda, of the Ramakrishna-Vivekananda Center in New York. I have referred to it extensively in writing these notes.

As we read M's book, we can begin to form some mental picture of a saint's daily life. It is certainly very strange; and, in this particular case, doubly remote from our experience. Firstly, because, as ordinary unregenerate human beings, our own behavior has an entirely different frame of reference; secondly, because the cultural background itself is alien and complex.

The Dakshineswar temple garden was, of course, a stronghold of tradition and religious orthodoxy. Yet its northern wall was bounded, symbolically enough, by a powder magazine belonging to the British government; and the nearby city of Calcutta was the center of Western influence in India. Nearly all Ramakrishna's followers were men who had come into some contact with European ideas. Keshab advocated the abolition of the caste system and of child marriage; and he had been to England, where he was the guest of Queen Victoria. Even M would quote English philosophers and expound the latest discoveries of modern science.

Amidst these ideological contrasts sat Ramakrishna, the living embodiment of a wisdom that transcended and reconciled them all. Mother is everywhere. What else, on this earth, do we need to know? In the presence of his smiling certainty, the scholar and the reformer became silent; their own doubts and anxieties ceased. One is reminded of another great prophet who lived as a member of a subject race within a vast imperial system; but the parallel is misleading. Nobody ever asked Ramakrishna to head a nationalist movement, or to decide whether it is right to pay tribute to Caesar. His life was happier than that of the Galilean. Its very significance is in its quietness, its utter lack of external drama. Calcutta was at his doorstep; yet there were probably not a dozen Englishmen who were even aware of his existence.

Ramakrishna could scarcely read or write. But he knew the scriptures by heart and quoted them continually, with the comments of his own unique experience. His talk was a blend of sublime subtlety and homely illustration. He spoke with a slight stammer, in a country dialect, sometimes using coarse, vivid words with the innocent frankness of a peasant. Most of his parables are based upon the everyday circumstances of village life and the folklore of the people. A man of faith is compared to well-boiled sugar; a monk to a snake, which seldom stays long in one place and has no hole of its own. Greed and lust are likened to moisture in wood; they must be dried out by the flame of discrimination before the fire will burn. We are to walk through the world like the girl who carries five waterpots on her head, never losing her balance.

The few existing photographs of Ramakrishna show us a slender, bearded man of medium height. They were taken while he was in samadhi; the lips are parted and the eyes half-closed. In one picture he stands supported by a devotee, with the right arm raised and two fingers of the left hand rigidly extended—an attitude which somehow suggests the concentration of an intense, mysterious delight. The figure has an eager poise, a childlike unselfconsciousness. There is no trace of egotism here; no hint of a desire to dominate, to fascinate, to create an impression. What attracts us is precisely that absence of demand, that joyful openness, in a face which seems to promise the love that makes no reservations, and is without pathos or fear.

He was always smiling, laughing, crying aloud in his joy. Those who visited him felt as if they had arrived at a party which never stopped. A really happy party has no sense of past or future: life at Dakshineswar was lived in a perpetual present tense. The awareness of God's presence was always here and now. Sometimes there would be animated discussion. Sometimes musicians came, and Ramakrishna sang and danced, or clowned to amuse the boys. Often, he passed into samadhi, and the little room was filled with ecstasy and silence.

The experience of samadhi is, literally, a death to the things of this world. It is said that the body of an ordinary human being could not survive it for more than a few weeks. Ramakrishna had entered samadhi daily for many years. In the process, his whole physical organism had been transformed: it was extraordinarily sensitive and delicate. One night, in 1885, he had a hemorrhage of the throat. The doctor diagnosed cancer.

That autumn, he was moved into Calcutta for better nursing. Despite his weakness and terrible pain, he continued to teach his disciples, to laugh, to joke, and to sing. One of his attendants has even expressed a belief that Ramakrishna was not suffering at all. The eyes of the saint regarded the wasting body with a kind of calm, secret amusement, as though this horrible disease were only a masquerade.

His disciples begged him to pray that he might recover—for their sake, if not for his own. At last, Ramakrishna agreed to do so. A little later, he told them: "I said to her: 'Mother, I can't swallow food because of my pain. Make me able to eat a little.' But she pointed to you and said: 'What? Aren't you eating enough through all those mouths?' I was ashamed. I couldn't say another word."

Toward the end, his chief concern was for the future of his young disciples. Two he had especially loved. One of them, later to be known as Swami Brahmananda, he regarded as his own spiritual son. The other, Naren (afterwards Swami Vivekananda), he had trained to be the bearer of his message to the world.

One day, while Ramakrishna lay in the last stage of his illness, Naren was in a downstairs room, meditating. Suddenly, he lost consciousness, and went into samadhi. At first, the experience terrified him. Coming to himself, he cried, "Where is my body?" Another of the boys saw him, and ran upstairs in a fright to tell Ramakrishna. "Let him stay that way for a while," said the Master, calmly. "He has worried me long enough."

Much later, Naren himself came into Ramakrishna's room. He was full of delight and peace. "Now Mother has shown you everything," said Ramakrishna. "But I shall keep the key. When you have done Mother's work, you will find the treasure again."

On August 15, 1886, Ramakrishna uttered the name of Kali three times, in a clear ringing voice, and passed into the final samadhi. At noon, next day, the doctor found that life had left his body. There is a photograph, taken that same evening, in which we see the mourners grouped around the corpse before its removal to the cremation ground. The young faces are all somber and meditative, but there is no sign of frantic grief or despair. The disciples were worthy of their master. Their faith seems never to have left them, even at this supreme moment of loss.

Not long after, they resolved unanimously to enter the monastic life. And thus the group was formed which afterwards became the Ramakrishna Order.

The boys had little money and few friends. Their first monastery was a tumbledown old house, midway between Calcutta and Dakshineswar, with nests of cobras under the floor, which could be rented cheaply because it was supposed to be haunted. Here they lived, and often starved, in meditation and ecstasy. M, who went to visit them, marveled at their joy. So vivid was their awareness of Ramakrishna's presence that they could even joke about him. M records how, one evening, Vivekananda mimicked the Master going into samadhi, while his brother-monks roared with laughter.

Vivekananda and Brahmananda (or "Swamiji" and "Maharaj," as they were more familiarly called) were the group's natural leaders. The two had been friends from early boyhood; both were now twenty-three years old. Handsome and athletic, Vivekananda was the embodiment of physical and intellectual energy; impulsive, ardent, skeptical, impatient of all hypocrisy, conservatism, or sloth. His faith had not come to him easily. He had questioned Ramakrishna at every step, and would accept nothing on trust, without the test of personal experience. Well-read in Western philosophy and science, and inspired by the reformist doctrines of Keshab Sen, he brought to his religious life that most valuable quality, intelligent doubt. If he had never visited Dakshineswar, he might well have become one of India's foremost national leaders.

Brahmananda is a more mysterious figure. Few knew him intimately, and those few confessed to the inadequacy of their knowledge. He was a very great mystic and saint. His wisdom and his love seemed superhuman. His brother-disciples did not hesitate to compare him to Ramakrishna himself. "Whatever Maharaj tells you," said one of them, "comes directly from God." Brahmananda was elected head of the Ramakrishna Order in 1902, and held that office until the end of his life, in 1922.

For seven years, the young monks wandered all over India, visiting shrines and places of pilgrimage, passing months of meditation in lonely huts, preaching, begging. Sometimes, they were royally entertained by wealthy devotees. More often, they shared the rice and hard bread of the very poor. These experiences were especially valuable to Vivekananda. They gave him a standard of comparison, a true picture of India's hunger and wisdom, her economic misery and deep spiritual culture, which he carried with him on his journey to the West.

In 1893, a Parliament of Religions was to be held at the World's Columbian Exposition in Chicago. Vivekananda was anxious to attend it, and his disciples and friends raised the money for the passage. What followed was a typically Indian comedy of errors. He arrived much too early in the United States. His funds ran out. He lost the address of his Chicago hosts, did not know how to use the telephone or the directory, and spent the night sleeping in a box[car] in the freight yards. Next morning, after much walking, he found himself in a fashionable residential district, without a cent in his pocket. There seemed no point in going any further. He sat down on the sidewalk and resigned himself to the will of God. Presently, a door opened, and a well-dressed lady came out. "Sir," she asked, "are you a delegate to the Parliament of Religions?" A few minutes later, he was sitting down to breakfast, with all his difficulties solved.

The other delegates to the Parliament were prominent men, admirably representative of their respective creeds. Vivekananda, like his Master, was unknown. For this very reason, his magnificent presence created much speculation among the audience. When he rose to speak, his first words, "Sisters and Brothers of America," released one of those mysterious discharges of enthusiasm which seem to be due to an exactly right conjunction of subject, speaker, and occasion. People rose from their seats and cheered for several minutes. Vivekananda's speech was short, and not one of his best; but, as an introduction, it was most effective. Henceforward, he was one of the Parliament's outstanding personalities. The newspapers took him up. Invitations to lecture began to come in from all over the country. It was clear that he would have to remain in the United States for some time.

In those days, a foreign lecturer touring America found himself in a position midway between that of a campaigning politician and a circus performer. He had to face the rough-and-tumble of indiscreet publicity, well-meant but merciless curiosity, reckless slander, crude hospitality, endless noise, and hurry and fuss. Vivekananda was surprisingly well-equipped for all these trials. He was outspoken, quick at repartee, dynamic, witty, and courageous. Above all, he was a true monk; and only a monk could have preserved his inner calm amidst such a tumult. On one occasion, a party of cowboys fired pistols around his head during a lecture, for a joke. Vivekananda went on imperturbably. He said what he had to say, whether the audience liked it or not. "In New York," he used to remark, "I have emptied entire halls."

His main theme was the universality of religious truth, a dangerous topic in communities which still clung to a rigid Christian fundamentalism. To such listeners, the doctrine of the Atman must have sounded like the most appalling blasphemy: "Look at the ocean and not at the wave; see no difference between ant and angel. Every worm is the brother of the Nazarene. . . . Obey the scriptures until you are strong enough to do without them. . . . Every man in Christian countries has a huge cathedral on his head, and on top of that a book. . . . The range of idols is from wood and stone to Jesus and Buddha." Vivekananda is preeminently the prophet of self-reliance, of courage, of individual inquiry, and effort. His favorite story was of the lion who imagined himself to be a sheep, until another lion showed him his reflection in a pool. "You are lions, you are pure, infinite, and perfect souls. The might of the universe is within you. . . . After long searches here and there, at last you come back, completing the circle from where you started, and find that He, for whom you have been weeping and praying in churches and temples, on whom you were looking as the mystery of all mysteries shrouded in the clouds, is nearest of the near, your own Self, the reality of your life."

Vivekananda really loved America: that was part of his greatness. As few men, before or since, he stood between East and West impartially, admiring the virtues and condemning the defects of both. To Americans and Englishmen, he preached India's religious tolerance, her freedom of spiritual investigation, her ideal of total dedication to the search for God. To Indians, he spoke severely of their sloth, their timid conservatism in manners and customs, and held up for their imitation the efficiency of the American and the Englishman's energy and tenacity. "You have not the capacity to manufacture a needle and you dare to criticize the English! Fools! Sit at their feet and learn their arts and industries. . . . Without the necessary preparation, what's the use of just shouting in Congress?" With himself, he was equally ruthless. Some friends once unkindly tricked him into eating beef. When he discovered that he had done so, his involuntary disgust was so extreme that he vomited. "But I must overcome this ridiculous prejudice," he exclaimed, a few moments later. And he asked for a second helping.

In 1897, after two visits to England, he returned to India, where he witnessed the founding of the Ramakrishna Order, with its headquarters in Calcutta, and the establishment of several other monasteries. His progress through the country was triumphal; and his achievements in the West, real as they were, were wildly exaggerated by the enthusiasm of his Indian disciples. [The "wild exaggerations" were, in fact, the product of popular enthusiasm which were further dramatized by the press of his day.] Yet, amidst all this adulation, Vivekananda never lost his emotional balance. Again and again, he paid homage to Brahmananda, whose spirituality was the inner strength of the movement and the inspiration of its growth. The relation between these two men, the ardent missionary and the calm, taciturn mystic, remained deep and beautiful throughout their lives. *

In 1899, Vivekananda returned to America. His second visit was less spectacular than his first; it was concerned chiefly with the development of small groups and the training of devotees in different parts of the country. But it made great demands upon his already failing strength. He came back to India by way of England and Europe at the end of 1900, sick and exhausted. His mood, too, had changed. He was weary of talk, of letter writing, of the endless problems of organization. He was weary of activity. He longed for the Himalayas, and the peace of meditation. Through much struggle, he had learned resignation and acceptance. He was happier, perhaps, than at any other period of his life. Already, before leaving America, he had written to a friend: "I am glad I was born, glad I suffered so, glad I did make big blunders, glad to enter peace. Whether this body will fall and release me or I enter into freedom in the body, the old man is gone, gone for ever, never to come back again! Behind my work was ambition, behind my love was personality, behind my purity was fear, behind my guidance the thirst for power. Now they are vanishing and I drift."

---

*Ramakrishna himself was the real founder of the Ramakrishna Order of monks. Shortly before his death in 1886, Ramakrishna asked that ocher cloths be given to his young disciples who were planning to renounce the world. Ramakrishna entrusted the care of these young boys to Vivekananda, and charged him to make sure that the boys did not return to their families. After Ramakrishna's death, the young disciples took informal monastic vows on Christmas Eve in 1886.

Swami Vivekananda was the founder of the Ramakrishna Mission. His experience in foreign countries had brought him to the conclusion that an organization was necessary for the permanent great work he envisioned. To that end, he created the Ramakrishna Mission on May 1, 1897, its members consisting of monks, devotees, and the general public. The Mission's

His departure from this life, on July 4, 1902, had all the marks of a premeditated act. For some months, he had been quietly releasing himself from his various responsibilities and making final arrangements. His health gave no particular cause for alarm. He had been ill, and now seemed better. He ate his midday meal with relish, talked philosophy with his brother-swamis, and went for a walk. In the evening, he sat down to meditate, giving instructions that he was not to be disturbed. Presently, he passed into samadhi, and the heart stopped beating. It all happened so quietly that nobody could believe this was the end. For hours, they tried to rouse him. But his Mother's work was done. And Ramakrishna had set him free at last.

I HAVE ALREADY suggested that Vivekananda had two messages to deliver: one to the East, the other to the West. In the United States and in England, he preached the universality of religious truth, attacked materialism, and advocated spiritual experiment, as against dogma and tradition. In India, on the other hand, we find that he preferred to stress the ideal of social service. To each, he tried to give what was most lacking.

Vivekananda founded the first American Vedanta Society in New York City. Four direct disciples of Ramakrishna came from India to carry on his work. From that time onward, the Order has met an increasing demand for teachers. Each one of them has come to this country upon the invitation of some group of local citizens who wished to learn more about Vedanta philosophy. Although the Vedanta Societies are an extension of the Ramakrishna Mission of India, whose headquarters are at Belur, Calcutta, each center is a separate unit. Nearly all of them have their own boards of trustees, made up of local citizens.

goal was the spiritual, mental, and material service of mankind. Swami Vivekananda was its General President, and Swami Brahmananda was the President of the Calcutta Center.

During the years that Swami Vivekananda was abroad, the work of the Order remained in the forefront of his mind. His many letters to his brother-monks and disciples written during this period were filled with zeal and encouragement. The letters concerned themselves with the Order's goals, ideals, and day-to-day activities, and were a constant source of guidance and inspiration to the fledgling Order.

Christopher Isherwood's book, *Ramakrishna and His Disciples*, addresses these issues in depth.—Ed.

Editor's Note on the Introduction

SINCE THIS INTRODUCTION was written nearly fifty years ago, the work and influence of the Ramakrishna Order, both in India and abroad, has vastly increased; its ideals and activities are found in far-flung locations across the globe.

There are over 140 official centers of the Ramakrishna Order, and many more unofficial, or unaffiliated, ones. These centers not only cover the length and breadth of the Indian subcontinent, but can also be found in Europe, Russia, Japan, South America, Africa, Canada, and the United States.

Those branches of the Ramakrishna Order located outside India are generally known as Vedanta Societies, and are under the spiritual guidance of the Ramakrishna Order.

The work of the Vedanta Societies in the West has primarily been devoted to spiritual and pastoral activities, though many of them do some form of social service. Many of the Western Vedanta Societies have resident monks, and several centers have resident nuns. A monk who has taken his preliminary monastic vows is called a "brahmachari." After he has taken his final monastic vows, he is referred to as "swami." A nun who has taken her preliminary vows is called a "brahmacharini"; when she takes her final vows she is called "pravrajika." These Western monastics take their vows in the Ramakrishna Order, and generally remain residents in their own country .

On the Indian subcontinent, the Ramakrishna Order has been formed along two parallel lines: the Ramakrishna Math, which is primarily dedicated to spiritual development, and the Ramakrishna Mission, which is dedicated to social service. In a sense these twin efforts cannot be separated, since the goal of the Ramakrishna Order has been since its inception in 1897: "Liberation for oneself and service to mankind." The two goals go hand in hand. By serving others as a manifestation of the Divine, we worship God, and thus work towards our own spiritual growth.

From the beginning, the Ramakrishna Mission has been in the forefront of philanthropic activities. Its first social service efforts—inspired by Swami Vivekananda—began in 1897. Since that time, the Mission's activities have continued to expand up to the present day.

The Ramakrishna Mission has its own hospitals, charitable dispensaries, maternity clinics, tuberculosis clinics, and mobile dispensaries. It also maintains training centers for nurses. Orphanages and homes for the elderly are included in the Mission's field of activities, along with rural and tribal welfare work.

In educational activities, the Ramakrishna Mission has consistently been ahead of its time. It has developed some of the most outstanding educational institutions in India, having its own colleges, vocational training centers, high schools and primary schools, teachers' training institutes, as well as schools for the visually handicapped. It also has adult education centers throughout the country.

Whenever disaster has struck, the Ramakrishna Mission has been there to offer relief from famine, epidemic, fire, flood, earthquake, cyclone, and communal disturbances.

In founding the Ramakrishna Order in India, Swami Vivekananda envisioned an order of monks who would devote themselves to realizing God and serving humanity. At the same time, Swami Vivekananda had the idea of starting a similar order for women who would dedicate themselves to the ideals of spirituality and service.

A half-century after Swami Vivekananda's death, his dream became a reality when in 1954, Sarada Math, India's monastic order for women, was founded. Like the Ramakrishna Order, Sarada Math emphasizes both spiritual development and social welfare programs. Sarada Math, with a smaller work force than the Ramakrishna Mission, has accomplished an impressive record in education, medical service, and rural uplift. As of this writing, Sarada Math has seventeen centers in India, and one in Australia.

Real Religion

by Swami Vivekananda

RELIGION DOES NOT consist in doctrines or dogmas. It is not what you read, nor what dogmas you believe that is of importance, but what you realize. "Blessed are the pure in heart, for they shall see God," yea, in this life. And that is salvation. There are those who teach that this can be gained by the mumbling of words. But no great master ever taught that external forms were necessary for salvation. The power of attaining it is within ourselves. We live and move in God. Creeds and sects have their parts to play, but they are for children, they last but temporarily. Books never make religions, but religions make books. We must not forget that. No book ever created God, but God inspired all the great books. And no book ever created a soul. We must never forget that.

The end of all religions is the realizing of God in the soul. That is the one universal religion. If there is one universal truth in all religions, I place it here—in realizing God. Ideals and methods may differ, but that is the central point. There may be a thousand different radii, but they all converge to the one center, and that is the realization of God: something behind this world of sense, this world of eternal eating and drinking and talking nonsense, this world of false shadows and selfishness. There is that beyond all books, beyond all creeds, beyond the vanities of this world, and it is the realization of God within yourself.

A man may believe in all the churches in the world, he may carry in his head all the sacred books ever written, he may baptize himself in all the rivers of the earth, still, if he has no perception of God, I would class him with the rankest atheist. And a man may have never entered a church or a mosque, nor performed any ceremony, but if he feels God within himself and is thereby lifted above the vanities of the world, that man is a holy man, a saint, call him what you will.

As soon as a man stands up and says he is right or his church is right, and all others are wrong, he is himself all wrong. He does not know that upon the proof of all the others depends the proof of his own.

Love and charity for the whole human race, that is the test of true religiousness. I do not mean the sentimental statement that all men are brothers, but that one must feel the oneness of human life. So far as they are not exclusive, I see that the sects and creeds are all mine; they are all grand. They are all helping men towards the real religion. I will add, it is good to be born in a church, but it is bad to die there. It is good to be born a child, but bad to remain a child. Churches, ceremonies, and symbols are good for children, but when the child is grown, he must burst the church or himself. We must not remain children for ever. It is like trying to fit one coat to all sizes and growths.

I do not deprecate the existence of sects in the world. Would to God there were twenty millions more, for the more there are, there will be a greater field for selection. What I do object to is trying to fit one religion to every case.

Though all religions are essentially the same, they must have the varieties of form produced by dissimilar circumstances among different nations. We must each have our own individual religion, individual so far as the externals of it go.

Many years ago, I visited a great sage of our own country, a very holy man. We talked of our revealed book, the Vedas, of your Bible, of the Koran, and of revealed books in general. At the close of our talk, this good man asked me to go to the table and take up a book; it was a book which, among other things, contained a forecast of the rainfall during the year. The sage said, "Read that." And I read out the quantity of rain that was to fall. He said, "Now take the book and squeeze it." I did so, and he said, "Why, my boy, not a drop of water comes out. Until the water comes out, it is all book, book. So until your religion makes you realize God, it is useless. He who only studies books for religion reminds one of the fable of the ass which carried a heavy load of sugar on its back, but did not know the sweetness of it."

Shall we advise men to kneel down and cry, "O miserable sinners that we are!" No, rather let us remind them of their divine nature. I will tell you a story. A lioness in search of prey came upon a flock of sheep, and as she jumped at one of them, she gave birth to a cub and died on the spot. The young lion was brought up in the flock, ate grass, and bleated like a sheep, and it never knew that it was a lion. One day a lion came across the flock and was astonished to see in it a huge lion eating grass and bleating like a sheep. At his sight the flock fled and the lion-sheep with them. But the lion watched his opportunity and one day found the lion-sheep asleep. He woke him up and said, "You are a lion." The other said, "No," and began to bleat like a sheep. But the stranger lion took him to a lake and asked him to look in the water at his own image and see if it did not resemble him, the stranger lion. He looked and acknowledged that it did. Then the stranger lion began to roar and asked him to do the same. The lion-sheep tried his voice and was soon roaring as grandly as the other. And he was a sheep no longer.

My friends, I would like to tell you all that you are mighty as lions.

If the room is dark, do you go about beating your chest and crying, "It is dark, dark, dark!" No, the only way to get the light is to strike a light, and then the darkness goes. The only way to realize the light above you is to strike the spiritual light within you, and the darkness of sin and impurity will flee away. Think of your higher self, not of your lower.

Two birds of beautiful plumage, inseparable companions, sat upon the same tree, one on the top and one below. The beautiful bird below was eating the fruits of the tree, sweet and bitter, one moment a sweet one and another a bitter. The moment he ate a bitter fruit, he was sorry, but after a while he ate another and when it too was bitter, he looked up and saw the other bird who ate neither the sweet nor the bitter, but was calm and majestic, immersed in his own glory. And then the poor lower bird forgot and went on eating the sweet and bitter fruits again, until at last he ate one that was extremely bitter; and then he stopped again and once more looked up at the glorious bird above. Then he came nearer and nearer to the other bird; and when he had come near enough, rays of light shone upon him and enveloped him, and he saw he was transformed into the higher bird. He became calm, majestic, free, and found that there had been but one bird all the time on the tree. The lower bird was but the reflection of the one above.

So we are in reality one with the Lord, but the reflection makes us seem many, as when the one sun reflects in a million dew-drops and seems a million tiny suns. The reflection must vanish if we are to identify ourselves with our real nature which is divine. The universe itself can never be the limit of our satisfaction. That is why the miser gathers more and more money, that is why the robber robs, the sinner sins, that is why you are learning philosophy. All have one purpose. There is no other purpose in life, save to reach this freedom. Consciously or unconsciously, we are all striving for perfection. Every being must attain to it.

The man who is groping through sin, through misery, the man who is choosing the path through hells, will reach it, but it will take time. We cannot save him. Some hard knocks on his head will help him to turn to the Lord. The path of virtue, purity, unselfishness, spirituality, becomes known at last and what all are doing unconsciously, we are trying to do consciously. The idea is expressed by St. Paul, "The God that ye ignorantly worship, Him declare I unto you." This is the lesson for the whole world to learn. What have these philosophies and theories of nature to do, if not to help us to attain to this one goal in life? Let us come to that consciousness of the identity of everything and let man see himself in everything. Let us be no more the worshipers of creeds or sects with small limited notions of God, but see Him in everything in the universe. If you are knowers of God, you will everywhere find the same worship as in your own heart.

Get rid, in the first place, of all these limited ideas and see God in every person—working through all hands, walking through all feet, and eating through every mouth. In every being He lives, through all minds He thinks. He is self-evident, nearer unto us than ourselves. To know this is religion, is faith, and may it please the Lord to give us this faith!

When we shall feel that oneness, we shall be immortal. We are physically immortal even, one with the universe. So long as there is one that breathes throughout the universe, I live in that one. I am not this limited little being, I am the universal. I am the life of all the sons of the past. I am the soul of Buddha, of Jesus, of Mohammed. I am the soul of the teachers, and I am all the robbers that robbed, and all the murderers that were hanged, I am the universal. Stand up then; this is the highest worship. You are one with the universe. That only is humility—not crawling upon all fours and calling yourself a sinner. That is the highest evolution when this veil of differentiation is torn off.

The highest creed is oneness. I am so-and-so is a limited idea, not true of the real "I." I am the universal; stand upon that and ever worship the highest through the highest form, for God is Spirit and should be worshiped in spirit and in truth. Through lower forms of worship, man's material thoughts rise to spiritual worship and the universal infinite One is at last worshiped in and through the spirit. That which is limited is material. The Spirit alone is infinite. God is Spirit, is infinite; man is Spirit and, therefore, infinite, and the Infinite alone can worship the Infinite. We will worship the Infinite; that is the highest spiritual worship.

The Minimum Working Hypothesis

by Aldous Huxley

RESEARCH INTO SENSE-EXPERIENCE—motivated and guided by a working hypothesis; leading, through logical inference to the formulation of an explanatory theory; and resulting in appropriate technological action. That is natural science.

No working hypothesis means no motive for research, no reason for making one experiment rather than another, no way of bringing sense or order into the observed facts.

Contrariwise, too much working hypothesis means finding only what you already *know* to be there and ignoring the rest. Dogma turns a man into an intellectual Procrustes. He goes about forcing things to become the signs of his word patterns, when he ought to be adapting his word patterns to become the signs of things.

Among other things religion is also research. Research into, leading to theories about and action in the light of, nonsensuous, nonpsychic, purely spiritual experience.

To motivate and guide this research what sort and how much of a working hypothesis do we need?

None, say the sentimental humanists; just a little bit of Wordsworth, say the nature worshipers. Result: they have no motive impelling them to make the more arduous experiments; they are unable to explain such nonsensuous facts as come their way; they make very little progress in charity.

At the other end of the scale are the Catholics, the Jews, the Muslims, all with historical, one-hundred-percent revealed religions. These people have their working hypotheses about nonsensuous reality; which means that they have a motive for doing something about it. But because their working hypotheses are too elaborately dogmatic, most of them discover only what they were initially taught to believe. But what they believe is a hotchpotch of good, less good, and even bad. Records of the infallible intuitions of great saints into the highest spiritual reality are mixed up with records of the less reliable and infinitely less valuable intuitions of psychics into the lower levels of nonsensuous reality; and to these are added mere fancies, discursive reasonings and sentimentalisms, projected into a kind of secondary objectivity and worshiped as divine facts. But at all times and in spite of these handicaps a persistent few have continued to research to the point where at last they find themselves looking through their dogmas, out into the Clear Light of the Void beyond.

For those of us who are not congenitally the members of an organized church, who have found that humanism and nature worship are not enough, who are not content to remain in the darkness of ignorance, the squalor of vice or the other squalor of respectability, the minimum working hypothesis would seem to run to about this:

That there is a Godhead, Ground, Brahman, Clear Light of the Void, which is the unmanifested principle of all manifestations.

That the Ground is at once transcendent and immanent.

That it is possible for human beings to love, know, and from virtually, to become actually identical with the divine Ground.

That to achieve this unitive knowledge of the Godhead is the final end and purpose of human existence.

That there is a Law or Dharma which must be obeyed, a Tao or Way which must be followed, if men are to achieve their final end.

That the more there is of self, the less there is of the Godhead; and that the Tao is therefore a way of humility and love, the Dharma a living law of mortification and self-transcending awareness. This, of course, accounts for the facts of history. People like their egos and do not wish to mortify them, get a bigger kick out of bullying and self-adulation than out of humility and compassion, are determined not to see why they shouldn't "do what they like" and "have a good time." They get their good time; but also and inevitably they get wars and syphilis, tyranny and alcoholism, revolution, and in default of an adequate religious hypothesis, the choice between some lunatic idolatry, such as nationalism, and a sense of complete futility and despair. Unutterable miseries! But throughout recorded history the great majority of men and women have preferred the risk—no, the positive certainty—of such disasters to the tiresome whole-time job of seeking first the kingdom of God. In the long run, we get exactly what we ask for.

✳

The Starting Point

by Swami Ashokananda

RELIGION IS THE natural expression of man's being. We can no more get rid of it than we can do away with our very self. In our heart of hearts there is an inevitable craving for the eternal, the immutable. Man can never rest contented with the ephemeral. It can delude him for the time being, but it cannot suppress or subvert his inherent longing for the Truth. So long as there are changes in the world, so long as death and decay are the necessary conditions of life, this instinctive desire for the Real will force itself up time and again and set men on the quest of religion. Science, philosophy, and art have the same impulse behind them to discover the Truth. But while science, philosophy, and poetry end in a reasoned perception, a conceptual knowledge or an aesthetic apprehension of the Reality, religion leads to its immediate vision.

Through religion alone we come in direct contact with the Reality and feel our kinship and become one with it. It penetrates all the layers of our being and manifests itself in the whole range of life. We live the Truth. Man's eternal relation with the divine and his union with it have been the key words of all religions. In the storm and stress of life, these have been man's only hope, solace, and inspiration. This is why religion has been the strongest cementing force, the highest motive power, the greatest comforter, and the supreme illuminator of life. In all ages and all countries man has paid the greatest homage to religion. Saints and seers have commanded the highest veneration of mankind. The greatest sages were men with spiritual vision. Religion has proved the greatest cultural force. The best literature, architecture, music, and poetry have grown out of religious fervor. . . .

An urge towards perfection is the motive power behind all human aspirations and activities. Why should man feel a natural attraction for the Reality that is beyond phenomena? Why can he not remain satisfied with the finite and the evanescent? He is not contented even to grasp the Reality through intellect or aesthetic imagination; he wants to see it face to face, to touch it. Nay, he seeks to be united with it, to lose himself in it.

This feeling of affinity with the Real, the eternal, the divine, is the first blossoming of religious consciousness. Man longs for the eternal and the infinite and at the same time feels his littleness, weakness, and imperfection. This creates a sense of awe—a blended feeling of attraction and repulsion. It is not fear; for fear always repels, never attracts. Like attracts like. The human self is eternally related to the divine. Divinity is in its nature. The innate purity, eternity, luminosity, and blissfulness of the self have been acknowledged directly or indirectly by all great religions of the world. But in no other religion has this fact been given such prominence as in the Vedanta. . . .

The self is of all the most real to us. The reality of everything presupposes the reality of the self. A thing exists because *I* feel its existence. The reality of all other things is judged by referring it to the self. The self is the eternal seer. The external objects, body, and mind are all seen by it. The whole world of facts, the entire realm of ideas rest on the consciousness of the perceiver. It is the datum of all experience and knowledge. It is the ultimate reality. It cannot be seen, because it is the seer—everything is revealed to it. The self is this seer. It is consciousness itself. It cannot be seen, but it can be realized. It cannot be denied, for the denial presupposes another seer and conceives it as seen, which is absurd. The subject can never turn into the object.

The self is pure intelligence. It illumines everything. It is also bliss itself. It is the only true object of love. Whatever we love we love for the sake of the self. I like this body because I project my self on it, and everything favorable to the body becomes dear to me. The wife, children, parents, and friends are loved by me, because my self is reflected in them. The feeling of love is indissolubly connected with the "my" idea.

The more the self is expanded, the greater is the range of love. Love and bliss are inseparable. Where there is bliss, there is love. Where there is love, there is bliss. The self being bliss itself, evokes spontaneous love.

The pure, blissful, self-effulgent Atman is our true self. It is the knower of body and mind. The knower and the known are ever distinct. We perceive ourselves to be the knower, still we identify ourselves with the known, the body, mind, etc. This is absurd. Yet it is a fact. We cannot help it. We can neither conceive ourselves as pure spirit nor think of ourselves as gross matter. The two ideas are as it were woven into one. By identifying the self with body and mind, we have imposed on ourselves all the limitations and imperfections that belong solely to body and mind. Hunger, disease, growth, decay, birth, death, happiness, misery are the properties of body and mind. They are falsely ascribed to the changeless self, the witness of all. We live in mind and body, but we must be reinstated in the purity and blissfulness of self. The whole history of spiritual progress is simply a travel from the body idea to the spirit consciousness.

To uphold the pristine glory of the Atman is the supreme need of religion today. One can be religious without faith in God, but not without faith in the essential purity and eternity of the Atman. A true atheist is not he who disbelieves God, but he who has lost faith in the Atman. . . .

There can be no faith in God without faith in the self. He who does not believe in the divinity of the self cannot have any relation with God. Relation exists between what are alike and of the same nature. . . .

Faith in the Atman is the starting point of religion. The self offers the first clue to Reality. Turn to whichever direction you may, to the highest heaven or the farthest limit of the horizon, nowhere will you find a loophole to Truth. So you must have your foothold secure on the reality of the self, which is so apparent to you, before you can enter into the realm of light and bliss eternal. "This Atman is Brahman"—reiterate the whole Upanishads—pointing inward. We see God within us. Nobody ever realized God outside. Self-knowledge is always involved in God-consciousness. There can be no God-vision without Self-realization. The one is but a phase of the other.

To believe in the absolute purity of the self and to realize its divinity is the religion that demands acceptance by the scientific mind of today. Human nature is never against religion, the religious spirit is ingrained in man's very being. What man gets disgusted with, is the crystallized form, which, however appealing to the people of one age, fails to attract the men of a different age. . . .

This age requires a religion which does not depend on outer sanctities, but holds life and spirit as essentially sacred. It should not be confined in certain rites, objects, ceremonies, doctrines, or dogmas, but find adequate expression in thought and conduct. The reorientation of life has been the cry of the age. It is mankind's outlook on life that the world counts today, and not the particular act or belief however righteous it may be. The external distinction of the secular and the spiritual is fast fading away. The stress is laid on a higher conception of reality which should shape the judgment of values and transform human relationships, in fact the whole range of life.

Spiritual life, rightly understood, is not a life of isolation. It does not consist in mere disengagement of the spirit from the contagion of the flesh. The self should realize its aloofness from the physical and the mental being, and at the same time guide and restrain them according to its needs and ends. The spiritual consciousness must be infused into the whole system and expressed in concrete forms. Belief without conduct has no value. Our thoughts and acts are but expressions of self-consciousness. It is the greatest creative factor of life. We are what we believe ourselves to be. He who thinks that he is pure by nature, that wickedness and vice are foreign to him, pure he will be in no time. He who considers himself weak, his ideas and deeds will bear the impress of that mentality. Humanity progresses along the line of self-consciousness. Evolution of life means the evolution of consciousness. The higher the self-consciousness, the greater the life.

The more a man knows himself to be pure and perfect by nature, the more glorified will he be. The more he realizes that weakness, ignorance, and unhappiness are mere accretions on his ideal self, the greater will be the manifestation of divinity in him. His thoughts, views, aims, and sentiments will be colored by that consciousness . . . the world will appear to him in a new light. As he will feel his inward goodness and greatness, he will perceive the same in others as well. His attitude to the world will consist of the highest and the noblest feelings of love, respect, and service. The consciousness "I am He" must develop its necessary counterpart "Thou art That." The two views will grow side by side. Never was humanity so intensely realized as an organic whole as in the present age. . . .

With the knowledge of the self, man's vision of life will be clearer, wider, and deeper. He will feel that his self is at the same time the selves of others. It is one Self that exists in all. It is one Spirit that pervades the universe and shapes it from within. The immanence of a formative principle in the world system is more in conformity with modern thought than an extracosmic God. . . .

Faith in the self and the realization of the self are the religion of today. We do not mean thereby that that will be the only existing religion in the future, that other faiths will be obsolete or prove abortive. We only mean that this of all others will come into prominence, as it will be embraced by the advanced section of humanity. Different faiths are necessary for different minds, which cannot find inspiration from a single creed. It is the age of synthesis. The faith of the enlightened must harmonize all other faiths. The monism of the Vedanta which declares the Atman to be Existence-Knowledge-Bliss absolute, is the key to all other religions. It can receive all into its infinite bosom. All faiths, morals, and theories are according to it more or less perfect presentations of one Truth.

❈

Is Vedanta for the West?

by Swami Atmarupananda

FROM TIME TO time, it's good to ask basic questions: Where exactly am I going? Why? Is this conveyance *really* going to get me there? Had I rather be doing something else?

Since I sometimes am asked about Vedanta, I like to ask myself, Why would anyone want to study it? What good does it do? If any, how?

These questions arise with a special insistence when I see an audience of twenty to twenty-five people who have gathered out of a city of more than a million to hear about Vedanta. How tempting then to question Vedanta's relevance! But I don't. There's the constant certainty that someday the Western world will catch fire with the ideas of Vedanta, transforming the landscape: social, cultural, intellectual, educational, moral, and religious.

Why?

Because Vedanta provides a new paradigm which the world needs desperately. When the world will recognize the vast promise contained in that paradigm, great things will happen. This paradigm is vast and can work through all great traditions as well as outside all traditions. It respects diversity and individuality and is not concerned with membership.

A new paradigm: does that sound like an intellectual fad? What the phrase refers to certainly isn't. It's something profound and encompassing.

Or does it sound cold and bookish? It's not that, either. It is life-giving, uplifting.

So, what is this "new paradigm"?

Let's first ask what attracts people to Vedanta? That will tell us what people actually find of value there. Then we can look more carefully at the total picture of what Vedanta has to offer.

When asked, most Western Vedantins say what first attracted them was the universal outlook toward other religions: the teaching that all religions are different paths leading toward the same goal.

Others are attracted because in their prior experience, religion has been at war with science. Yet science demonstrates its truths right in front of our eyes, while religion seems to say, wait till after death and you'll find out that religion was true. How can a sensible person accept the latter and deny the former? Such religious claims appeal to our fears and not to our intelligence. But Vedanta is a religion in search of truth, based on experience rather than on creed, and therefore has no conflict with the thrust of science. Yet it offers an exquisite idealism and the chance of transcendence, which science cannot offer.

It is also the emphasis on personal transformation, on practice and realization, which attracts people. Religion for the Vedantin lies in being and becoming, not in believing and proclaiming. All religions, of course, emphasize personal growth to some extent, but for the Vedantin it is the only standard of measurement. It's not what we say we believe, but what we are that matters.

Some are attracted by great souls—the lives of great illumined beings like Sri Ramakrishna and Sri Sarada Devi and Swami Vivekananda—or perhaps by a living exemplar of Vedanta. In either case they find someone who has attained something they want, something of obvious value which they haven't seen elsewhere. It is fire that generates fire: one burning candle can pass its flame to countless other candles. An unlit candle can't do that. And so it is life that generates life: one great life ignites other lives with a vision of something heretofore unimagined, of priceless value.

Such are some of the elements that attract newcomers to Vedanta. But the value of Vedanta goes much farther. It is something much more encompassing, affecting all aspects of our being in ways that we often don't see till much later. It is only with the passage of years that we begin to understand the true significance of Vedanta to the Western world. Even then we perhaps are catching only a glimpse of what history will reveal. And the benefits are not just individual: they are social, cultural, "civilizational."

Let us now approach this "new paradigm" more systematically.

First, what do we mean by paradigm in this context?

Every civilization has a mythic basis or paradigm. "Mythic" doesn't mean "false." It refers to a comprehensive worldview that is deeper, more primal than intellectualized philosophy, and includes ideas of space, time, purpose, male and female roles, heroism, selfhood, duty, human relationships, a person's relationship to society, to the natural world, and so on. These elements can be philosophically analyzed with great benefit, but they exist even in the absence of any philosophical statement.

Why do we need a new paradigm?

Because the old one isn't working. It's not that it's ill and in need of treatment. It's dead. A strong statement? Look at the facts:

What's dead? The six days of creation. Traditional ideas of time and space. The earth as the center of the universe. Euro-centrism. Man's separation from the natural world. Man's dominion over woman. Chivalry. The idea of God as Patriarch. The idea of God as King. The certainty that "our" race, "our" nation, "our" religion, "our" culture, is *the* race, *the* nation, *the* religion, *the* culture. The certainty that God is on our side in every conflict. Morality as a covenant with God based on what he likes and doesn't like. The view that man is a sinner by nature. The view of God as Judge. The view that man exists to glorify God. The willingness to accept tradition because it is tradition. The willingness to accept doctrine and dogma because authorities tell us that they know what's what. The willingness to accept a sacred book as the infallible Word of God.

It's this mythic basis of Western civilization which is dead. And it's this death which is the cause of the individual and social "identity crisis" we see all around us. (Is this only a Western problem? No, it's a global problem; but it has become a global problem with the spreading influence of Western civilization.) All over the world there has been a return to religious fundamentalism, apparently in an attempt to find security in an absolute viewpoint in the midst of so much change and uncertainty. This revival of fundamentalism, however, doesn't solve anything because the problem is the death of those old myths and values. Returning to them is like the young pup returning to its dead mother again and again, hoping she'll respond and get up. We can sympathize, but certainly can't encourage it.

Some may say that science has already replaced this mythic basis with its own rational worldview, and so there is no need for a new paradigm. It already exists: the truth of science as opposed to the myths of religion.

Others would say, and I agree, that science has not provided an acceptable foundation for human civilization. Science cannot provide values or purpose, nor can it provide for transcendence. All human values are actually rooted in spiritual values. When the spiritual is taken from life, values continue for some time by their own momentum, but eventually they die. We see that happening all around us. Science can tell us *how* we live, but not *why we should* live, and so it can't address purpose either. Science extends the senses, it doesn't transcend the senses; yet there is something inside of us which can never be satisfied with sense life, however comfortable.

Science and religion have fought each other now for several centuries in a quest to control the mythic foundation of society. But the two are tied together more closely than most scientists and theologians think. For instance, our view of scientific progress—the gradual conquest of all the evils of life through technological progress—is rooted both in a linear view of time and in the conviction that good and evil are separate, distinct quantities. These views of time and of good and evil are religious in origin: time had a beginning and is moving steadily toward a crowning end point or millennium; God is good and his creation is good, but evil entered into the picture through man's disobedience, abetted by Satan.

These mythic ideas are dead, and most recognize them as dead, but they continue to control our thought and behavior more than we think. As yet there is nothing to replace them.

Let me add here that our religious traditions are greater than their mythic foundations. It is not Christianity and Judaism which are dead, but the old paradigm which they use to support and explain their experience. They are vital, and their great vitality is partly shown by the search within their own ranks for a new paradigm. Every great tradition has something of value to contribute to the world at large. What Vedanta has to contribute, perhaps, above all else is a clear vision of the essence of spirituality. That can help all traditions to find what is essential and what is circumstantial, what can be sacrificed without harm.

Let's look briefly at a few of the points raised above.

The story of creation according to Genesis is beautiful and profound if taken as myth, but if taken as history it is contradicted at every step by science. It is, unfortunately, as a literal historical document that the Genesis account has shaped the mythic basis of our civilization. How common has been the belief among the devout that "we aren't supposed to know everything . . . there are some things we just can't understand and shouldn't inquire into"! That can be traced to the belief that Adam and Eve fell from grace because they wished to know as much as God. Science was obstructed at every step by this attitude, until religion itself lost face. Unfortunately, when institutional religion lost face, so did genuine spiritual values which are so essential for human well-being.

Our Western preoccupation with sin comes from the ideas associated with the fall of Adam and Eve. Swami Prabhavananda said after having spent many years in America that the major problem he found in Westerners was chronic guilt, that is, chronic sin-consciousness. A major reassessment in this area is taking place in certain Western religious circles now, showing the vitality and adaptability of the tradition. But the old view is still a primary part of our mythic background. Its pervasive influence can be seen not just in religious thought and practice but even in the thought of people like Sigmund Freud and Karl Marx. The weight of this sin-consciousness is felt by many people today, and yet a satisfactory basis for a new image of humanity hasn't been found.

Woman was made subservient to man by God himself, according to the biblical account. The challenges to this view are so evident today that no comment is needed. And yet a profound basis for equality between the sexes has not been found, a basis which sees unity in the midst of difference. The unity espoused now is only socio-political and emotional. People *feel* that there should be equality. But that, perhaps, is not enough to effect the change desired, a change where women are equal as women, and not because they can do everything a man does in the same way a man does it.

The image of God as Father came naturally to pastoral people like the ancient Jews, but that image also, though beautiful, is now seen as limited. It is also seen as a factor contributing to the inferior position of women in society. Not that it needs to be replaced—it will always be appropriate for some—but it does need to be balanced. Many are now seeking to revive the ancient Mother Goddess, but the effort is largely intellectual and artificial. That is, God the Mother is not experienced as a reality which people encounter and then worship; rather "it" is seen as a good idea which people try to construct into a viable psychological archetype. No one, however, is going to worship for long an intellectually constructed psychological archetype.

During the age of kingly rule it was common for people to think that the king was the value and people existed to glorify and serve the king. Similarly it was natural for people to think that God the heavenly King was the value and humans existed to glorify him. But now when democracy is ascendant *people* have become the value, and the image of God the King has lost relevance. The primary questions are no longer, Who is God and how do I serve him and please him? but, Who am I and how do I find completion? Yet there is no spiritual basis for this change from a God-centered universe to a self-centered universe; in fact, "self-centered" is itself a derogatory term. It seems, according to the old paradigm, you can't be "self-centered" without being selfish and self-indulgent.

Morality as a covenant with God, where what pleases God is moral and what displeases him is immoral, is also untenable today. People want to know *why* certain actions are wrong. In the meantime morality itself is dying for lack of a sure foundation.

For these and other reasons, people have willingly or unwillingly become alienated from the old, and yet have no basis for a new understanding of the world, of self, of God, and of purpose. There has probably never been such a deep and widespread identity crisis in the history of humanity.

Heroes past and present have been debunked and are replaced by rock stars. Loyalty is dead for lack of a worthy object, and devotion is squandered on TV screens.

All of these factors point to the need for a new paradigm, a "unified field theory" of human existence, much broader than the unified field theory sought by some physicists. These physicists seek a theory which would unify our understanding of all the various physical forces, by showing their interrelatedness. What humanity at large needs is a new understanding of self, God, world, purpose, which can serve as the basis for creative action and discovery; that is, it can't be a dogmatic creed which claims to answer all questions and thereby deaden all creative thought and action. It needs to be open-ended, dynamic, releasing human potential, and yet harmonizing, unifying while respecting diversity.

That, I think, is beautifully provided in Vedanta as interpreted by Swami Vivekananda. It is not a paradigm which destroys or replaces all other traditions, but one which calls out the potential of other traditions, *from within* those traditions. It doesn't answer all possible questions so that there is nothing left to think, but rather opens the mind and heart to new and promising possibilities, all pointing toward the infinite. It provides a spiritual foundation for the highest aspirations of the age: democracy, equality, freedom, the dignity of all. And it does this while providing a new basis for morality, not in the likes and dislikes of a deity but by pointing to a universal principle; in other words, morality is not imposed from without, but is sought and found within the very nature of things.

The grand message of the Atman, the divine Self of man, is the source of Vedanta's harmonizing power. It is the basis for Vedanta's vision of unity in diversity, the equality of all people, the equality of man and woman. It thus gives a spiritual basis to democracy and to the belief in the dignity of all beings. It shows us the way to harmonize unselfishness with the desire for self-knowledge and self-discovery and thus overcome the self-alienation which is so characteristic of Western society. No longer does man exist to serve the needs of something outside of himself, whether God or church or king. As Swami Vivekananda said, "The old religions said that he was an atheist who does not believe in God. The new religion says that he is the atheist who does not believe in himself."[1] And yet, worship and devotion are not negated: God is within your own heart, the soul of your own soul, and so worship and devotion can continue without self-alienation.

And what a wonderful conception of God! God is not limited to one idea. Rather the infinite divine Being has infinite manifestations, infinite faces so that God approaches each person according to that person's needs. To some, God is Mother, to some, Father; to some God is Friend, to some, Beloved, to still others, Child.

Then there is the path. Yoga means spiritual path. Each of the four main yogas as taught by Swami Vivekananda can be expanded to include and enhance, and eventually to spiritualize, all of humanity's endeavors. In Western thought as in Indian, three supreme human values are recognized: Truth, Goodness, and Beauty, known in Sanskrit as Satyam, Shivam, and Sundaram. Jnana yoga—the path of knowledge—can be expanded to include the search for the True in any field, whether through science or philosophy or religion. Karma yoga—the path of action—can be expanded to include the search for the Good through work, through service, through sacrifice. Bhakti yoga—the path of devotion—can be expanded to include the search for the Beautiful, which includes the search for love and the search for joy, through art, through religion, through any worshipful action, through all acts of love. And raja yoga is the science of searching itself—the method of search in any field for the Good, the True, and the Beautiful.

Heroism? Sri Ramakrishna, Sri Sarada Devi, Swami Vivekananda, and the other disciples of Sri Ramakrishna have all shown that true heroes do exist. Of course, not everyone will be attracted to the same personalities. But these great people have not set themselves up as objects of worship before which all must bow. Through their example they have also made spiritual heroes of the past believable once again. And they have shown us where to look for heroism in the people around us. As Swami Vivekananda said, "Every one of you is a Prophet, bearing the burden of the world on your own shoulders. Have you ever seen a man, have you ever seen a woman, who is not quietly, patiently, bearing his or her little burden of life? The great Prophets were giants. . . . Compared with them we are pygmies, no doubt, yet we are doing the same task; in our little circles, in our little homes, we are bearing our little crosses."[2]

What does Vedanta offer to the Western world? I think it offers nothing less than a new basis for civilization. And for the individual: a path opening into the infinite.

1. *Complete Works of Swami Vivekananda* (Calcutta: Advaita Ashrama, 1972), 2: 301.
2. Ibid., 4: 152.

The Problem of Evil

by Swami Prabhavananda

THE PROBLEM OF evil is a central one in every system of philosophy or religion, a problem that is usually explained away instead of itself being explained; and the difficulty of reconciling the conception of a God who is all good with the existence of evil remains. Monists of the West, in order to be consistent with their philosophy of absolutism, tend to deny the reality of evil; for, they declare, what we call evil is evil only because we do not view our lives *sub specie aeternitatis.* What appears to be evil is in reality good when viewed in this manner.

And yet we must ask, can evil really be changed into good merely by viewing it in a special manner? Can pain be labeled pleasure provided we view it absolutely? It is true that pain may be borne gracefully if we fix our gaze upon the ultimate goodness of God, but pain is a positive experience of suffering, at least during the duration of the experience. How then can a philosophy be at one with itself simply by denying evil or even more simply by affirming that it can be transformed into good when it is viewed "under the aspect of eternity"? The question remains unanswered in Western attempts to dodge this gravest of all ethical problems.

Vedanta meets the issue in a different way. In the first place, it asserts that, when viewed from the point of view of the Absolute, there is neither good nor evil, neither pleasure nor pain. Then evil no longer exists, not because the magical power of the Absolute changes evil into good, but because both good and evil have ceased to exist. So long, however, as we are experiencing pleasure and pain, so long do both good and evil exist as empirically real. The experience of evil is indeed as much a positive fact as the experience of good. Vedanta thus recognizes both good and evil, and pleasure and pain, as positive facts of experience in our empirical lives, they being in effect the play of *maya,* neither real nor unreal. They cannot be said to be real, for we no longer experience them when we touch absolute experience; and they cannot be said to be actually unreal, for they are experienced in our empirical lives.

Thus, if we accept finite experiences as but the play of maya, the perfection of the Absolute is in no way tarnished. The experiences of pleasure and of pain within maya are in fact due to the good and evil deeds of an individual's past; they are the direct result of karma operating in an individual's life. Shankara compares God to the giver of rain. As rain falls to the ground, various plants ripen and grow and differ from one another, not because the rain is partial but because the seeds are different. *Ishvara* (God) in like manner is the dispenser of the Law, and individuals experience pleasure and pain according to the seeds of merit and demerit they have sown in themselves from a beginningless past.

So, again, the all-goodness of God is not contradicted by our own individual experiences of suffering and evil. Good and evil, that is to say, as they exist as maya, are relative—in the sense that the one without the other is meaningless. Shankara, therefore, distinguishes maya as being of two kinds—*avidya* (evil) and *vidya* (good). Avidya is that which causes us to move away from the real Self, or Brahman, drawing a veil before our sight of Truth; vidya is that which enables us to move towards Brahman by removing the veil of ignorance. As we receive illumination and come to know the Self, we transcend both vidya and avidya and cease to submit to the dominion of maya.

A Meaningful Life

by Pravrajika Vrajaprana

SITTING IN HIS science class, a junior high school student was listening as his teacher explained the biology of organisms. In the final analysis, the teacher observed, life—including that of mankind—was nothing but the process of oxidation and combustion. Some inner rebellion forced that student out of his chair. Springing to his feet, he burst out, "If that's so, then what kind of meaning does life have?"

That boy's cry can be seen as the cry of Everyman. At some point a time comes when we can no longer paper over the larger issues of human existence; is life, we ask, merely an intricate web of chemical processes? Has our life no more significance than a candle which slowly burns and sputters its way into oblivion? Is it "a tale told by an idiot, full of sound and fury, signifying nothing"?

If there is one thing that we fear—and fear it more desperately than death itself—it is the dread of living a life without significance. A life smaller than the sum of its parts is intolerable to the human spirit.

Yet this dread has become more prevalent as we advance technologically, careening fast forward in a struggle to master the external world. We chase goals that evade us, disappoint us, turn to ashes in our hands. Our interior world—unexplored, uncultivated—is left barren. There's no doubt that we've enjoyed remarkable technological success. But the psychic cost has been great: in our search for comfort and prosperity, we've dangled ourselves over the edge of an existential cliff.

Mankind, in earlier, simpler years, was not inclined to believe that his existence was a haphazard event, an accident without a goal or purpose. There was security in the assumption that society was a microcosm of the harmonious universe it mirrored; God's well-ordered creation had an intimate niche for everyone and everything.

The security mankind once knew is now long gone. The faith that knit our lives together slowly unravelled with the intrusion of science. The universe, we discovered, hummed along quite nicely by itself: God wasn't necessary to turn its wheels. The shift in the West's worldview over the past century rendered God, if not dead, at least cooly marginalized.

Faith in God shifted to a faith in various demigods, Marxism and Freudianism being the two most influential of the century. These quasi-religions offered their votaries a worldview that was satisfying in its rigidity, their respective dogmas being as zealous in their orthodoxy as any bona fide creed. According to Marx, a human being was nothing more than a socio-economic entity at the mercy of economic forces and ongoing class struggles. Man was defined by his or her place in the labor force.

Freud, by contrast, saw humanity as a mass of seething, repressed sexual desires. A person's life was dictated by his or her desire for pleasure. Later psychoanalytic schools expanded upon Freud's basic premise: Adler, for example, posited that man was motivated by the will for power.

But neither science nor any political, social, or psychological doctrine offer us the peace that we crave. None answer the larger questions that life presents. The psychiatrist Viktor Frankl observed, "Some of the people who nowadays call on a psychiatrist would have seen a pastor, priest, or rabbi in former days. Now they often refuse to be handed over to a clergyman and instead confront the doctor with questions as, 'What is the meaning of my life?'"

This is the question that brought most of us to Vedanta's doorstep.

MANY OF US turn to spiritual life only when nothing else *works*. Being creatures of habit, we first try the techniques which have always patched things up for us before: we manipulate people and situations, pull a stitch here, move a stitch there, in the hopes that we can salvage a little happiness out of our lives. But it doesn't work. Things fall apart. Our solutions are jerry-rigged, bandaids over tectonic plates.

Why don't our solutions work? Because we are seeking external solutions to spiritual problems. Dr. Carl Jung—whose career spanned several decades and included patients from every corner of the globe—wrote:

> There has not been one [patient] whose problem in the last resort was not that of finding a religious outlook on life. It is safe to say that every one of them fell ill because he had lost that which the living religions of every age have given their followers, and none of them has really healed who did not regain his religious outlook.

It is the "religious outlook" that gives meaning to life. *Religious* in this sense "has nothing to do with a particular creed or membership in a church" as Jung hastened to say. It is a spiritual approach to life which recognizes that our lives have meaning—a purpose and a goal.

The central fact of our existence is the divinity that lies at the core of our being. Divinity is our real nature, our birthright. Nothing can change it, nothing can take it away from us. True, for many of us that divinity is unmanifest; we are unaware, or only dimly aware, of its presence. But that doesn't make it any less real. If clouds hide the sun, we don't doubt the sun's existence. We know that the sun is there in all its glory, ready to shed its warmth and light. Similarly the Atman, the divinity within us all, is shadowed by clouds of ignorance. But these clouds do not affect the Atman: our real Self is pure, eternal, perfect, blissful. It is unaffected by our miseries, untouched by our failings. Within every one of us lies the source of all goodness and strength. Humanity, Swami Vivekananda said,

> stands on the glory of his own soul, the infinite, the eternal, the deathless—that soul which no instruments can pierce, which no air can dry, no fire burn, no water melt, the infinite, the birthless, the deathless, without beginning and without end, before whose magnitude the suns and moons and all their systems appear like drops in the ocean, before whose glory space melts away into nothingness and time vanishes into nonexistence. This glorious soul we must believe in. Out of that will come power. Whatever you think, that you will be.... All knowledge is in me, all power, all purity, and all freedom.

Unfolding our divinity, removing the clouds of ignorance, is the goal that gives meaning to life.

What exactly is this ignorance? It is the illusion that we are separate from God and from one another. Oneness is the great truth that Vedanta has to teach. We are all one—the universe and all its living beings are all manifestations of the one Brahman. Unity is the sole reality of the universe. Brahman—eternal, infinite existence—cannot be divided. The nature of Brahman is bliss absolute: the law of unity is the law of love.

When we see ourselves as separate from the One, suffering is the inevitable result. "He who says he is different from others," Swami Vivekananda said, "even by a hair's breadth, immediately becomes miserable."

But wait a minute. There are not many people who walk around attuned to the divine unity which pervades all things. Does this mean that everyone is miserable? Everyone who thinks of himself or herself as a limited being certainly suffers. When ignorance blinds us to our divine nature, we feel alone and helpless, at the mercy of external and internal forces beyond our control. Clinging to our egos, we suffer the demons of fear, loneliness, and insecurity. The more egocentric a person is, the more insecure and selfish he is. The more selfish and insecure, the more vulnerable and miserable that person is. He or she feels that he must compete to survive. Fearful that others are taking advantage of him, he is in fact his own worst enemy. Only when we rid ourselves of the ego, do we flow with the natural law of the universe: the law of unity and the law of love. We have to get ourselves, our prickly egos, out of the way. "When the ego dies," Sri Ramakrishna said, "all troubles cease." The ego, the root of all ignorance, is the cloud which hides the sun of our true Self.

The goal, then, is to remove that ignorance so that we can attain the only goal worth having: realization of God, realization of the Self within.

Is it possible? Certainly. We've made our bed, and we can unmake it just as well. Just as our past actions have created the life that we are living now, so can our present actions create what we will be tomorrow. We are the masters of our own fate. There are no victims in the cosmos: whatever we see around us is the inevitable result of past actions.

Nothing happens to us by the whim of an outside agency. Our experience in the world is not haphazard. What may superficially appear to be absurd is in fact the effect of seeing the results of past actions in progress. We're seeing only one frame of a movie, without seeing what comes before or after the isolated freeze frame. For example: a child is struck by a car and is killed instantly. Is this the hand of fate, randomly selecting a victim here, a victim there, leaving grief in its wake? No, Vedanta says. We're only seeing the effect of an action that began long, long ago. Whatever actions a person has committed must take effect sometime or other. As we sow, so we reap. If we are reaping, there must have been some sowing somewhere along the line.

Does this make Vedanta a coldhearted, fatalistic religion? Isn't Vedanta saying that if a person suffers, he or she must have deserved it? Never.

Experience has shown that the more a person advances on the spiritual path, the more his heart broadens in love and sympathy for others. No one could love a Mary Magdalene more than a Jesus Christ; no one but a Ramakrishna could transform—through the sheer power of love—the debauched Girish Ghosh. Who but a Sarada Devi could say with utter conviction that the Muslim thief Amjad was as much her son as the monk Sarat, a beloved disciple of Ramakrishna? And who but a Buddha, overcome by pity, could offer his life for a goat? It is axiomatic that the more a person reflects the light of God, the less he condemns his fellow beings. Only an illumined soul can really love others with a full and open heart. The illumined soul, united with God, is freed from the bondage of egotism. With his or her "I" out of the way, he can truly feel the sufferings of others. "May I be born again and again," Swami Vivekananda declared,

> and suffer thousands of miseries so that I may worship the only God that exists, the only God I believe in, the sum total of all souls—and above all, my God the wicked, my God the miserable, my God the poor of all races, of all species, is the special object of my worship.

Hardly cold words of indifference. The illumined soul rejoices in others' happiness and intensely feels for them in their sorrow. Yet, in the core of his being, the illumined soul is free—detached from both happiness and misery, pleasure and pain. And he knows that those who suffer can—and eventually will—be as free as he or she is.

Having rid himself of the ego, the illumined soul has found the mine of bliss within himself. Anger, hatred, lust, ambition, and pettiness of every variety, can never trouble him. Peace is his permanent treasure; peace is his abode.

"What kind of meaning does life have?" the junior high school student asked. Its meaning is found in how we live it. Our goal is to manifest our innate divinity through every deed we do, every word we speak, every thought we think.

It is not an easy task, but no worthwhile endeavor ever is. What is important to remember is that no effort is lost. There is no failure in spiritual life. Every step that we take in the right direction is a permanent gain. Every one of us, whether we know it or not, has greatness within; every human being's life is infinitely precious. A meaningful life begins when we add a spiritual base to life's equation. "If you put fifty zeros after a one, you have a large sum," Sri Ramakrishna said. "But erase the one and nothing remains. It is the one that makes the many."

Life without an awareness of our innate divinity is a stack of zeros. Add the "1" of the divine Self, and a meaningful life is ours.

The Wisdom Teachings of India

by Richard Schiffman

"NEVER FORGET THE glory of human nature!" Vivekananda thundered to his American audience just before the turn of the century. "We are the greatest God . . . Christs and Buddhas are but waves on the boundless Ocean which *I AM.*" These words have echoed down through the decades, and they thrill us still. But the great Swami's words were themselves the echoes of much more ancient words, words that had been spoken at the dawn of history by sages whose names we have forgotten, but whose realizations have been blazoned into the spiritual memory of the human race.

What these realizations were can at best be hinted at but not communicated in words, however lofty; they can only finally be disclosed to us through the disciplines of jnana yoga in which we systematically detach ourselves from ever more subtle levels of our identification with thoughts, feelings, and objects. This practical philosophy was first spelled out in the Upanishads—there are a dozen major ones and numerous minor ones—a series of thematically connected expositions by unknown authors of the millennia before Christ. In these scriptures, which are regarded by scholars as the sourcebook of Indian philosophy, the seminal ideas which would be considerably developed in the various schools of Hindu and Buddhist thought are encountered, often for the first time and in the purity of their original conception. Nevertheless, the intention of their authors was far from polemical; the Upanishads are not compendiums of philosophy, but workbooks on the nature of the absolute Reality and the path to its attainment. Above all, the *rishis*—the ancient Indian sages—wished to evoke something of the experience itself—the ineffable breakthrough to that Ground of all existence, which the sages called, with refreshing simplicity, "the Self."

These spare treatises of great beauty, intensity, and revelatory power are set for the most part in the form of dialogues of spiritual guidance between youthful seekers and their enlightened masters, the immortal rishis. (The technique of dialogue in which the disciple questions the guru and is questioned in turn by the guru in a pointed effort to lay bare the hidden suppositions and sense of egohood which lie behind the disciple's own questioning remains one of the mainstays of jnana practice.) About these semimythical founding fathers of wisdom yoga, the rishis, we know very little save that they were jungle ascetics who had retired, often together with their wives and their disciples, to remote hermitages called *ashrams*, where they sustained themselves by herding cattle and gathering forest roots and fruits while experimenting with radical new modes of prayer, introspection, philosophical inquiry, and the rigorous control of body, mind, and emotions. The approaches pioneered by the rishis remain to this day the mainstays of Hindu mystical practice.

Living far from the concerns of the larger society, these sages nonetheless initiated a revolution in thought and spiritual practice which would spread throughout Asia and beyond, setting the basic agenda for the development of over two millennia of Eastern civilization—and just now sparking some interesting fireworks along the cutting edge of our own evolving Western civilization as well! They inaugurated an era of inward exploration which has continued until the present day. And they charted in breathless and enigmatic words—the only words possible for describing such a mystery!—the rough outlines of a realm as wide as the cosmos and equally as wondrous. For had not the sage of the Chandogya Upanishad declared: "The little space within the heart is as great as this vast universe. The heavens and the earth are there, and the sun and the moon, and the stars; fire and lightning and winds are there; and all that now is and all that is not: for the whole universe is in Him and He dwells within our heart."[1]

With words such as these, the rishis were the first to proclaim the virtually unlimited potential of consciousness, not as an abstract theoretical possibility, but as an experiential reality. They alone had gazed deep within the crystal ball of themselves to that placeless place where boundaries dissolve, shapes fall in on themselves and, instead of there being a person, all is a tissue of formless radiance within a boundless expanse of radiance. "I am the first-born of the world of truth, born before the gods, born in the center of immortality. I have gone beyond the universe and the light of the sun is my light."[2] Thrilled by such ecstatic declarations, generations of seekers have set out to prove for themselves the central contention of the Upanishads—that the physical creation which we perceive all around us, and that conventional figment of an identity which I call "myself" are but the fleeting shadows of an immaterial Absolute which alone is real and worthy of our striving.

This primal insight into the dreamlike nature of the world of appearances has an oddly contemporary resonance given the direction of modern scientific thought. Long before post-Newtonian physics "discovered" that matter is essentially energy in drag—$E=Mc^2$—the sages had already intuited that the physical universe is an emanation of that omnipotent Force, which they called *Shakti*. "By Primal Energy, all that exists is born; by Primal Energy all that exists is sustained; and into Primal Energy all that exists returns in the end."[3] Creation, according to this view, is neither static, nor at base even material, but a dynamism of ceaseless transformation, the ecstatic dance of the Divine Mother, Kali. The astrophysicist, the molecular biologist, the subatomic physicist could only agree! These investigators are now telling us that matter only appears solid and continuous from the vantage point of our narrowly time-bound and sense-bound mind, as the set for a Hollywood western only appears like a real town if we do not bother to look behind the facade; when we do take the trouble to investigate, however, we discover behind the solid-seeming front of matter a madly whirling array of virtually massless particles which themselves behave in ways more akin to forces than to independently existing things.

The sages would have found nothing to be surprised at in this! But unlike the material scientist, who has still proceeded no further than seeing the physical creation as a complex fabric of transmutation—vibratory energy in different modes and frequencies of expression—the ancients did not stop there. They went on to trace the ceaselessly arising waves and currents of Shakti, divine force, back to their origin, the shoreless expanse of oceanic Consciousness, the supersubstance of creation itself. And then they went still further, tracing Consciousness back to its transcendent Source, the incomprehensible fullness of the Absolute, the "region beyond darkness where there is neither day nor night, nor what is, nor what is not."[4]

Today such statements about a radically nondual and relationless Absolute as abound in the Upanishads will perhaps be hard for minds weaned on far more earthy food to digest, and we might wonder if they amount to little more than the airy dream of navel-gazing philosophers cut off from the grounding of material realities. But we should remember that the Absolute was not, for the rishis, a merely hypothetical *terra incognita* roughly scrawled upon some spiritualized mental map, but a place where they had actually been. The Upanishads are before all else the account of an actual journey. And as if making the ultimate journey to this "no-man's-land" beyond the apparent self were not enough, these sages were the first ones to attempt to describe the final destination by way of a sublime and an enigmatic poetry possessed of an uncanny power to arouse the intuition sleeping fitfully within modern women and men quite as much as it was fully awake and active within these inspired ancients.

A wise proverb states: "In each person there dwells a King. Speak to the King, and the King will come forth." The poetry of the Upanishads is speech directed to the King within all of us. It is kingly speech—lofty, sovereign, unassailable—speech whose unearthly cadences are as a "breath of the eternal" come down to our world of strife and division to awaken us from out of a bad dream. This arousing breath does not so much endeavor to describe the indescribable as it strives to *incite* the unthinkable leap, or perhaps we should say *to insight*. It was not explanation that the sages were aiming for, but in-sight, the direct seeing within the heart which sparks ecstasy and propels awareness explosively beyond all charts, all maps, all guides, all descriptions, all explanations whatsoever to the blazing core of Reality itself.

It should be clear, therefore, that for all the philosophical precision and uncompromising purity of their nondualism, tracing all phenomena back to a single transcendent Source, the rishis were far from being dry theoreticians; it was not ideas as such which interested them, nor the hairsplitting theological warfare which comes to dominate religious traditions during the centuries of their decline, but facts. And clearly, for them, the greatest fact of all, and the most self-evident, is the fact of the Atman. All other facts pale in comparison with this supreme fact. All other facts would collapse in an instant if it were not for this singular fact which, like the central pole of a circus tent, supports and sustains the provisional architecture of all created things. "Who could live, who could breathe, if that blissful Self dwelt not in the lotus of the heart?"[5]

But it was not this fact alone which concerned the sages, but also an act. Of equal importance with the fact of the Atman is the act of remembrance (*Atma-nishtha*) which makes it real for us. The Upanishads are nothing so much as a sustained exhortation to remember. "When there is a constant and unceasing remembrance of the Self, all bonds are loosed and freedom is attained," proclaims the Chandogya Upanishad.[6] It is crucial to remember the Self, for at the moment, nothing is so certain as the fact that we have forgotten it. "Forgetfulness is death," asserted the Jillellamudi Mother, a sage of modern India. And, by implication, you and I are the living dead who exist in a chronic state of forgetfulness of our true nature. Not only have we forgotten, but we have forgotten that we have forgotten. Not only are we lost, but we imagine that we are found. And to be lost and yet imagine that you are found is, the sages tell us, both here and hereafter to be beyond all hope of return.

So the Upanishads begin with the bottom-line reality that we are lost. They remind us time and again that our true Home is elsewhere. They spell out no detailed program for our return, for they were convinced that to consistently and deeply remember one's true Home is itself to return. All spiritual practices have no other aim than to foster this remembrance. But for these sages, who always emphasize the clear lines of spiritual first principles over and against the labyrinthine ways and means by which they get worked out in practice, all mechanical questions of technique were evidently of secondary importance, and they do not dwell on them.

Instead of getting bogged down in the nuts-and-bolts details of the plethora of spiritual paths, the masters of wisdom yoga speak to us words of remembrance. They do not advocate one approach over another approach; they feed the root of all paths by urging us to remember our true nature. Their statements are like so many fingers pointing towards the moon of the ultimate Reality. "Awake, arise! Strive for the Highest, and be in the Light."[7] Because of the generic nature of these teachings, they are capable of inspiring us on whatever spiritual path that we may have chosen to follow.

And yet we should not imagine, on account of their universality, that there is anything bland or watered down about the exhortations of the rishis. They speak to us words incandescent with the power of their own realization, words which bound like Durga's tiger over the chasm of the centuries and of civilizations, and of diverse spiritual traditions, words that are at one and the same time both inspirational and yet intensely practical and experiential in nature. And words almost monomaniacal in their unwavering purity of focus. For those who are temperamentally incapable of connecting with the living quality behind these words of power, the Upanishads are bound to seem repetitive, even monotonous. But others, those whose hunger for such refined "soul food" is keen, will find the wavelike nature of these repetitions richly evocative.

Much stress has traditionally been laid upon the value of repetition in the spiritual culture of India. In the West, by contrast, we tend to view repetition as being wearisome and mindless. We value novelty of thought and freshness of expression, often at the expense of depth of penetration. Traditional thinkers, however, are much more likely to appreciate the fact that there really is "nothing new under the sun." They also know that truth is not in its nature complex or convoluted, but transparently simple. And they know, moreover, that it is not intellectual comprehension or the nuanced subtlety of our mental grasp, but deep penetration into the core of that timelessly simple truth which really counts for something. The brunt of their effort therefore is not laboriously to convince the mind, and still less to indulge the mind's predilection for endless elucidation and elaboration, but rather to touch the soul where it lives. And these spiritual thinkers understood instinctively, what every poet knows from the gut, that nothing equals the power of cadenced and subtly repetitive speech to touch the soul and to open it out to its own innate Truth.

The Upanishads are a living expression of that understanding. They are full of repeated refrains, rhythmic devices, rhymes, puns, thoughts, and sentiments reiterated in slightly different ways, whose cumulative effect is to draw us gently out of ourselves and into the vital heart of their revelation. Sanskrit has long been regarded as a spiritually onomatopoetic language. That is to say, the sound of the words themselves are actual verbal equivalents of subtle spiritual states which correspond to (and indeed help to awaken, when they are properly recited) the experiences to which they refer. It is for this reason that the act of chanting the sacred language, which is believed to have been superconsciously revealed to the sages in their meditation, has a special potency. This potency is further amplified when the words in question were those of inspired scriptural texts, such as the Upanishads, which have overflowed into our human world from out of the intensities of direct spiritual experience.

We said before that the Upanishads are a tool to foster remembrance. To remember is an inward act of recollection by which we return to ourselves. It is often the case, however, that this subtle inward act of remembrance is prompted by that most explicit of outward acts, the act of memorization. As a first step toward remembering their true nature, the gurus of traditional India instructed their pupils to commit to memory the seminal texts which treat of it. This was of course a practical necessity in those days when books were not readily available, and the wisdom teachings were passed along verbally. But on a deeper level, there is a sense in which memorizing a text and reciting it out loud nourishes a special sort of intimacy which it is difficult to feel for the written word. To recite is a resonant act which involves the voice and also, by extension, the heart; whereas, to read, as often as not, takes place almost exclusively in the airless precincts of the mind alone. The English word "inspiration" refers to the breath and the voice (to inspire is also to breathe in). Reading a book is an abstract act—reciting a text most assuredly is not.

It is for this reason that the air of the Indian ashram rings to this day with the almost continual chanting of scriptural texts. Those who have been fortunate enough to experience this for themselves will attest to the remarkable energizing and purifying influence which chanting has on the very atmosphere. It goes without saying that what is called for here is not so much a rote and thoughtless repetition of sacred formulas as an alert and personal declaration of vital truths which one is in the process of making one's own. The spiritual aspirant recites words which are not the dead letters of still more dead sages, but a living, breathing presence within the heart. A presence which evokes in the chanter an ever-widening resonance of feeling, as well as a deepening intuitive appreciation for their import. Such conscious recitation of texts, prayers, and words of power—mantras—remains one of the cornerstones of the yoga of the Upanishads. "Let us learn the art of recitation, which calls for knowledge of letters, accent, measure, emphasis, sequence, and rhythm."[8]

As a start to the remembrance of the Self, we remember the words of the Self—chanting them, singing them, meditating upon them in silence, repeating them as mantras—allowing them to wash over the mind again and again in successive waves of expansion and purification. This repetition has a wondrous power to take the mind out of itself. For the sacred words of power are not like other words frozen into small conventional meanings like ice cubes in their tray. And the thoughts which they embody are not, like other thoughts, living quite obediently, quite securely and monotonously within their own four walls of significance as suburbanites in their tract homes. They are words and thoughts of power that are so wide no mind can ever embrace them or claim them as its own, so fluid that no conceptual framework can possibly contain them, no definition define them, no boundaries confine them, even including their own ostensible verbal bounds. For their very nature is to flow beyond all conceivable limits, including their own.

The words of scripture are fiery with the heat of their own inconceivable transcendence. Like molten lava, they respect none of the conventional divisions which reason thrives upon and logic demands. They just flow ever outward, inundating the fences which we construct around things, incinerating all of the crystallized structures of mind and form which stand in their path. The teachings of the sages are replete with such "megawords": Eternity, Atman, One, Deathless, Immutable, Freedom, Bliss, Light, Truth . . . words that are so absurdly large and unwieldy that they become almost meaningless, in a strictly intellectual sense. But words which exercise a powerful undertow upon the mind, nevertheless. Repeating them over and over again, even if at first only in a mechanical way, these wide, weird and wonderful, stark and unthinkable words begin to grip us with a strange fascination. They come to swell and glow at the peripheries of consciousness. And we come to feel their constant pressure on the mind. Not that we *understand* them, of course, or even so much as try to understand them except perhaps in the original sense of the term, which is to "stand under." We do indeed stand under these sublime words, these vast thoughts, and allow them to envelop us in their pervasive and oceanic power.

❊

1. Juan Mascaro, trans., *The Upanishads* (Baltimore: Penguin Books, 1965), Chandogya 8.1., p. 120.
2. Ibid., Taittiriya 3.10. 6., pp. 111-12.
3. Swami Prabhavananda and Frederick Manchester, trans., *The Upanishads: Breath of the Eternal* (Hollywood: Vedanta Press, 1947), Taittiriya, p. 89.
4. Mascaro, Svetasvatara 4.18., p. 92.
5. Prabhavananda, Taittiriya, p. 85.
6. Ibid., Chandogya, pp. 118-19.
7. Mascaro, Katha 1. 3. 14., p. 61.
8. Eknath Easwaran, trans.,*The Upanishads* (Petaluma, CA: Nilgiri Press, 1987), Taittiriya 1. 2., p. 137.

Meditation according to the Upanishads

by Swami Aseshananda

TRULY HAS THE poet said, "Our sincerest laughter with some pain is fraught." There is no abiding joy in all the multicolored experiences of life. In spite of our best efforts we cannot hold on to happiness. In the midst of enjoyment all of a sudden a crisis comes in the form of a painful disease or the death of a dear and near one.

Misgivings sway the mind. We seriously doubt the existence of the benevolent Being whom the theologians designate as God. Where is the proof? The problem becomes more complicated when we view the dark episodes, the hell of suffering, which good and righteous people have had to experience in their checkered lives.

The answer to this fundamental problem comes from a realm beyond reason. According to Vedanta, the mind is a storehouse of enormous energy. There are three faculties of the human mind which can be used for the apprehension of truth and the gathering in of knowledge. They are styled by the teachers of the Upanishads as instinct, reason, and intuition. Through instinct, by the urge of the subconscious, man performs his automatic and reflex actions. In instinctive deeds man is bereft of I-consciousness. Instinct develops into reason.

Reason functions on the conscious plane. Our intellectual pursuits and rational activities are associated with I-consciousness. Reason finds its fulfillment and highest consummation in the pure awareness of intuition. Intuition functions on the superconscious plane. Instinct acts with precision and accuracy in a limited sphere. The province of the intellect is better, but it cannot lay claim to infallible knowledge.

In the deeper problems of life only the light of intuition illumines the path and works as an unerring guide. Sometime or other we ask these fundamental questions: Who am I? Where do I come from? What is my destiny? But answers to these perplexing riddles cannot be found as long as we remain clogged within the bounds of the plodding intellect.

Doubtful conjectures and intellectual pastimes must be hushed into silence. Goethe rightly says: "Man's highest happiness as a thinker is to have fathomed what can be fathomed, and to bow down in reverence before the unfathomable."

Problems of God, the immortality of the soul, and the origin of the universe cannot be solved until we transcend the realm of the intellect. We must go to the other side of the prism in order to envisage the white light of unity which has not been disintegrated into parts and fragments. The Vedas speak of the futility and utter inadequacy of the mind in probing into the depths of the Reality which is at the back of the universe:

> Formless is He though inhabiting form. In the midst of the fleeting He abides forever. All-pervading and supreme is the Self. The wise man, knowing Him in His true nature, transcends all grief.

> The Self is not known through the study of the scriptures, nor through subtlety of the intellect, nor through much learning, but by him who longs for Him is He known. Verily, unto him the Self reveals His true being.

Religion does not consist in subscribing to this creed or that creed, but in actual realization, in coming face to face with God. Paying allegiance to a particular dogma or doctrine has only a secondary value. The substance of religion is not blind faith or intellectual understanding, but in being and becoming.

What counts most in spiritual life is character and a way of life molded by inner experience. The divinity within must be brought to one's perception.

The ultimate proof of God's existence is a unique spiritual experience. Our different senses and mind fail to apprehend Him because He is not an object. He is the eternal subject, the witness of the changing phenomena of the universe. Sri Ramakrishna used to tell the parable of the salt doll which went to the sea to measure its depth. As soon as it touched the water it melted and was fully absorbed in it. How then could it measure the depth of the sea? Similarly all descriptions of God by the limited mind are vain attempts to express the inexpressible.

Hence the Upanishads say:

> He who knows the joy of Brahman, which words cannot express and the mind cannot reach, is free from fear. He is not distressed by the thought, "Why did I not do what is right? Why did I do what is wrong?" He who knows the joy of Brahman, knowing both good and evil, transcends both.

All definitions of God by the human mind must be anthropomorphic. Silence is the homage that is to be paid in order to be able to describe the ineffable. The same truth was reiterated by Meister Eckhart when he said, "Why dost thou prate of God? Whatever thou sayest of him is not true."

God is the essence of bliss, the fount of eternal joy. All beings have sprung from bliss; they are maintained by bliss, and in the end they enter into the heart of bliss. Who could live, who could breathe, if the indwelling Self were not rooted in untrammeled felicity?

God is the repository of all blessed qualities. He is the immutable Spirit residing in the cave of the heart, drawing all people together. Beauty of form is only a dull reflection of the indescribable beauty of the Spirit. A physical body, however attractive it may appear, is dead insentient matter. The power of attraction does not belong to it: we must look for the pull of attraction elsewhere.

If nature, which is a mere patchy reflection, a shadow, is so beautiful, how marvelously beautiful must be the source, the mighty Spirit that pervades every atom of our being, every particle of the universe. There is a fascinating passage in the Brihadaranyaka Upanishad which says that the true basis of love is spiritual and divine.

After fulfilling the duties of the householder, when the evening of life approached, Yagnavalkya, in accordance with the ancient tradition of the Hindus, proposed to enter into monastic life. He called his wife, Maitreyi, apprised her of his intention, and gave her all the wealth and property that he possessed. Maitreyi was a spiritual woman given to thoughts of the evanescence of the world. She said to her husband, "My lord, if this whole earth belonged to me, with all its wealth, should I through its possession attain immortality?" Yagnavalkya replied, "No. Your life would be like that of the rich. None can possibly hope to attain immortality through wealth." Maitreyi said, "Then what need have I of wealth? Please, my lord, tell me what you know about the way to immortality." Then Yagnavalkya, in words of profound wisdom, explained the significance of human life:

> It is not for the sake of the husband, my beloved, that the husband is dear, but for the sake of the Self. It is not for the sake of the wife, my beloved, that the wife is dear, but for the sake of the Self. It is not for the sake of the children, my beloved, that the children are dear, but for the sake of the Self.

But how to attain the vision of God and realize one's divine destiny? The Vedas say, through yoga. The word yoga means "yoke" or "union"— union of the individual soul with the Supreme Soul.

Yoga has been erroneously interpreted as crystal gazing, fortune telling, fire eating, and other types of miracle-mongering. Yoga has nothing to do with any kind of miracles or occult practices. Yoga is a rational method of self-discipline and purification of the heart. "Blessed are the pure in heart, for they shall see God," says Christ.

The Upanishads preach that the best way of purifying the heart is through contemplation and meditation. Meditation has been defined as an unbroken stream of thought focused on an object, like oil which is poured from one vessel to another in a continuous flow. The purpose of meditation is to still the modifications of the mind. The mind may be compared to a lake. It is full of waves created by multifarious desires which are perpetually rising to the surface. On account of the agitated condition of the surface, we do not perceive our inmost Self, which is pure and divine. By the steady practice of meditation one can quell the waves and attain to perfect calmness, which nothing in the world can disturb.

The Upanishads speak of the heart, shaped like a lotus bud, as the most appropriate place for divine contemplation. It is also called *Brahmapura*, the abode of Brahman. As meditation deepens, the aspirant is blessed with subtle perceptions which make his mind tranquil like the unflickering flame of a lamp burning in a windless spot. At the culmination, the seeker after truth reaches the highest peak of realization in nirvikalpa samadhi—an all-annihilating experience in which space melts away and time stands still. The phenomenal world is totally obliterated from the consciousness of the meditator, and knowledge of Brahman saturates every fiber of his being. There is no more distinction of subject and object, and the seer is engulfed and absorbed in the bliss of Self-knowledge, transcending the bounds of sorrow and grief. Then all the fetters of the heart are broken, and all the doubts of the mind are resolved by the light of knowledge which dispels all gloom of ignorance forever.

The value of meditation cannot be overemphasized. Every Upanishad has a special chapter dealing with the method and means of meditation as an important practical discipline. Meditation is the *sine qua non* of spiritual realization. The daily practice of meditation is an essential prerequisite for a student of Vedanta, who views life as a sacred trust to be used for the emancipation of the soul, and for the service of humanity as the symbol and expression of God.

As one becomes absorbed in meditation, one realizes that the Self is separate from the body and for this reason will not be affected by disease, old age, or death. The first signs of progress in meditation are health, a sense of physical lightness, clearness of complexion, a beautiful voice, an agreeable odor of the person, and freedom from craving. "As a soiled piece of metal, when it has been cleaned, shines brightly, so the devotee in the body, when he has realized the truth of the Self, is freed from sorrow and attains to bliss."

Visions and voices and the supersensuous perception may be milestones on the road to realization, but they are not the whole story. They may be met with on the way, but one must not be attracted by their fascinating power. It is a precious saying—"Power corrupts." This saying is true in secular matters as well as in spiritual matters. It is best to ignore the visions and voices and keep perpetual vigil until the goal is reached.

The Upanishads constantly remind us that the path is sharp as a razor's edge and that slackening of effort due to inadvertence or self-complacency will mean disaster. One must practice meditation with unwavering zeal and inflexible determination till the veil is lifted and the face of Truth shines effulgent. As the Mundaka Upanishad says:

> Affix to the Upanishad, the bow incomparable, the sharp arrow of devotional worship; then, with mind absorbed and heart melted in love, draw the arrow and hit the mark—the imperishable Brahman. Om is the bow, the arrow is the individual being, and Brahman is the target. With a tranquil heart, take aim. Lose thyself in him, even as the arrow is lost in the target.

How long does it take to hit the mark and arrive at the goal? This cannot be answered categorically. Realization of the highest good and attainment of freedom is not a question of time. Emancipation refers to an experience that implies timelessness. It cannot be attained at any given moment. No time limit can be set. Everything depends upon *shraddha*, which means sincerity, intense longing, and an affirmative attitude towards life.

Negative thoughts are more deadly than a deadly poison. God is the searcher of our hearts. He knows all our inner motives. We can draw his sympathy only through self-surrender and humility of spirit. We cannot move him by eloquence or fine words. To the proud and the arrogant he is an all-exacting master. But to the meek and the gentle he is the ever-forgiving Father, kind and generous beyond human understanding. One who approaches him with bended knee and perfect resignation will surely be uplifted and brought within the orbit of his grace.

The experiences of all great men tell us that nothing but strenuous effort and dogged determination can remove the insurmountable barriers that we are to face in spiritual life—the barriers of egocentric tendencies and negative thoughts. What stands between man and God is of man's own making—his stubbornness of mind and his destructive doubts.

The only key that can unlock the door to divine realization is steady and persistent meditation. In the beginning, meditation will be dull and uninteresting, but if one continues even for a few days one will feel better and find some joy in it. This experience is due to the thrill of a new adventure which may be described as "beginner's luck." But it does not last. Instead, there will come a spell of dryness and dull monotony. The mind lapses into a state of torpidity. A kind of inertia sets in, and the aspirant feels a great abhorrence for contemplation. He is unwilling to make any fresh effort, and his spiritual life suffers a great setback. This experience is caused by an upsurge of emotions which were lying hidden in the subconscious mind. The residuals of past impressions are legion; in mystic literature they are referred to as "little imbecilities of the mind." As Swami Vivekananda says, "Some days or weeks when you are practicing, the mind will be calm and easily concentrated and you will find yourself progressing fast. Then, all of a sudden, the progress will stop, and you will find yourself as it were stranded. Persevere. All progress proceeds by such rise and fall."

There is no shortcut to spiritual progress. It is all uphill work. If the seeker after God can hold on and struggle with unremitting zeal and patience for three years, he will surely meet with some tangible results. His labor will never go in vain. The flame is to be kept burning by the sheer force of will.

The value of meditation will be felt when the mind is wholeheartedly and continuously absorbed in the thought of God. In the depth of meditation the senses will be stilled and there will come the sweetness of union. The aspirant will then feel the presence of the almighty Being in the inner sanctuary of his heart, and all his desires and aspirations will find their highest fulfillment in the joy of divine communion. In God alone he finds repose, and nothing can assail the peace and equanimity which will remain with him as an abiding possession.

Never again can the grim specter of depression invade his soul; his life will be a song to sustain and cheer him to the end of his days, and in the height of his spiritual experience he will truly know that: "From joy all beings are born; once born, by joy they are sustained, and into joy they enter after death."

Idolatry

by Aldous Huxley

EDUCATED PERSONS DO not run much risk of succumbing to the more primitive forms of idolatry. They find it fairly easy to resist the temptation to believe that lumps of matter are charged with magical power, or that certain symbols and images are the very forms of spiritual entities and, as such, must be worshiped or propitiated. True, a great deal of fetishistic superstition survives even in these days of universal compulsory education. But though it survives, it is not regarded as respectable; it is not accorded any kind of official recognition or philosophical sanction. Like alcohol and prostitution, the primitive forms of idolatry are tolerated, but not approved. Their place in the accredited hierarchy of spiritual values is extremely low.

Very different is the case with the developed and civilized forms of idolatry. These have achieved, not merely survival, but the highest respectability. The pastors and masters of the contemporary world are never tired of recommending these forms of idolatry. And not content with recommending the higher idolatry, many philosophers and many even of the modern world's religious leaders go out of their way to identify it with true belief and the worship of God.

This is a deplorable state of affairs, but not at all a surprising one. For, while it diminishes the risk of succumbing to primitive idolatry, education (at any rate of the kind now generally current) has a tendency to make the higher idolatry seem more attractive. The higher idolatry may be defined as the belief in, and worship of, human creation as though it were God. On its moral no less than on its intellectual side, current education is strictly humanistic and antitranscendental. It discourages fetishism and primitive idolatry; but equally it discourages any preoccupation with spiritual reality. Consequently, it is only to be expected that those who have been most thoroughly subjected to the educational process should be the most ardent exponents of the theory and practice of the higher idolatry. In academic circles, mystics are almost as rare as fetishists; but the enthusiastic devotees of some form of political or social idealism are as common as blackberries. Significantly enough, I have observed, when making use of university libraries, that books on spiritual religion were taken out much less frequently than in public libraries, frequented by persons who had not had the advantages, and the disadvantages, of advanced education.

The many kinds of higher idolatry may be classified under three main headings, technological, political, and moral. Technological idolatry is the most ingenuous and primitive of the three; for its devotees, like those of the lower idolatry, believe that their redemption and liberation depend upon material objects, namely machines and gadgets. Technological idolatry is the religion whose doctrines are explicitly or implicitly promulgated in the advertising pages of newspapers and magazines—the source from which millions of men, women, and children in the capitalist countries now derive their philosophy of life. In Soviet Russia, during the years of its industrialization, technological idolatry was promoted almost to the rank of a state religion. . . .

Military success depends very largely on machines. Because this is so, machines tend to be credited with the power of bringing success in every sphere of activity, of solving all problems, social and personal as well as military and technical. So wholehearted is the faith in technological idols that it is very hard to discover, in the popular thought of our time, any trace of the ancient and profoundly realistic doctrine of hubris and nemesis.

To the Greeks, hubris meant any kind of overweening and excess. When men or societies went too far, either in dominating other men and societies, or in exploiting the resources of nature to their own advantage, this overweening exhibition of pride had to be paid for. In a word, hubris invited nemesis. The idea is expressed very clearly and beautifully in "The Persians" of Aeschylus. Xerxes is represented as displaying inordinate hubris, not only by trying to conquer his neighbors by force of arms, but also by trying to bend nature to his will more than it is right for mortal man to do. For Aeschylus, Xerxes' bridging of the Hellespont is an act as full of hubris as the invasion of Greece, and no less deserving of punishment at the hand of nemesis. Today, our simple-hearted technological idolaters seem to imagine that they can have all the advantages of an immensely elaborate industrial civilization without having to pay for them.

Only a little less ingenuous are the political idolaters. For the worship of tangible material objects, these have substituted the worship of social and economic organizations. Impose the right kind of organizations on human beings, and all their problems, from sin and unhappiness to sewage disposal and war, will be automatically solved. Once more we look almost in vain for a trace of that ancient wisdom which finds so memorable an expression in the Tao Te Ching—the wisdom which recognizes (how realistically!) that organizations and laws are likely to do very little good where the organizers and lawmakers on the one hand, the organized and law-obeyers on the other, are personally out of touch with Tao, the Way, the ultimate Reality behind phenomena.

It is the great merit of the moral idolaters that they clearly recognize the need of individual reformation as a necessary prerequisite and condition of social reformation. They know that machines and organizations are instruments which may be used well or badly according as the users are personally better or worse. For the technological and political idolaters, the question of personal morality is secondary. In some not too distant future—so runs their creed—machines and organizations will be so perfect that human beings will also be perfect, because it will be impossible for them to be otherwise. Meanwhile, it is not necessary to bother too much about personal morality. All that is required is enough industry, patience, and ingenuity to go on producing more and better gadgets, and enough of these same virtues, along with a sufficiency of courage and ruthlessness, to work out suitable social and economic organizations and to impose them, by means of war or revolution, on the rest of the human race—entirely, of course, for the human race's benefit. The moral idolaters know very well that things are not quite so simple as this, and that, among the conditions of social reform, personal reform must take one of the first places. Their mistake is to worship their own ethical ideals instead of worshiping God, to treat the acquisition of virtue as an end in itself and not as a means—the necessary and indispensable condition of the unitive knowledge of God.

"Fanaticism is idolatry." (I am quoting from a most remarkable letter written by Thomas Arnold in 1836 to his old pupil and biographer-to-be, A.P. Stanley.) "Fanaticism is idolatry; and it has the moral evil of idolatry in it; that is, a fanatic worships something which is the creation of his own desires, and thus even his self-devotion in support of it is only an apparent self-devotion; for in fact it is making the parts of his nature or his mind, which he least values, offer sacrifice to that which he most values. The moral fault, as it appears to me, is the idolatry—the setting up of some idea which is most kindred to our own minds, and the putting it in the place of Christ, who alone cannot be made an idol and inspire idolatry, because he combines all ideas of perfection, and exhibits them in their just harmony and combination. Now, in my own mind, by its natural tendency—that is, taking my mind at its best—truth and justice would be the idols I should follow; and they would be idols, for they would not supply *all* the food which the mind wants, and whilst worshiping them, reverence and humility and tenderness might very likely be forgotten. But Christ himself includes at once truth and justice and all these other qualities too. . . . Narrow-mindedness tends to wickedness, because it does not extend its watchfulness to every part of our moral nature and the neglect fosters the growth of wickedness in the parts so neglected.''

As a piece of psychological analysis this is admirable, so far as it goes. But it does not go quite far enough; for it omits all consideration of what has been called grace. Grace is that which is given when, and to the extent to which, a human being gives up his own self-will and abandons himself, moment by moment, to the will of God. By grace our emptiness is fulfilled, our weakness reinforced, our depravity transformed. There are, of course, pseudograces as well as real graces—the accessions of strength, for example, that follow self-devotion to some form of political or moral idolatry. To distinguish between the true grace and the false is often difficult; but as time and circumstances reveal the full extent of their consequences on the personality as a whole, discrimination becomes possible even to observers having no special gifts of insight. Where the grace is genuinely "supernatural," an amelioration in one aspect of personality is not paid for by atrophy or deterioration in another. Virtue is achieved without having to be paid for by the hardness, fanaticism, uncharitableness, and spiritual pride, which are the ordinary consequences of a course of stoical self-improvement by means of personal effort, either unassisted or reinforced by the pseudograces which are given when the individual devotes himself to a cause, which is not God, but only a projection of one of his own favorite ideas. The idolatrous worship of ethical values in and for themselves defeats its own object—and defeats it not only because, as Arnold rightly insists, there is a lack of all-round watchfulness, but also and above all because even the highest form of moral idolatry is God-eclipsing, a positive guarantee that the idolater shall fail to achieve unitive knowledge of Reality.

❋

Faith

by Pravrajika Bhavaprana

FAITH. WE COULD not live a day without it. We cross a street corner with the faith that the stopped cars will not run over us; we submit ourselves to the surgeon's knife with the faith that he will cure our disease; we rely on our friends with the faith that they will help us in our time of need. The examples of faith as a dynamic and constructive force in our lives are limitless and they demonstrate the truth of Tolstoy's statement, "Faith is the force of life."

Yet, ironically, when it comes to having faith in God, a multitude of doubts surface. We question the validity of having faith in the unseen and unknown. When the same faith that moves our everyday life is directed toward God, it is called "blind faith." But isn't all faith blind? "Has faith an eye?" asked Sri Ramakrishna. "Speak either of faith or of direct knowledge."

Nevertheless, the label of "blind faith" remains and carries with it all sorts of undesirable connotations. The classic example of blind faith is the individual who accepts, without question, every word in the scriptures as the literal truth, even though it may directly contradict scientifically proven facts. With the mind closed to doubt and reason, faith becomes rigid, unyielding, and easily demolished. Such faith is usually a product of laziness, ignorance, or fear. This faith is indeed "blind" and is worthy of the derision it often receives.

But to cover all faith in God under a blanket of irrationality and rigidity is unjust. The implication is that reason and faith in God do not and cannot coexist, when in fact one must first open the door to doubt and reason before genuine faith in God can be cultivated. We are fools to accept whatever we read or hear as the truth without first subjecting it to critical scrutiny in the light of reason. If it passes this test, if it satisfies reason, it should be accepted and held onto with unswerving faith. If not, it should be discarded as mere superstition. Swami Vivekananda once said, "Be an atheist if you want, but do not believe in anything un-questioningly."

Although real faith is founded upon reason, it is not limited to reason. Faith often takes us where reason cannot penetrate, such as to the belief in the existence of God.

Intellectual conviction is essential, but this in itself is not faith. It is merely rational belief. When conviction in the mind is followed by a response in the heart, when our beliefs touch our hearts and change our lives, only then do we begin to have true faith.

How can we attempt to understand lofty spiritual truths with our limited intellect? The finite cannot comprehend the infinite. Reason can lead us only to a certain point after which faith must take over and carry us to the final realization of God.

Faith in God develops gradually. It often begins with a feeling of interest in an aspect of God or in a spiritual teaching we have heard or read. The idea intrigues us at first, and we inquire further into its meaning and import. After delving into it, reasoning upon it, and discovering that it satisfies reason, we reach the stage of intellectual acceptance. But this is not enough. We still feel unfulfilled and restless. When we begin to feel intuitively that the Lord is present within us, the seed of faith is beginning to mature.

Intuitive knowledge transcends intellectual knowledge. For example, someone has told you that your friend is in the next room. Upon entering the room, you find it completely dark and not a sound is heard. Since you were told your friend was there, you intellectually believe it. Yet doubt comes finding the room dark and silent. Then you begin to feel the presence of someone else in the room. The feeling is an intuitive one since you cannot see or hear anything. Yet it is strong enough to eliminate many of your doubts. Then at last, the light is turned on and you find yourself face to face with your friend. All doubts vanish with this direct perception.

Once we see the Lord, once we experience that ultimate Reality, nothing can shake our faith. If I see a table before me, nothing or no one can convince me that the table does not exist. My faith in the existence of the table is unshakable because I directly perceive it. If my friend writes to me of a table she has bought, I accept her word, believing she now has such a table. But the table becomes truly real for me when I have seen it and touched it. This is the epitome of faith—belief based on direct perception. Complete faith in God comes only after one has directly perceived and experienced him.

But until the faith of experience comes, we need a working faith, a faith in the unseen. In the Bible we read, "Blessed are they that have not seen, and yet have believed." This faith, this firm belief in the living presence of God, is the essence of spiritual life. Faith is something which on the surface appears so easy to obtain. Yet as we strive to acquire it, we realize how difficult and how rare it is to have real faith in God having never seen him. After years of conditioning in a society that measures intelligence by cynicism about belief in anything outside direct sense perception, acquiring simple, childlike faith in the unseen becomes arduous.

Sri Ramakrishna once said, "Unless a man is guileless, he cannot so easily have faith in God. God is far, far away from the mind steeped in worldliness. Worldly intelligence creates many doubts and many forms of pride—pride of learning, wealth, and the rest." We find ourselves faced with the task of getting rid of the intellectual jargon in our minds and the emotional turmoil in our hearts, which only serve as breeding grounds for doubts, and replacing them with guileless, childlike faith in God. The faith of a child is such that if his mother says there is a bogeyman or a ghost, there *is* one. And there is no doubt in his mind that such an entity does indeed exist.

Childlike faith is different from blind faith. The faith of the child is open, spontaneous, and receptive, without motive or thought of self. In contrast, the faith of a fanatic is closed, willed, and unsympathetic. Blind faith is usually motivated by fear, a need for security, or a desire for acceptance.

Firm faith and absolute trust in the Lord within is necessary before surrender to him is possible. Would you think of resigning yourself to the will of someone you did not trust wholeheartedly? Our faith in the Lord must be so great that we are ready and willing to entrust our body, mind, and soul to him. When we reach this lofty point in spiritual life, self-surrender will follow naturally.

To have faith when everything is going well is not too difficult. But the true test of genuine faith is to have complete trust in the Lord in the midst of trials, troubles, and temptations. In the words of Sri Ramakrishna, "The stone may remain in water for numberless years and yet the water will never penetrate it. But clay is soon softened into mud by coming in contact with water. So the strong heart of the faithful does not despair in the midst of trials and persecutions, but the man of weak faith is shaken, even by the most trifling cause."

From time to time, through prayer and spiritual discipline, we may get glimpses of the beauty and majesty of God, and every now and then we may feel a particle of his tremendous love for us. These glimpses serve to restore and build our faith in God.

Obstructions, disappointments, and dry periods are bound to come and with them doubts creep into the mind. But in the midst of these trials, we should try to recall the glimpses we have had and try to feel again that faith and love that accompanied them. By regaining our faith through recollection, we are able to overcome or at least endure the hard blows in life. By exercising patience and a healthy sense of perspective, we are able to ride out the turbulent tide of events without being capsized.

Most of us have assumed since childhood that God exists. Why then do we continually allow ourselves to be caught in the clutches of the world, to be consumed by our own petty little desires, to be ruled over by the materialism of our society? Because we lack faith. Our belief in the existence of God is only in the mind and has not yet reached the heart.

If we really had faith that the very source of all love, knowledge, and joy was within us and was attainable, we would go mad to get it. Our longing would be unbearable and would know no bounds. The story is told of a thief who knows there is gold in the next room and he stays up all night thinking of nothing else but how to get it. His entire mind is riveted to the gold. So it is with faith, having which our only desire would be to see God face to face, to experience and become one with that Reality.

These Shackles Must Be Broken

by George Fitts

EVERY GREAT TEACHER, every scripture has impressed upon us again and again the necessity of belief. What must we believe? Whom shall we believe—and why?

We are repeatedly told that "whoso believeth shall never thirst—shall have everlasting life." We read these words in the scriptures, we hear them from spiritual teachers, we repeat them over and over, we try to meditate upon their meaning, yet still there remains for many of us that cloud of doubt, that cloud of incomprehension, that cloud of unbelief.

Is it that we intellectually grasp the significance of the words, but that the feeling of their reality and of their attainability and of their present immediate practicability seems so lifeless to our world-trained senses, our outgoing desires, and our educated ignorances?

We live and are apparently controlled by the misconception that the spiritual world is a world of illusion. The mass mind has accepted the physical, outer, apparent world as the reality, and the spiritual inner real world as the illusion. Hence comes our unbelief. We instinctively refuse the truth. Our feelings are attached to the illusions of ignorance.

These shackles must be broken. This can be done by creating the right feeling toward God, the right feeling toward the promises of the scriptures and the spiritual teachers. The Upanishads tell us: "With the thought, 'why do I fear' disappears all fear, for fear comes of duality." In the same way it would seem that by questioning "why do I disbelieve," by realizing the intensity of our ignorance, this unbelief is gradually lessened, and finally it disappears.

Through discrimination, we no longer ignore the fundamental truth—the supreme principle of existence, bliss, and knowledge which lies within each and every one of us. It is attainable and to be known even in this very life. This attainment may be experienced by all who have a living faith in God, in the spiritual teacher, in the scriptures, and a living faith in the permanently unblemishable purity of one's own soul—concealed though that purity is, temporarily, by the mask of materialism.

It is then only, through the grace of the Lord, the grace of the guru, and the grace of the individual mind, that the multiples of the One are realized to be but different aspects of the same substance—the one unchanging principle of light, of consciousness, of bliss.

The Self in one is the Self in all. The Lord in one is the Lord in all. We have to seek to find the shadowless light, the silent light of eternity. And by this light we shall consciously realize that the light, the lighted, and the lighter are one. The omnipresent light of consciousness is the omnipresent presence of God, the source of all.

May we nourish and intensify our belief in the Word, and by so doing may we conquer our racial, inherited, and acquired beliefs. May we realize God here and now. May we seek God wholeheartedly. May we consciously dwell in him, even as he dwells in us. May our famished souls be nourished by that bread of life, which is our very Self.

Peace

by Swami Swahananda

THROUGHOUT THE AGES, mankind has yearned for peace—world peace, national peace, community peace, and peace of the individual soul. This coveted yet elusive goal has been relentlessly pursued on the international level through peace talks, peace treaties, peace summits, and so forth. In a letter written by Leo Tolstoy, which was enthusiastically endorsed by Mahatma Gandhi, he expressed doubt that peace could be achieved by these methods. He wrote: "One thing only is needful: the knowledge of the simple and clear truth which finds place in every soul that is not stupefied by religious and scientific superstitions—the truth that for our life one law is valid—the law of love, which brings the highest happiness to every individual as well as to all mankind."

International peace can come only if there is national peace, and national peace can come only if there is individual peace. If the world is in turmoil today, it is because its inhabitants are in turmoil. World peace begins with each one of us. As the well-known Russian painter and thinker Nicholas Roerich said, "Every man, every member of the human family, carries the responsibility for the peace of the whole world."

A society is the summation of individuals. The values of a society are determined by its individuals, and the force of inequality in society, strengthened by selfish considerations, has to be kept under control.

The force that can hold society together is moral force, *dharma*, the consideration for the other person. This deep value in mankind, which enhanced becomes altruism, is possible only in an atmosphere of "toned-down materialism" and assertion of the Spirit. If the individuals value sense gratification and money, the society will be materialistic; if the individuals value intellectual pursuits, the society will be advanced in science and technology; if the individuals value the arts, the society will be cultured. Only if the individuals place the highest value on spiritual awakening, will the society be a peaceful one.

The jewel of everlasting peace is within each one of us, only waiting to be discovered. It is futile to try to find peace outside if we have not found it inside. As Swami Vivekananda said, "It is only with the knowledge of the Spirit that the faculty of want is annihilated forever. . . . Spiritual knowledge is the only thing that can destroy our miseries forever; any other knowledge satisfies wants only for a time."

Lasting peace cannot be found in the external world. In fact, it is our identity with the external world that causes inner conflict and anxiety. Peace comes through detachment and renunciation. It is not an emotion but the suspension of emotions. We can feel this temporary absence of emotion, and the peace associated with it, during an aesthetic experience. Aristotle said that the fine arts act as a catharsis. What is left after the outpouring of an emotion? An inner feeling of peace and harmony, at least until another emotion arises.

The only way to achieve lasting peace, however, is to detach ourselves from our emotions and transcend the ego. We read in the Bhagavad Gita: "The man who lives completely free from desires, without longing, devoid of the sense of 'I' and 'mine' attains peace."

The path to eternal peace is not an easy one. It requires self-sacrifice and self-control. To quote Thomas à Kempis, "All men desire peace, but very few desire those things that make for peace." In order to achieve inner peace, we must restructure the way we now think and feel. Peace, to be a part of our character, must be continually practiced. For, as Swami Vivekananda said, "Character is repeated habits." "Blessed are the peacemakers," said the Bible. But the peace must be a victory that defeats none. To quote Abraham Lincoln, "With malice towards none, with charity for all."

Peace and truth are interrelated. Mahatma Gandhi said:

> The way of peace is the way of truth. Truthfulness is even more important than peacefulness. Indeed, lying is the mother of violence. A truthful man cannot long remain violent. He will perceive in the course of his search that he has no need to be violent and he will further discover that so long as there is the slightest trace of violence in him, he will fail to find the truth he is searching.

The fundamental nature of man, says Vedanta, has two important characteristics: freedom and equality. These two aspects have found expression in man's urge for freedom and equality in the social realm as well. Each of the two main ideals of social and political systems of the world, democracy and socialism, emphasizes one of these fundamental urges of mankind.

The world has dreamt of unity in humankind. As Tennyson expressed in *Locksley Hall*: "Till the war-drum throbbed no longer, and the battle flags were furled . . . in the Parliament of man, the Federation of the world." The idea of glory through destruction must be replaced by positive efforts towards peaceful cooperation. "Peace hath her victories," wrote Milton to Cromwell, "no less renown'd than war."

There are two classes of people working for peace. One strives to uplift humanity by eliminating tension, rivalry, and confrontation which culminate in skirmishes and war. They advocate peace as a necessity, especially in these times of nuclear development. The other class just *lives* peace by putting into practice the principles of peace. They are the deeply spiritual souls who have become identified with peace in their attitude and conduct. They exude peace. We honor the people who labor for peace because of its urgent need in this world of strife and tension, but we love the souls who *live* peace. That is why saints are so much loved and venerated.

Modern science now accepts the theory that the essence of all matter is energy, a theory which unifies the physical world. Long before the birth of Einstein, this unity was declared by the sages of the Upanishads who realized this through inspiration, or intuition. Their philosophy, Vedanta, teaches that the essence of all existence is the eternal, changeless Brahman—Existence, Knowledge, Bliss absolute. In the Chandogya Upanishad we read, "All this is verily Brahman." That is, not merely mankind, but all creation is the manifestation of the same Reality.

Everlasting peace can be found only by becoming one with the infinite, blissful Brahman. In order to experience this unity we must transcend all differences and limitations. "Here, on earth," said Swami Vivekananda, "we strive to enclose little spaces and exclude outsiders. . . . our aim should be to wipe out these little enclosures, to widen the boundaries until they are lost sight of."

Beauty, philosophy, and science, when taken to their highest point, break the boundaries that separate us and lead the way to unity. The greatest value of artistic, intellectual, and spiritual culture is that it inspires us to expand beyond ourselves. Leo Tolstoy said: "Human life . . . is always striving for divine perfection that it is able to attain only in infinity. . . . Only the aspiration towards this perfection is enough to take the directions of man's life away from the animal condition . . . towards the divine condition."

Our awareness should expand from consideration of the self to those of the family, to community, to country, to mankind, and ultimately to all of existence. Such expansion leads to greater appreciation of the diversity in the world. We cannot appreciate this diversity if we are self-centered and assume that our way is the best and only way. When we realize our unity with all existence, we realize that diversity is merely a change in appearance. Swami Vivekananda said, "Nature is unity in variety—an infinite variation in the phenomenal—as in and through all these variations of the phenomenal runs the Infinite, the Unchangeable, the Absolute Unity."

All the differences that cause discord have their origin in our perceptions of name and form, perceptions we have superimposed upon the essential unity of the universe. We have separated ourselves so much from the unity which pervades this world that we have become enemies of nature. This situation has reached crisis proportions. While civilization evolved from man's attempt to control nature, he became isolated from it. He has forgotten that he is one with nature. Ecological considerations get the fullest support from this idea of the unity of existence. Rabindranath Tagore wrote, "When we become merely man, but not man-in-the-universe, we create bewildering problems. . . . But this cannot go on forever. Man must realize the wholeness of his existence, his place in the infinite." Thus we see that in unity alone is lasting peace.

"This idea of oneness is the great lesson India has to give," said Swami Vivekananda,

> and mark you, when this is understood, it changes the whole aspect of things, because you look at the world through other eyes than you have been doing before. And this world is no more a battlefield where each soul is born to struggle with every other soul and the strongest gets the victory and the weakest goes to death. It becomes a playground where the Lord is playing like a child, and we are His playmates, His fellow-workers.

In this exalted state, eternal peace is ours.

Our efforts to attain peace should be approached on different fronts. Social and political measures will directly facilitate efforts for peace. Cultural and religious movements and institutions will create the climate for peace. In all types of groups—regional, national, and international—stress will have to be given to harmony and not to difference.

An awareness of different cultures and religions will have to be made with an effort to find the unity behind all. Spiritual and cultural communities will thus lessen tension and bring about understanding and peace.

Higher virtues conducive to individual and collective peace will have to be practiced. Altruism and selfless service will have to be encouraged.

May strength and conviction grow in us as we proceed with our own personal struggle for peace, and may they also unite our efforts towards world peace.

Shanti Shanti Shanti
Peace   Peace   Peace.

The Gita and War

by Christopher Isherwood

IN THE COURSE of a year spent studying the Bhagavad Gita, I have talked about its philosophy to a considerable number of people. Whatever else they had to say, I found them, almost without exception, agreed on one point: that the Gita "sanctions" war. Some were glad of this. Others were sorry. But all, I think, were puzzled. Educated in the Christian tradition, they were accustomed to a gospel which is uncompromisingly pacifist. However deeply they might be convinced of the justice or necessity of some particular conflict, they didn't like what they regarded as a general approval of the use of military force. They themselves, mere human beings struggling in the everyday world, might be driven to fight and kill one another, but they wanted Krishna, like Jesus, to stand for a higher ideal. That was their reaction.

I do not wish to sound superior or conceited when I say that I myself do not put this interpretation upon the teaching of the Gita. I will try to explain why I do not: not merely for the information of the few people who may be interested, but because I want to straighten out my own ideas. The question is of the greatest importance to me, because I am myself a pacifist, and because I believe the Gita to be one of the major religious documents of the world. If its teachings did not seem to me to agree with those of the other gospels and scriptures, then my own system of values would be thrown into confusion, and I should feel completely bewildered.

Briefly, the circumstances of the Gita dialogue can be described as follows:

Two factions, closely bound to each other by ties of blood and friendship, are about to engage in a civil war. Arjuna, one of the leading generals, has Krishna for his charioteer. Krishna has told Arjuna that he will not fight, but has promised to accompany him throughout the battle. Just before it begins, Arjuna asks Krishna to drive his chariot into the no-man's-land between the two armies. Krishna does so. Arjuna looks at the opposing army, and realizes that he is about to kill those whom he loves better than life itself. In his despair, he exclaims: "I will not fight!"

Krishna's reply to Arjuna occupies the rest of the book. It deals not only with Arjuna's immediate personal problem, but with the whole nature of action, the meaning of life, and the aims for which man must struggle, here on earth. At the end of their conversation, Arjuna has changed his mind. He is ready to fight. And the battle begins.

Before trying to analyze Krishna's arguments, I must mention two points which certain commentators have raised with regard to the battle itself. In the first place, it is sometimes said that the battle of Kurukshetra cannot possibly be compared to a battle in modern war. It was, in fact, a kind of tournament, governed by all the complex and humane rules of ancient Indian chivalry. A soldier mounted upon an elephant may not attack a foot soldier. No man may be struck or shot at while running away. No one may be killed who has lost his weapons. And we are told, in the *Mahabharata*, that the opposing armies stopped fighting every evening, and even visited each other and fraternized during the night. In the second place, it is sometimes said that the whole battle is to be regarded allegorically. Arjuna is the individual man, Krishna is the indwelling Godhead, the enemies are man's evil tendencies, and so forth.

All this is interesting, of course. But it has nothing to do with our problem. If Krishna is only talking figuratively, or only about war under certain conditions, then the Gita is just a fable, an archaic curiosity: we need not discuss it. Personally, I prefer to forget Kurukshetra and ancient India altogether, and imagine a similar dialogue taking place today. . . .

To understand the Gita, we must first consider what it is and what it is not. We must consider its setting. When Jesus spoke the words which are recorded as the Sermon on the Mount, he was talking to a group of followers in the most peaceful atmosphere imaginable, far from the great city, far from all strife and confusion. He was expressing the highest truth of which man's mind is capable, in general terms, without reference to any immediate crisis or problem. And even in the Garden of Gethsemane, when he told Peter to sheathe his sword, he was addressing a dedicated disciple, a monk, a man who was being trained to preach and live the spiritual life. For Peter, there could be no compromise. He must learn to accept the highest and strictest ideal, the ideal of nonviolence.

The Gita is very different. Krishna and Arjuna are on a battlefield. Arjuna is a warrior by birth and profession. He corresponds to the medieval knight of Christendom. His problem is considered in relation to the circumstances of the moment. The Gita fits into the narrative of an epic poem, the *Mahabharata*, and must be read in the light of previous happenings. It is not simply a sermon, a philosophical treatise.

This, I believe, is the cause of much misunderstanding. We all tend to remember most clearly the part of a book which we read first. The opening chapters of the Gita deal with a particular case: they are concerned with a soldier and the duties of a soldier. Later on, Krishna passes from the particular to the general, and utters those same truths which were afterwards taught by Jesus and the Buddha. But the first impression is apt to remain. The superficial reader closes the book and remembers only Arjuna and the battle. He says to himself: "Krishna tells us that we must fight."

Krishna, it must be repeated, is not talking to a monk. We ought to be glad of this, not sorry. The vast majority of mankind are not monks, but householders. What a great teacher has to say to a married man, a soldier, is of immediate interest to the world at large.

We must realize, also, that Krishna, in teaching Arjuna, employs two sets of values, the relative and the absolute. This duality is inherent in the circumstances of the story. For Krishna is both Arjuna's personal friend and his illumined teacher. He is a fellow-mortal and he is God. As God, he expresses the absolute truth, the highest ideal. As a fellow-man, he presents the relative values which apply to Arjuna's particular condition. Considered superficially, this duality of attitude may seem to produce contradictions. Carefully studied, it will be seen to compose into a complete and satisfying philosophical picture. For life itself is double-faced, and any attempt at simplification will only bring us to ultimate confusion.

One circumstance renders Arjuna's compassion suspect: its occasion. Arjuna himself is dimly aware of this. "Is this real compassion I feel," he asks Krishna, "or only a delusion? My mind gropes about in darkness. I cannot see where my duty lies." Up to this moment, Arjuna has not hesitated. He has accepted the necessity of the war. He has assumed responsibility for its leadership. Then, suddenly, he sees the other side of the picture: the bloodshed, the horror. And he recoils.

In the years that followed the 1914-1918 war, much pacifist propaganda was based on gruesome narratives of battle and books of photographs showing mutilated corpses. "This is what war is like," said the authors. "Isn't it horrible? Do you want to go through this again?" And nearly everybody agreed that they didn't. But this sort of revulsion is always short-lived, because it appeals, fundamentally, to our cowardice.

When a new war situation develops, most of us react in the opposite direction, and rightly. Men can never, ultimately be deterred from any course of action by cowardice alone. Otherwise we should never have evolved from the jellyfish. We have to go forward, and the path is always dangerous, in one way or another. Arjuna has to go forward. Krishna tells him so. Arjuna must accept the sum of his actions up to that moment— and the sum is this battle.

Krishna's reply begins by dealing with Arjuna's feelings of revulsion, on general grounds. Arjuna shrinks from the act itself, the act of killing. Krishna reminds him that, in the absolute sense, there is no such act. The Atman, the indwelling Godhead, is the only reality. This body is simply an appearance: its existence, its destruction, are alike illusory. In the absolute sense, all talk of killing or being killed is meaningless.

> Some say this Atman
> Is slain, and others
> Call It the slayer:
> They know nothing.
> How can It slay
> Or who shall slay It?

Therefore, if Arjuna is objecting to the act of killing, as such, he need have no scruples. For he only seems to kill.

Then, with one of those changes of viewpoint which may bewilder and shock a reader who opens the Gita for the first time and takes only its surface meaning, Krishna begins to talk to Arjuna as man to man:

"Even if you consider this from the standpoint of your own caste-duty, you ought not to hesitate; for, to a warrior, there is nothing nobler than a righteous war. . . .

"But if you refuse to fight this righteous war, you will be turning aside from your duty. You will be a sinner, and disgraced. People will speak ill of you throughout the ages."

For Arjuna, a member of the warrior caste, the fighting of this battle, in defense of his family and property, is undoubtedly "righteous." It is his duty. In the Gita, we find that the caste system is presented as a kind of natural order. People are divided into four groups, according to their capacities and characteristics. Each group has its peculiar duties, ethics, and responsibilities; and these must be accepted. It is the way of spiritual growth.

A person must go forward from where he stands. He cannot jump to the Absolute: he must evolve toward it. He cannot arbitrarily assume the duties which belong to another group. If he does so, his whole system of values will be upset, his conscience can no longer direct him, and he will stray into pride or doubt or mental confusion. "Prefer to die doing your own duty," Krishna teaches: "The duty of another will bring you into great spiritual danger."

Socially, the caste system is graded. The merchants are above the servants. The leaders and warriors are above the merchants. The priestly brahmins are highest of all. But, spiritually, there are no such distinctions. Krishna is very clear on this point. Everyone, he says, can attain the highest sainthood by following the prescribed path of his own caste-duty. In Southern India, we are told of seven saints who belonged to the lowest caste of all, the untouchables. And the same principle, of course, holds true if we apply the caste-classification to the social pattern of Europe. Men have grown into spiritual giants while carrying out their duties as merchants, peasants, doctors, popes, scullions, or kings.

In the purely physical sphere of action, Arjuna is, indeed, no longer a free agent. The act of war is upon him: it has evolved out of his previous actions. He cannot choose. "If, in your vanity, you say 'I will not fight,' your resolve is vain. Your own nature will drive you to the act." At any given moment in time, we are what we are; and our actions express that condition. We cannot run away from our actions, because we carry the condition with us. On the highest mountain, in the darkest cave, we must turn at last and accept the consequences of being ourselves. Only through this acceptance can we begin to evolve further. We may select the battleground. We cannot avoid the battle.

Arjuna is bound by the law of karma, the law of cause and effect which has brought him face to face with this particular situation. Now he is compelled to act, but he is still free to make his choice between two different ways of performing the action. Krishna introduces this great theme—the principal theme of the Gita—in the passage which immediately follows. He proceeds to define the nature of action.

In general, mankind almost always acts with attachment: that is to say, with fear and desire. Desire for a certain result, and fear that this result will not be obtained. Attached action binds us to the world of appearance, to the continual doing of more action. We live in a delirium of doing, and the consequences of our past actions condition the actions we are about to perform. According to the Gita, it is attached action which compels us to revisit this world, to be reborn again and again.

But there is another way of performing action; and this is without fear and without desire. The Christians call it "holy indifference," and the Hindus "nonattachment." Both names are slightly misleading. They suggest coldness and lack of enthusiasm. That is why people often confuse nonattachment with fatalism, when, actually, they are opposites. The fatalist simply does not care. He will get what is coming to him. Why make any effort? Fatalists are apt to get drunk or spend most of the day in bed.

The doer of nonattached action, on the other hand, is the most conscientious of men. He does not run away from life: he accepts it, much more completely than those whose pleasures are tinged with anxiety and whose defeats are embittered by regret. No matter whether he is sweeping out a room, or calculating the position of a star, or taking the chair at a meeting, he does it to the utmost limit of his powers—so carefully, so devotedly, so wholeheartedly, that the dividing line between the chosen activity and the necessary chore disappears altogether. All work becomes equally and vitally important. It is only toward the results of work that he remains indifferent. Perhaps a dog runs across the clean floor with muddy paws. Perhaps his researches are recognized by Harvard University. Perhaps somebody throws a rotten egg at him. It doesn't matter. He goes right on with his job.

We find something of this spirit in the lives of all truly great men and women, including the professed atheists and agnostics. Madame Curie refuses the Legion of Honor with the matter-of-fact words: "I don't see the utility of it." Lenin, in 1921, with the White armies converging on Moscow, his regime apparently doomed, his work brought to nothing, calmly sits down and writes the order: "The peasants in the localities of Gorki and Ziianova are immediately to be supplied with electric light." This, in its highest development, is the attitude of the saint.

When action is done in this spirit, Krishna teaches, it will lead us to true wisdom, to the knowledge of what is behind action, behind all life: the ultimate Reality. And, with the growth of this knowledge, the need for further action will gradually fall away from us. The law of karma will cease to operate. We shall realize our true nature, which is God.

It follows, therefore, that every action, under certain circumstances and for certain people, may be a stepping-stone to spiritual growth—if it is done in the spirit of nonattachment.

All good and all evil is relative to the individual point of growth. For each individual, certain acts are absolutely wrong. Indeed, there may well be acts which are absolutely wrong for every individual alive on earth today. But, in the highest sense, there can be neither good nor evil.

> The Lord is everywhere
> And always perfect:
> What does He care for man's sin
> Or the righteousness of man?

Because Krishna is speaking as God himself, he can take this attitude, and advise Arjuna to fight. Because Arjuna has reached this particular stage in his development, he can kill his enemies and actually be doing his duty.

There is no question, here, of doing evil that good may come. The Gita does not countenance such opportunism. Arjuna is to do the best he knows, in order to pass beyond that best to better. Later, his fighting at Kurukshetra may seem evil to him, and it *will* be evil—then. Doing the evil you know to be evil will never bring good. It will lead only to more evil, more attachment, more ignorance.

How, in this complex world, are we to know what our duty is? There is no greater problem. Yet, somehow, we have to find our position and make our stand. For the majority, much self-analysis, much trial and error, would seem to be the only way. But, having found that position, we must accept it in its entirety. The soldier has many responsibilities and duties besides fighting. The pacifist has much else to do besides refusing to fight. These duties and responsibilities extend equally over wartime and peace: they cover our whole life. But, in every case, the final ideal is the same.

The Gita neither sanctions war nor condemns it. Regarding no action as of absolute value, either for good or evil, it cannot possibly do either. Its teaching should warn us not to dare to judge others. How can we prescribe our neighbor's duty when it is so hard for us to know our own? The pacifist must respect Arjuna. Arjuna must respect the pacifist. Both are going toward the same goal. There is an underlying solidarity between them which can be expressed, if each one follows, without compromise, the path upon which he finds himself. For we can only help others to do their duty by doing what we ourselves believe to be right. It is the one supremely social act.

Symbols In Hindu Spirituality

by Swami Swahananda

A SYMBOL REPRESENTS or recalls a thing by possession of analogous qualities or by association in fact or thought. The original Greek word *symbolon* means a sign by which one knows or infers a thing. Symbols express the invisible by means of visible or sensory representations—the immaterial via the material.

All our contact with the outside world is based on symbols. The symbol-making tendency is innate in man. Languages are nothing but symbols. "We think in symbols, we act in symbols, we live in symbols, we learn in symbols." As Carlyle's professor in *Sartor Resartus* put it: "The universe is but one vast symbol of God; nay, if thou wilt have it, what is man himself but a symbol of God?"

"In a symbol," as Carlyle pointed out, "there is concealment and yet revelation." The symbol partly conceals the essential content from an ordinary person and partly reveals it by suggesting it. When the abstract is quite clear to a discerning mind, a symbol loses its concealing quality, but even then it may be used to suggest the abstract.

Because of its allegoric nature, a symbol gives rise to esoterism. This is true of every branch of learning. But this tendency is most evident in religion. Religious truth, being intangible, has given rise to much symbology. Every religion has its own body of symbols which suggest the ultimate Reality and other spiritual truths.

Hinduism has made use of symbolism profusely with a definite purpose, that of setting forth in visible or audible likeness what cannot be really or fully expressed or conceived. The highest reality in Hinduism is Brahman, the all-pervading divine Ground, which is absolute and indefinable. Symbols are used as intermediaries between the inadequate and limited capacity of man and his created language, and the incommunicable nature and fullness of Brahman.

Symbols of Brahman are regarded as a portion or aspect of the truth. They provide objects of reverence, but Hinduism does not consider them as ultimate. They are stepping-stones to higher conceptions, signposts or guides to better or higher thoughts. That is why Hinduism does not look askance at so-called idols, totems, or fetishes. It considers them to have a valid function since they remind the worshiper of the Reality. Swami Vivekananda explained this viewpoint on an occasion when he was asked to condemn the fetishism of the Hottentot: "Don't you see that there is no fetishism? Oh, your hearts are steeled that you cannot see that the child is right! The child sees person everywhere. Knowledge robs us of the child's vision. But at last, through higher knowledge, we win back to it. He connects a living power with rocks, sticks, trees, and the rest. And is there not a living power behind them? It is *symbolism*, not fetishism! Can you not see?"

For worship, various symbols of Brahman have been accepted— symbols which have become living because saints and holy men have visualized them and meditated on them. Of the most important ones a few may be mentioned. Brahman has been described as Satchidananda, Existence-Knowledge-Bliss absolute, or as *Svayambhu*, the self-created and self-existent one. But even these conceptions are difficult and elude our comprehension. So the Upanishads have prescribed for meditation the more tangible symbols of *prana*, the vital energy; *vayu*, the wind; *akasha*, the all-pervading ether; *aditya*, the sun; and so forth. Though the Vedic seers worshiped many deities, such as Indra, Varuna, Mitra, Savita, and others, they had even in those ancient times the knowledge of the supreme Brahman as the divine substratum of these deities. This is evident from sayings like the following one from the Rig Veda: "Truth is one; sages call it by various names."

For the realization of the impersonal aspect of Brahman, meditation is enjoined considering the soul as a spark rising from a blazing fire, or as a river flowing into the sea, or as a fish swimming in the ocean of the Absolute, or as a bird flying through infinite space.

But the impersonal aspect of Brahman is too abstract for the ordinary person. Therefore most spiritual aspirants choose one or another of the innumerable form symbols of the personal aspect of Brahman which appeals to their particular temperament. Usually the chosen ideal of God is conceived as seated on the lotus of the heart of man. This conception is based upon the yogic principle that spiritual nerve centers, resembling the lotus flower in shape, exist in the human body within the *sushumna*, the path in the spinal column through which spiritual energy rises from the base of the spine to the brain. The lotus of the heart is considered one of the centers of spiritual consciousness most favored for the purpose of meditation. As the devotee meditates on the chosen deity seated on the lotus of the heart, the center of his very life, so externally also the deities are conceived as sitting on lotuses.

Worship of the incarnations of God is very common in Hinduism; Krishna and Rama are examples of divine incarnations of great popular appeal. The incarnations are regarded as veritable manifestations of God on earth.

All the gods in the Hindu pantheon have some identifying marks, some representing animal symbols placed beneath the deities, called "vehicles" or mounts, others representing articles upon their person. Each vehicle is a duplicate representation of the energy and character of the god. Thus the goose of Brahma, the eagle of Vishnu, the bull of Shiva, the elephant of Indra, the owl of Lakshmi, the swan of Saraswati—all are vehicles by which we can identify the respective deity.

The images of the deities themselves and the articles they carry also signify particular qualities or powers. Thus Brahma—God in his creative aspect—has four faces to give out the four Vedas. From the *Bhagavatam* we learn that Vishnu—God in his aspect as Preserver—has a discus, a club, and a conch shell, thus indicating his authority and power. The auspicious mark, *srivatsa*, usually represented on his breast in the form of a curl of hair, signifies his brilliance and capability. The garland he wears symbolizes the variegated maya—the universe of name and form—and his sacred thread the Om, the sound-symbol of Brahman.

Shiva is one of the most popular deities in Hindu worship. In one of his forms he is depicted with his three-pronged trident with which he has killed the demon of ego. The trident bespeaks his government and authority. The three prongs represent nonattachment, knowledge, and samadhi—that is, spiritual absorption. Shiva has three eyes with which he sees the past, present, and future. His third eye is the eye of knowledge.

Shiva as the Lord of the universe rides on the bull of dharma, whose four feet represent truth, purity, kindness, and charity. His symbol of destruction is the battle-ax. Shiva is the chosen ideal of the yogis; to the devotees of Shiva the constantly burning *dhuni* fire* symbolizes the fire of dispassion which burns all worldly attachments and desires. Shaivites—devotees of Shiva—besmear their bodies with the ashes of the dhuni fire as the Lord Shiva is said to do himself. The ashes represent what is left after the universe of diverse names and forms dissolves in the realization of the underlying Unity. Shiva here is the all-destroyer, for he dissolves all diversities in the one absolute Existence.

---

* A fire lighted by wandering monks, beside which they meditate and sleep.—Ed.

As Nataraja, Shiva dances. Nataraja means "Lord of the stage of this transitory world." His dance represents his five activities: *shrishti*, creation and evolution; *sthiti*, preservation and support; *samhara*, destruction and evolution; *tirobhava*, veiling, embodiment, and illusion; *anugraha*, release from transmigration, grace, and salvation.

Shiva is the real guru, the teacher, for he teaches by being what he teaches. This idea is the keynote to the Nataraja symbol. The drum in the upper right hand means that God, or guru, holds in his hand the cause of the world—sound. The fire in the upper left hand represents the light of the Atman. The Ganges on his head represents wisdom, which is cooling and refreshing; and the moon represents the ethereal light and bliss of the Atman, the Self.

One foot crushes the demon Muyalaka (or maya, the great illusion which is the cause of birth, death, and rebirth); the other foot, to which the remaining left hand is pointing, is raised upward and represents turiya—the superconscious state, beyond waking, dreaming, and dreamless sleep, beyond the mind and the world.

The second right hand bestows fearlessness and peace. The place of the dance, the theater, is the body—of the individual as well as of the cosmos. The body is spoken of as a forest because of its many components. The platform of the theater is the cremation ground, where all passions and all names and forms, which constitute the vision of this illusory world, are burnt away. The circle of flames within which Shiva dances has been interpreted by some to be the dance of nature contrasted with Shiva's dance of wisdom. Others have identified Shiva's dance with the mystic syllable Om, the fiery arch being the hook of the ideograph of the written symbol.

According to the conception of the Nataraja symbol, God the teacher teaches that maya, illusion, should be crushed, that egoism must be destroyed, and that man should ascend to the regions of pure, unconditioned consciousness and enjoy the blissful peace which is the Atman. Viewed in the light of this inner meaning, the image of Nataraja is a symbol of the highest teaching, one that can inspire and elevate.

The form of Kali, the Divine Mother, has given rise to much symbolic interpretation. She dances on the breast of the inert Shiva, her husband. Shiva here represents the transcendent aspect of Spirit and Mother Kali, the world-producing supreme Power, the dynamic aspect. Kali's dance indicates that the whole universe of ever-changing diversities is an appearance of the one immutable supreme Spirit. Amidst all changes, Shiva remains unchanged. Mother Kali is worshiped in order that man, amidst all the vicissitudes of life, may realize the Absolute within himself. Usually Mother Kali is represented with four arms stretched out over all the four directions. She holds the bleeding head of a demon in the lower left hand, a sharp dazzling sword in the upper left; she bestows fearlessness with the upper right hand and offers boons with the lower right. Thus she destroys evil and ignorance, preserves world order, and grants salvation to her devotees. She is both the just Ruler and the affectionate Mother. She subdues evil forces and bestows her grace. Both are her aspects. The former is necessary to lead her creatures to the latter, so that ultimately they may be released from all bondage and find eternal peace.

In addition to form symbols, sound symbols or mantras play an important part in the Hindu religion. The sound symbols, like the form symbols, are embodiments of consciousness through which God may be communicated. In the scriptural teachings concerning mantras, it is pointed out that every form has a corresponding sound, and every sound must have a corresponding form.

The most important mantra is the Om, or Aum. It represents the undifferentiated Brahman. As the personal God, its three letters A, U, M, represent his aspects of Brahma, Vishnu, Shiva, and their powers. The vibration of Om is the sound-Brahman or the first manifestation of the primordial Person. Om is the ground sound and ground movement of nature. Out of Om everything else has evolved. It is a symbol of universality. Every uttered sound is particular, produced from the strokes of the vocal organs and broken into parts. But Om is the universal unstruck sound behind all broken sounds. As an effective spiritual practice, repetition of the sacred syllable Om with steady and lengthened utterance is prescribed.

In the yogic tradition the mantras are regarded as the special manifestations of the supreme Power. The essence of mantra yoga—the way to God by means of the mantra—is the constant repetition of the divine name, which leads to illumination.

For spiritual progress, a mantra of a chosen ideal of God is prescribed. This sacred formula of the chosen deity is selected by the spiritual teacher in accordance with the nature of the devotee and his or her emotional disposition. The mantra is infused with the teacher's own spiritual power and the power of the propounder who discovered it. While chanting the divine name, the devotee should contemplate the spiritual meaning of the mantra. [This idea is discussed in depth in Swami Shraddhananda's article "Mantra Yoga."]

Halfway between the sound symbols and the anthropomorphic symbols there is another type called the aniconic symbols. The Shiva *lingam*, a symbol of Shiva, and the *Narayanasila* or the *salagrama*, a symbol of Vishnu, are examples of these.

Lingam means symbol, or sign. It also means the place of mergence, in which all manifestations are dissolved and unified. Some scholars have tried to trace the origin of the lingam to phallus worship. However, no such association exists in the minds of devotees, and Swami Vivekananda strongly repudiated this view. He said that the lingam originated in the famous hymn in the Atharva Veda Samhita sung in praise of the *Yupa Stambha*, the sacrificial post.

Some have endeavored to identify the conceptions of lingam and *yoni*—the latter forming the base of the image with the former rising from its center—in Tantra with fatherhood and motherhood of the universe. The tapering Shiva lingam situated on the base also represents Purusha and Prakriti of the Samkhya system of philosophy. Lingam here means the unchanging axis round which the whole creation moves. It has also been pointed out that the temples of Shiva are generally built in imitation of Himalayan peaks with their bases on the earth and summits soaring toward the transcendent sky. Similarly, a devotee, although he lives in the world, should keep his mind on Shiva.

The salagrama represents the Absolute with attributes. It is a black and egg-shaped stone, and represents *Hiranyagarbha*, or the primordial Golden Egg, the undifferentiated Totality. The idea is that out of Hiranyagarbha the whole universe has become differentiated in course of time.

A Hindu temple itself is a symbol of the body: the human body is considered to be the temple of God. "This body of ours is a temple of the divine," says the Maitreyi Upanishad. God resides in the heart of man, and the sanctum sanctorum of the temple represents his heart. The heart is a cave, and the king of the dark chamber is God. Hence the sanctum sanctorum is purposely kept dark without any windows. Lights in the temple represent the light of the soul. The clarified butter often supplied to the lamp stands for regular spiritual practice.

Spiritual growth comes through intense thought of God. With these and many more symbolic representations, Hinduism and other religions try to bring the divine within the grasp of the devotees and help them to keep their minds recollected in God. As the devotees' spiritual life deepens, their vision of the Deity changes. God, who was first considered to be outside of oneself is next seen as the indwelling Spirit, then as immanent in all creation, and ultimately as the transcendental Brahman. Thus the devotee gradually climbs the ladder of spirituality and finally attains the vision of the Supreme.

Perspectives

Religion in the Twenty-First Century

by Huston Smith

THE SKIES ARE clearing after a major storm, and the future of religion looks bright—even assured. From another weather station, however, we hear a different report. A tornado is approaching that could level religion forever.

My aim in this essay is to align these opposite reports in the manner of binocular vision. If we close our right and left eyes alternately, different images oscillate; but with both eyes open we see things in depth. Comparably here. Perhaps aligning the conflicting forecasts of religion's future can add depth to our understanding of what that future might be. I begin with those who see religion as on its way out.

God Is Dead. In the sixteenth and seventeenth centuries the West hit upon a new way of knowing. We call it the scientific method, and it quickly replaced revelation, its predecessor, as the royal road to knowledge. Conceptually, it spawned the scientific *worldview*, and its technology created the modern *world*. The citizens of these physical and conceptual environments constitute a new human breed whose beliefs correspond to very little in the heritage of their forebears. As a consequence, religion—the kingpin of that heritage—has been marginalized, both intellectually and politically.

First, politically. Fresh continents to occupy and easier travel have introduced a new phenomenon into history: cultural pluralism. The result has been to edge religion from public life, for religion divides whereas politics seeks unity. Concurrently, religion has been marginalized intellectually. Science has no place for revelation as a source of knowledge, and as moderns tend to think with science on matters of truth, confidence in revelation has declined. Marx considered religion "the opiate of the people," "the sob of an oppressed humanity," and Freud saw it as a symptom of immaturity. Children who cannot accept the limitations of their actual parents dream up Fathers in Heaven who are free of those limitations. Theism is wish fulfillment—a pandering to "the oldest, strongest and most urgent wishes of mankind,"[1]—and the religious experience ("the oceanic feeling") is regression to the womb.

For religion to be marginalized socially and forced to the wall intellectually is no small event. Some see it as substantial enough to warrant the pronouncement that God has died.* Sociologists compile statistics on the change, but for the intellectual historian two developments suffice. First, on the question of God's existence the burden of proof has shifted to the theist; and as proofs of the supernatural are difficult in any case, the classic proofs for God's existence have pretty much collapsed. The second sign, though, is more telling. Whereas atheists and theists used to agree that God's existence is an important issue, now even that common ground has vanished. The tension between belief and disbelief has slackened. "It leaves no mark on intellectuals now," a cultural historian has observed, adding: "we have witnessed a decline in the urgency of the debate."[2] The atheism of indifference or apathy simply refuses to take the question of God seriously.

Such, a French psychiatrist has written, "has become the common lot of at least a considerable portion, if not the majority, of our contemporaries."[3] Their number has given rise to a distinction between secularization and secularism. The word "secularization" is now typically used to refer to the cultural process in which the area of the sacred is progressively diminished, whereas "secularism" denotes the reasoned stand that favors that drift. It argues on grounds that are cognitive, moral, or both, that the desacralizing of reality and consequent recession of the God idea is a good thing. Whether favored or merely accepted, though, the change itself seems undisputed. *The Chronicle of Higher Education* condensed it into a single sentence: "If anything characterizes 'modernity,' it is a loss of faith in transcendence, in a reality that encompasses but surpasses our quotidian affairs."[4]

How, in the face of these seemingly irrefutable signs of faith's decline— "its melancholy, long, withdrawing roar" in Matthew Arnold's memorable phrase—is it possible to argue that the future of religion is promising?

The Eyes of Faith. One of the interesting recent developments in physics has been the realization that at its frontiers the observer must be included in the experiment. It's not just that we can't know where a particle is until we perform an experiment to locate it. The particle literally isn't anywhere until (by collapsing its wave packet) an experiment gives it its location. Whether or not this Copenhagen reading of the matter will prevail, it at

---

*From a famous passage in *Thus Spake Zarathustra* in which Nietzsche has a madman running through the streets announcing that God is dead.

least highlights the active component in knowing. Knowing is not a passive act. If seeing is believing, believing is also seeing, for it brings to light things that would otherwise pass unnoticed.

> The Life's dim windows of the Soul
> Distorts the Heavens from Pole to Pole
> And leads you to Believe a Lie
> When you see with, not thro' the Eye.
> William Blake[5]

How does this affect the question of religion's future? The Death-of-God prediction of religion's demise was reported through eyes that register data that is available to everyone. Religion, though, sees through the eyes of faith, and in doing so sees a different world. Or better, it sees the same world in a different light.

In this new light things look different in a way that is commanding. Arguments are irrelevant here, as they are when a rope that was mistaken for a snake is recognized for the rope that it is. The sacred world is the truer, more veridical one, part of the reason being that it includes the mundane world. It also redeems that world by situating it in a context that is meaningful—completely so. The whole (of which the visible world is part) is not only more inclusive than the visible world. It is better than the visible world—infinitely better in being able to shine its glory on everything. Because its power is ineluctable, it cannot be gainsaid, for (as William James put the point) "religion says that the best things are the more eternal things, the things in the universe that throw the last stone, so to speak, and say the final word."[6]

Backed by its ineluctable authority, religion's future (seen from this second perspective) is secure. As long as there are human beings there will be religion, for the sufficient reason that the self is a theomorphic creature—one whose *morphe* (form) has God (*theos*) built into it. Having been created in the image of God, every human being has a God-shaped vacuum built into its heart. We know that nature abhors vacuums, so people keep trying to fill theirs. Searching for an image of the divine that will fit, they paw over images as if they were pieces of a jigsaw puzzle, matching them successively to the gaping hole at the puzzle's center. (We call the wrong images idols to underscore their inadequacy. Calvin likened the human heart to an idol factory.) They keep doing this until, the right "piece" having been found, it slips into place and life's puzzle is solved.

The sight of the picture that then comes to view is so commanding that the soul finds its attention riveted to it completely; so completely that no attention remains for it to notice itself as the person who is *seeing* the picture. This sublime self-forgetfulness, this ecstatic release from ego-encasement, is salvation, or enlightenment. It is the complete and only possible liberation from the bondage of human finitude—the cord is cut, the bird is free. Achieving this freedom amounts to graduating from the human condition, but the passage in no way threatens the human future. Other generations are always waiting in the wings, eager to have their go at life's curriculum.

The gulf that separates this faith-oriented projection of religion's future from the worldly one this essay opened with is vast; but we live in the *uni*-verse, so in some way we must try to bring the two together. If we are religiously "unmusical" (Max Müller's phrase) and its account leaves us cold, the situation is simple: the worldly prognosis tells the tale. Others, though, have a problem on their hands. The religious forecast carries weight, but so does the secular one. This is where binocular vision enters. How does the future of religion look when we take into account both what social scientists tell us—our first reading—and what the eyes of faith report?

To bring the two together we need to look again at the historical developments of this century, this time with eyes that are peeled for signs of their spiritual significance.

The Ground Is Cleared. Those signs come to light when we remember the vacuum in the human heart that was mentioned a few paragraphs back, and the jigsaw pieces with which people try to fill it. None of the pieces the modern world has reached for have fit.

The two most important pieces have been Marxism in the East and Progress in the West, these being the principal gods of modernity. Of course Marxism believes in progress too, but it stresses its ideological program for effecting that progress. As for East and West, I use those words to refer to the poles that polarized the twentieth century politically, though of course Marxism began in the West.

Go back to the point I began this essay with: the new way of knowing that Europe hit on in the sixteenth and seventeenth centuries. We call it the scientific method, and with it, knowledge began to proliferate; for science houses the controlled experiment, the controlled experiment proves, and proven knowledge snowballs. The eighteenth century's Industrial Revolution established these points historically, for by applying the knowledge that was ballooning, it raised Europe's living standards dramatically. Together these scientific and industrial revolutions produced a third and psychological one: the Revolution-of-Rising-Expectations which has powered modernity ever since. It spawned three heady dreams which coalesced in the Enlightenment Project. Thanks to its new and reliable way of knowing, modernity would send ignorance packing. Applying its new knowledge to nature, it would send scarcity packing. And it would send superstition packing. The superstitions the Enlightenment had in mind were principally those of the Church, and as the Church's back was being broken, it seemed that mankind was ready to step into the Age of Reason. This reason spelled Progress, the hope that has powered the modern world since it swung to view.

As for Eastern Europe and subsequently China, its version of that hope has been, for the bulk of this century, Marxism. To set it in perspective we need only go back to the Revolution-of-Rising-Expectations that the scientific and industrial revolutions gave rise to. Hegel cashed in on that revolution's forward-looking stance and fashioned from it a metaphysics. From the seeming fact that things were getting better and stood a good chance of continuing to do so, Hegel extrapolated backwards to infer that they had always been improving. Progress is the name of the game for being inscribed in the structure of the cosmos. (In Hegel's vocabulary, Being is the necessary unfoldment of its Idea in ever-increasing consciousness and freedom.) Support for this heady scenario was welcome from every quarter, and Darwin supplied it from science. Himself inspired by Hegel, he painted the natural history of life on earth in strokes that fitted perfectly into Hegel's version of an evolution that is cosmic in sweep.

So far so good. But when we come to human history, Darwin's engine of progress—natural selection working on chance variations—chugs too slowly to explain. A principle was needed to account for progress in centuries, not eons, and Marx supplied it with his theory of class struggle. "Just as Darwin discovered the law of development of organic nature, so Marx discovered the law of development of human history," Engels intoned by Marx's grave at Highgate Cemetery.

One last step was needed, and though Marx assumed it, Engels (with Lenin's assistance) articulated it explicitly. To inspire not just hope but conviction, Communism's happy ending—the classless society—needed to be assured, and that required metaphysics. For science is never enough, not even natural and social science together. To inspire conviction, hope needs to be anchored in the very nature of things. So Hegel's cosmic vision was reaffirmed, but with an important change. Its inclusive and forward-looking features were in place, but its vocabulary needed to be converted from idealism to materialism. This had the double advantage of making the theory sound scientific and at the same time directing attention to the politico-economic scene; specifically to the means of production as the place where the gears of history grind decisively.

This is the package that in this century persuaded the Eastern half of humankind—the world's largest nation (the USSR) and its most popu-lous one (the People's Republic of China). With its "jigsaw piece" (Communism) placed beside the piece the West reached for (Progress), we can proceed to the point for which they were introduced. Neither filled the spiritual hollow in the human makeup.

To begin again with the West, Progress has turned into something of a nightmare. The campaign against ignorance has expanded our knowl-edge of nature, but science can't get its hands on values and life-giving beliefs. That's disappointing. It's discouraging to discover that not only are we no wiser (as distinct from more knowledgeable) than our forebears were; we may be less wise for having neglected value questions while bringing nature to heel. That possibility is frightening; for our vastly increased power over nature calls for more wisdom in its use, not less. The Enlightenment's second hope, of eliminating poverty, must face the fact that more people are hungry today than ever before. As for the belief that the Age of Reason would make people sane, that now reads like a cruel joke. In the Nazi myth of a super-race (which produced the Holocaust), and the Marxist myth of a classless utopia (which produced the Stalinist Terror), our century fell for the most monstrous superstitions the human mind has ever embraced.

With this last point we have already moved to the Eastern half of our twentieth century where Marxist hopes have not just declined but collapsed. The Soviet Union has disintegrated, and while Maoism re-mains nominally in place in China, no one believes it anymore—capitalism is advancing there faster than anywhere else on the planet. In its heyday, Marxism inspired commitment by claiming that its idealism was grounded in truth. This is indeed the winning formula, but our century has falsified both halves of its Marxist version. All of Marx's major predictions have turned out to be wrong. (1) The European model of production has not spread throughout the world. (2) The working class has not progressively grown more miserable and radical. (3) Nationalism and religious zeal have not declined. (4) Communism does not produce goods more efficiently than free enterprise, nor distribute them more equitably. (5) And in communist countries the states show no signs whatever of withering away. Faced with this predictive shamble, apologists regularly switched their appeal from truth to idealism—are we to forget the suffering masses? But the Marxist record on compassion is no better than its record on truth. In justifying Communism's (often vicious) means by the humanitarian end Marx expected them to lead to, he saddled his movement with a bloody-mindedness history has rarely seen.

Modernity's coming to see its gods for what they are—idols in their inability to deliver what was expected of them—is the most important religious event of the twentieth century. With the ground cleared of its illusions, we can now examine that ground to see if it shows signs of new life.

Re-nascence. At least we can say that religion weathered its winter. On his seventy-fifth birthday, Malcolm Muggeridge looked back over his long worldwatch as editor of *The Manchester Guardian* and concluded that the most important single fact of the twentieth century is that the USSR, with every totalitarian means at its disposal, was unable to destroy the Russian Orthodox Church. The same can be said of the People's Republic of China respecting its religions. Confucian ethics are back in the schools, and a new church is opening in China every day.

Even intellectuals who are not themselves believers now speak respectfully of religion's durability. Having discovered no society that is without religion, anthropologists (riding their "functionalist" theory that pointless institutions fall by the wayside) now agree that religion is "adaptive." Neuroscientists trace its utility to the very structure of the human brain. Without going into details,** "once the left-brain interpreter was fully in place and reflexively active in seeking consistency and understanding, religious beliefs were inevitable."[7] Alex Comfort, a gerontologist, writes that "religious behaviors are an important integrator of man's whole self-view in relation to the world."[8] Carl Jung reached the same conclusion as

---

**They can be found in Michael Gazzaniga, *The Social Brain: Discovering the Networks of the Mind* (New York: Basic Books, 1985).

a psychologist. His conclusion "that human beings have a built-in religious need grew out of observing actual dreams of his patients."[9] A leading authority on Freud draws all this together by likening faith to the glue that holds communities together; adding ominously that the weakening of this glue in the twentieth century has changed Dostoyevski's question, "Can civilized men believe?" to "Can unbelieving men be civilized?"[10]

As that second question is an oblique way of affirming religion's importance, informed observers (as was noted) have returned to the pre-Enlightenment position of taking it seriously. That, though, does not touch the question of its truth. On balance, intellectuals now believe in religion. Do they believe in God?

Some do and some don't, of course. What follows is an assessment of the general scene, with special attention to changes that are now occurring.

The New York Review notes that "a revival of theism seems to be taking place among intellectuals."[11] One evidence of this is the founding (in the 1970s) of the Society of Christian Philosophers. In the middle half of our century philosophy was cool (where not hostile) toward religion, whereas in this closing quarter the just-mentioned Society—whose journal, *Faith and Philosophy*, carries Tertullian's epigraph, "Faith seeking intelligence"—boasts over a thousand members and is by far the largest subsidiary organization in the American Philosophical Association.

Things like this could not happen if the three-hundred-year tension between science and religion had not begun to ease; for science continues to be what modernity believes in, so new life for the spirit requires its imprimatur. That (unofficial, of course) endorsement is coming through the realization that science is not omnicompetent. Its powers respecting nature and technology are awesome, but its parade of marvels proceeds from a line of inquiry that is powerful and at the same time limited. The usual way to register its limitation is to say that science can't deal with values and existential meanings, but the more important likelihood is that there are *things* it cannot connect with—things that are as real as material objects, and that affect us as much if not more, but which scientific instruments don't register.***

***It is important to see that science no longer opposes these possibilities. Quantum physics now plays freely with the possibility that not only matter but space and time derive from something that eludes their restrictions. There is also the surprising discovery that at the level of particle physics, power increases rather than decreases with smallness. To produce a million million protons would require a light pulse a million times *smaller* than one that can produce a million protons. This line of thought leads logically (though no experiment could prove it) to the possibility that if there is something of zero size, its power would be infinite.

This withdrawal of science to its important but not omnicompetent domain allows religion more intellectual room than the twentieth century accorded it, for religion specializes in the invisibles that science cannot touch. The stage is being set, it seems, for the twenty-first century to accept religion (and its ally, art) as equal partners to science in discerning the full range of reality.

That assessment seems secure, but another prospect is so recent that one cannot foresee its prospects. Is it possible that science, which today is still working on according religion scope and respect, will tomorrow actively endorse it?

Focally this is not possible, for as the preceding footnote indicated, controlled experiments cannot register spirit's workings. Indirectly, though, there is a way that science could eventually underwrite religion's claims. If there were not slightly more matter than anti-matter in the universe, the two would cancel each other out and the universe wouldn't exist. And if the forces of contraction and repulsion were not exactly balanced in the way they are, the universe could not support life. The list of such "coincidences" is so long that Stephen Hawking says flatly that the probability of there being a universe in which life is possible is in the order of absolute zero.

Why, then, in the face of this near-zero probability, *does* it exist? In a televised interview, the mathematical physicist Freeman Dyson answered as every theist would: "Of course there has to be a mind behind it all."[12]

It is going to be interesting if the very project that has gotten where it has by excluding final causes—explaining things via their author, or the purposes they serve—finds itself ending by proclaiming them. That would be more than a just and durable peace; it would be the final resolution to the warfare between science and religion that has troubled the modern era. It could also spell hope for the future—not just the future of religion, but the human future. For as Whitehead once observed, the future of civilization depends, more than on anything else, on the way the two most powerful forces of history, science and religion, settle into relationship with each other.

It stands to reason, moreover, that if there are things that are greater than we are—where "greater" refers not to size or brute power but to what is superior to us in value-aspects, such as intelligence—science cannot detect them. This follows from the fact that science's mode of detection is the controlled experiment, and we can control only what is inferior to us. If there are things that exceed us in every respect—angels? God?—they are not going to fit into our experiments because, as we don't know what their variables are, there is no possibility of our controlling those variables.

Conclusion. The conclusion that we have reached—that the twenty-first century will be religious; very likely more religious than our own—leaves untouched the question of the form(s) that religion will assume. Will new religions replace the traditional ones? If the great historical religions retain their vitality, will they also retain their separate identities, or will they phase into one another in the way certain Christian denominations are dropping their differences? If a world civilization emerges, will there be a single world religion? And there is the question of whether the evils that have plagued religion in the past can be mitigated—superstition, dogmatism, bigotry, oppression, neuroses, and the like. Now that Marx, Nietzsche, and Freud have brought them forcibly to our attention, can we heed the warnings of these secular prophets without ejecting the baby with its bath water?

These questions are already very much with us and will continue into the next century. But they are beyond the scope of this statement.

1. Sigmund Freud, "The Future of an Illusion," in Vol. 12 of the Pelican Freud Library (Pelican, 1985), p. 212.

2. Alaisdaire MacIntyre in (with Paul Ricoeur) *The Religious Significance of Atheism* (New York: Columbia University Press, 1969), p. 5.

3. Ignace Lep, *Atheism in Our Time* (New York: Macmillan Co., 1963), p. 11.

4. January 9, 1978, p. 18.

5. William Blake, *Complete Poetry* (New York: Random House, 1941), p. 614.

6. *The Varieties of Religious Experience* (New York: Longmans, Green & Co., 1902).

7. Michael Gazzaniga, *The Social Brain: Discovering the Networks of the Mind* (New York: Basic Books, 1985), p. 166.

8. Alex Comfort, *I and That* (New York: Crown Publishers, 1979), pp. 69-70.

9. Mary Ann Mattoon, *Understanding Dreams* (Dallas: Spring Publications, 1984), p. 97.

10. Philip Rieff, *The Triumph of the Therapeutic* (New York: Harper and Row, 1968), p. 4.

11. Martin Gardner in *The New York Review*, May 8, 1986, p. 25.

12. "The more I examine the universe and study the details of its architecture, the more evidence I find that the universe in some sense must have known that we were coming." Freeman Dyson, *Disturbing the Universe* (New York: Harper and Row, 1979).

Harmony of Religions

Swami Tyagananda

THE OLDEST RELIGIOUS sentiment ever expressed by mankind may perhaps be the statement on religious harmony in the ancient Vedas: "Truth is one; sages call It by various names."

The same sentiment has since then echoed and reechoed in the corridors of time, amplified by enlightened persons of different religions in different parts of the world. One may remember here the reply given by the pagan Roman thinker Quintus Aurelius Symmachus to St. Ambrose, the dogmatic bishop of Milan. "The heart of so great a mystery," said Symmachus, "cannot ever be reached by following one road only." And Ibn 'Arabī, the great Sufi mystic of thirteenth-century Spain, wrote in his book *Tarjumān al-Ashwāq* ("The Interpretation of Divine Love"):

> My heart is capable of every form,
> A cloister of the monk, a temple for idols,
> A pasture for gazelles, the votary's Kābā,
> The tables of Torah, the Koran.
> Love is the creed I hold: wherever turn
> His camels, love is still my creed and faith.

Apuleius, a Platonic philosopher of second century A.D., had the firm conviction that the Divine "is adored throughout the world, in divers manners, in variable customs, and by many names."

Though the truth of religious harmony has been affirmed and proclaimed by the enlightened few in every generation, humanity as a whole has not yet come to terms with it. In today's world, religious differences still rankle and continue to produce disharmony, misunderstanding, and mutual distrust.

Questions arise: How do we deal with all these differences? Would these vanish in course of time or are they here to stay? Are they in any way reconcilable? Is it possible to discover some thread of harmony connecting them? What is the significance of the presence of so many religious traditions in the history of the world? Such are the questions that every serious student of religion has to reckon with.

A number of approaches are possible to deal with these questions. Only a brief, general description of a few major approaches is attempted here.

Exclusivistic Approach. The easiest way to dispose of all the questions concerning the plurality of religions is to deny it altogether. Only one religion is true. The other so-called religions are false or misguided, and so do not really deserve to be called "religions." Always the underlying message is that "my religion" is the one "true religion." An implied corollary to this is the idea that if the world were to be united by one religion, that religion could only be "my religion."

Every religious tradition has at least a few adherents holding such views. The Archbishop of Canterbury refused to attend the World's Parliament of Religions at Chicago in 1893 because, he said,

> the Christian religion is the one religion. I do not understand
> how that religion can be regarded as a member of a Parliament
> of Religions without assuming the equality of the other
> intended members and the parity of their positions and
> claims.[1]

The destruction of the places of worship belonging to other religions by Muslim zealots was also due to the belief that Islam was the only true religion and so the destruction was supposed to be an act of faith. There certainly were political and economic factors involved in the wars that took place in the Middle Ages, but in many of them it was the exclusivistic approach toward religion that provided the justification and motivation. The aggressive proselytizing undertaken by the followers of Christianity ("saving" the souls of heathens from hellfire) and Islam are based on the belief that only one religion ("my religion") is true and hence universally applicable and enforceable. The claim of the Jews that their religion, Judaism, is the only true religion springs from the faith that they are the people especially chosen by the Lord. It cannot be denied that the exclusivistic approach was followed even by certain sects of Hinduism and Buddhism.

In a council held at Buffalo in 1805, Sagoyewatha (lit. "Red Jacket"), a Seneca Indian chief, is reported to have asked a missionary, "Brother, if there is but one way to worship and serve the Great Spirit, if there is but one religion, why do you white people differ so much about it?" The same question was asked by Vivekananda in 1900 in his Pasadena lecture:

> If the claims of a religion that it has all the truth and God has
> given it all this truth in a certain book were true, why are there
> so many sects? Fifty years do not pass before there are twenty

sects founded upon the same book. If God has put all the truth in certain books, He does not give us those books in order that we may quarrel over texts....Take the Bible, for instance, and all the sects that exist among Christians; each one puts its own interpretation upon the same text, and each says that it alone understands that text and all the rest are wrong. So with every religion. There are many sects among the Muslims and among the Buddhists, and hundreds among the Hindus. Now, I bring these facts before you in order to show you that any attempt to bring all humanity to one method of thinking in spiritual things has been a failure and always will be a failure.[2]

Syncretistic Approach. While admitting the limitations of the existing religions in their present forms, some thinkers feel that a new religion will eventually emerge, or can be created, by combining the best aspects of every religion and omitting their weak points. Those who follow this syncretistic approach do not emphasize the common ground of religions. They recognize the diversities in religion but hold that these are not antagonistic to one another. They try to combine some good elements from all religions to form a new religion. The most well-known example of this is the religion *Din-ilahi* created by Akbar, the sixteenth-century Mughal emperor of India. He summoned a General Council and invited to it scholars and leaders from his kingdom. He told them of his desire to unite all his people

> in such a fashion they should be both "one" and "all"; with the great advantage of not losing what is good in any one religion, while gaining whatever is better in another. In that way honor would be rendered to God, peace would be given to the people, and security to the empire.[3]

Akbar's syncretism produced a religion which was a pantheistic monotheism—a hotchpotch of elements borrowed from Islam, Christianity, Hinduism, Jainism, and Zoroastrianism. As a religion it failed, but it had a few short-term beneficent political results. Its failure as a religion for all is understandable. For, as said earlier, it is impossible to tie down humanity to just one way of approaching God.

The syncretistic approach has not succeeded at the collective level, but at the personal level many people are trying to follow it in modern times.

Teleological Approach. The teleological approach is based on the belief that one religion (and, as before, this is almost always "my religion") is the fulfillment of what is best and true in others. There must be some divine purpose in the existence of so many religions and it would be wrong to question the utility of their existence. The "other religions" are not totally false or misguided; they do have some element of truth the fullness of which, however, is most clearly revealed in only "my religion." Other religions are based on natural knowledge, not on divine revelation, and are incomplete. They will eventually have to come to "my religion" which is complete and revealed. In recent years some Christian theologians have put forward a subtler form of this argument which accepts a kind of progressive or "hidden" revelation in all religions. R.C. Zaehner, a Catholic professor at Oxford, is a well-known propounder of this view.[4]

Muslim theologians, on the other hand, argue that since their religion has most recently appeared in history, Judaism and Christianity are not false religions, but were rather "preparations" for the final revelation of the Prophet Muhammad. This "preparations"-theory was put forward by a bishop as early as 1893 before the Chicago Parliament of Religions began. He wrote:

> One result [of the Parliament of Religions] will be to show that the Christian faith was never more widely or more intelligently believed in, or Jesus Christ more adoringly followed. Civilization, which is making the whole world one, is preparing the way for the reunion of all the world's religions in their true center—Jesus Christ.[5]

Pluralistic Approach. The pluralistic approach not only acknowledges religious diversity, but seeks to come to grips with it in a positive way. It accepts that each religion is valid according to its own terms and concerns. This is the only approach acceptable to thoughtful, reasonable men and women of today's world. But this approach also poses serious challenges at both individual and collective levels. In countries which have adopted a secular constitution, religious pluralism has become one of the most serious socio-political problems. Owing to its comprehensiveness, the pluralistic approach allows several attitudes or approaches within its fold. Some of these approaches, which are now being actively followed, are mentioned below.

Many people today prefer to follow what may be called a noncommittal approach. They say that since we have to live together anyway, we must develop mutual respect and the spirit of toleration for the sake of collective peace and welfare. Let religion remain every individual's personal affair. There is no need to make a parade of it in society, where it is almost certain to clash with other religions. Let us be religious at home and secular outside. In pluralistic countries like the United States and India, this is the approach followed by the government and it has been incorporated in the constitutions of these countries.

Another way of responding positively to religious diversity is through the dialogic approach. There are many thinkers and scholars who hold that it is better not to have predetermined, fixed answers concerning the truth or superiority of any religion or concerning the relation between different religions. What is essential is to undertake dialogue with those of other faiths in a spirit of mutual respect, fellowship, and creative openness. We must learn the art of listening to the viewpoints of others with unprejudiced minds. It is such dialogic interaction that may, in course of time, produce greater understanding of one another, and the future relationship between religions may be quite different from that anticipated now.

The mass influx of Oriental teachers and ideas into Western society in the 1960s and 1970s, and the consequent depletion of monasteries and church communities, have forced the Western churches—both Catholic and Protestant—to adopt the method of dialogue, partly to enrich themselves but mainly to create a new image of a liberal and enlightened church.

Perhaps the best among the options provided by the pluralistic approach is the one that is available through Vedanta reinterpreted and exemplified by Sri Ramakrishna and Swami Vivekananda. Their approach toward plurality of religions may be called the harmonious approach. This approach has the unique advantage of fulfilling the aspirations of all concerned without destroying anyone's innate faith.

Harmonious Approach. Sri Ramakrishna's harmonious approach developed not through scholarship but through direct spiritual experience. He did not set out to "prove" the harmony of religions. He was a God-intoxicated soul. Having tasted supreme, transcendent bliss as a result of his intense longing for God as the Divine Mother, he became eager to know how God was worshiped in different ways. His all-consuming love for God made him take up the disciplines of different Hindu sects and also of other religions. This was a unique experiment and its results were extraordinary. Sri Ramakrishna found to his childlike wonder and joy that all these paths led to the ultimate awareness of God as the Supreme Spirit. Thus through direct experience Sri Ramakrishna proved the equal validity of all religions. This led him to formulate the following three fundamental principles which form the cornerstone of his harmonious approach to the phenomenon of religious plurality.

1. All religions have the same ultimate purpose, namely, God-realization; everything else in religion is secondary. Stripped of all theological trappings, every religion has for its goal the transcending of human limitations to contact the Reality beyond.

2. There is only one transcendent, ultimate Reality which manifests in various forms, with various attributes, and even as formless, and is known by various names. (This, of course, is an ancient Indian truism. What was intuited by the Vedic sages thousands of years ago has been reconfirmed in our own times by Sri Ramakrishna through direct experience.)

3. The ultimate Reality can be realized through various ways developed by the world religions. Every religion has the inherent power to take its followers to the supreme consummation of human life.

In practical terms, these three principles mean that religions of the world are not contradictory or antagonistic to one another but complementary. No one need change one's religion for another or persuade others to change their religion for one's own. Every religion is equally true and authentic.

Saying that all religions are equally true and authentic does not, of course, mean that "all religions are the same" or that "the differences are merely superficial." Every religion has a special bent, a characteristic feature, a unique trait. For instance, the dominant characteristic of Islam is its spirit of equality and brotherhood; of Christianity—its emphasis on love and sacrifice exemplified by Christ; of Buddhism—its stress on renunciation, compassion, and rationality; of Hinduism—its principle of the basic unity of the universe in consciousness, the insistence on the need for direct mystical experience, the spirit of acceptance, and its extraordinary power of assimilation.

At the same time, saying that every religion has its own uniqueness does not mean that religions have nothing at all to share. There are a great many things to share and learn, and if we really put our minds to this, we shall find that the religions of the world have a lot more in common than is normally recognized. In spite of the diversity and the differences, no one can deny that religions do share certain common characteristics such as concern for the existential problems of humanity, transcendence, ultimacy, holiness, fellowship, and symbolic expression of inner experience. The harmonious approach consists in recognizing this common ground, and enriching one's own spiritual life by absorbing the best elements of other religions but all the while remaining steadfast in one's own religion. Swami Vivekananda put it succinctly when he said: "The Christian is not to become a Hindu or a Buddhist, nor a Hindu or a Buddhist to become a Christian. But each must assimilate the spirit of the others and yet preserve his individuality and grow according to his own law of growth."[6]

Sri Ramakrishna gives the illustration of a daughter-in-law who serves all the members of her husband's family with love, but the nature of her relationship with her husband is special. Similarly, it is possible to be aware of the harmony underlying all religions and yet maintain a special relationship with one's own. This also implies that we recognize the privilege of everyone to maintain a special relationship with his or her own religion. It's time we learned that love for "my religion" does not become greater if it is accompanied by hatred for all the others. When true love sprouts in the heart, it doesn't leave any room for hatred. The two can never stay together. Thus, following the harmonious approach we can all live together in the global family of religions with mutual sharing, love, and cooperation.

The different religious traditions—or "labels" such as Christianity, Islam, Judaism, and Hinduism—are really walls dividing the total religious consciousness of humanity. These walls are necessary, for they do have their utility. Sri Ramakrishna explains this with the example of a hedge to protect a tender, growing plant from stray cattle. Once the plant grows up into a sturdy tree, the hedge is no more necessary. Indeed, it could then even be a hindrance. Similarly, religious traditions protect the neophyte from antireligious forces. Soon, however, the neophyte must evolve and outgrow the necessity of this confinement. Beyond the walls separating one religion from another lies the realm of religion without frontiers, the limitless expanse of the Religion beyond religions.

From Harmony to Universality. Every religion of the world is merely an expression of the transcendent aspect of religion, just as the truth every religion represents is an expression of the absolute, transcendent Truth.

The Religion beyond religions not only transcends all religions but also pervades every one of them. It is the totality of religions. Swami Vivekananda explains:

> Man has an idea that there can be only one religion, that there can be only one Prophet, and that there can be only one Incarnation; but that idea is not true. By studying the lives of all these great Messengers, we find that each, as it were, was destined to play a part, and a part only; that the harmony consists in the sum total, and not in one note. . . . The sum total is the great harmony.[7]

It is this "great harmony," the sum total, that expresses itself in different ways:

> That one eternal religion is applied to different planes of existence, is applied to the opinions of various minds and various races. There never was my religion or yours, my national religion or your national religion; there never existed many religions, there is only the one. One infinite religion existed all through eternity and will ever exist, and this religion is expressing itself in various countries in various ways.[8]

Since all religions are expressions of the Religion beyond religions, they not only are true and authentic but also have a thread of harmony connecting them. This thread can be discovered and the underlying harmony can be experienced by truly religious people. By "religious" is not meant those who merely believe in some dogma or accept some savior. True religion

> is not talk, or doctrines, or theories; nor is it sectarianism....It is the relation between soul and God....Religion does not consist in erecting temples, or building churches, or attending public worship. It is not to be found in books, or in words, or in lectures, or in organizations. Religion consists in realisation....[9] [We] must realise God, feel God, see God, talk to God. That is religion.[10]

Doctrines, dogmas, rituals, books, temples, churches are important and have their utility, but they are only "secondary details" of religion. The primary aspects of religion are the supersensuous experience of God, and our efforts to get this experience and to live by the implication of our relationship with God. Thus religion is not a bunch of attitudes or beliefs to be accepted on faith, but an active search for one's own spiritual roots which culminates in the direct experience of God.

This experience can come to everyone through a sincere, intense practice of his or her own religion. It is at an advanced stage of such practice that the seeker rises above his or her own religious tradition and begins to derive nourishment directly from the Religion beyond religions. The harmony underlying all religions becomes palpable in that supernal realm. There one intuits all religions to be "only a travelling, a coming up, of different men and women, through various conditions and circumstances, to the same goal."[11]

Here it may be argued: truth can be only one, so how can all religions be true at the same time? Vivekananda answers:

> We must learn that truth may be expressed in a hundred thousand ways, and that each of these ways is true as far as it goes. We must learn that the same thing can be viewed from a hundred different standpoints, and yet be the same thing.[12]

He explained the idea with an example in a lecture he gave at the Universalist Church, Pasadena, in 1900:

> Take four photographs of this church from different corners: how different they would look, and yet they would all represent this church. In the same way, we are all looking at truth from different standpoints, which vary according to our birth, education, surroundings, and so on. We are viewing the truth, getting as much of it as these circumstances will permit, coloring the truth with our own heart, understanding it with our own intellect, and grasping it with our own mind. We can only know as much of truth as is related to us, as much of it as we are able to receive. This makes the difference between man and man, and occasions sometimes even contradictory ideas; yet we all belong to the same great universal truth.[13]

The intellectual understanding of this idea may come much earlier, but the actual experience of it comes only when one enters the domain of the Religion beyond religions. The process is hastened considerably if the awareness of the transcendent aspect of religion is cultivated right from the beginning. Those who have succeeded in establishing contact with the Religion beyond religions are found to be absolutely free from fanaticism, narrow-mindedness, suspicion, and fear. They see the play of one Religion everywhere. They see that every prayer—no matter in what language, done in what place of worship, accompanied by what rituals, addressed to what form or name of the Divine—reaches the same God who is the Father or Mother of us all. They also see that it is possible to reach the Religion beyond religions even without rituals or prayers, for there are other paths like those of yoga, Zen, etc. The all-merciful God does not withhold His love, grace, and blessings from any of His children just because he or she is not "labeled" as belonging to some particular religion.

A study of other religions throws open before us a wide variety of practices and disciplines, and we have the freedom to choose and pick what we need without the formality of swapping our religious affiliation for another. Thus we can carve out a path for ourselves by integrating the best elements of other religions into our own religious life. A conscious effort must be made to see the thread connecting all religions, forming, as it were, a beautiful garland adorning the Supreme Being, who is neither a Hindu, nor a Christian, nor a Muslim, nor a Buddhist, nor belonging to any religion whatsoever. All belong to Him, but He transcends all.

When the spirit of religious harmony animates our soul and the awareness of the Religion beyond religions pervades our consciousness, life will hold a new, richer meaning for us. We can then team up with Swami Vivekananda and say, "I accept all religions that were in the past, and worship with them all; I worship God with every one of them, in whatever form they worship Him. I shall go to the mosque of the Mohammedan; I shall enter the Christian's church and kneel before the crucifix; I shall enter the Buddhistic temple, where I shall take refuge in Buddha and in his Law. I shall go into the forest and sit down in meditation with the Hindu, who is trying to see the Light which enlightens the heart of everyone.

"Not only shall I do all these, but I shall keep my heart open for all that may come in the future. Is God's book finished? Or is it still a continuous revelation going on? It is a marvelous book—these spiritual revelations of the world. The Bible, the Vedas, the Koran, and all other sacred books are but so many pages, and an infinite number of pages remain yet to be unfolded. I would leave it open for all of them. We stand in the present, but open ourselves to the infinite future. We take in all that has been in the past, enjoy the light of the present, and open every window of the heart for all that will come in the future. Salutations to all the prophets of the past, to all the great ones of the present, and to all that are to come in the future!"[14]

1. Marie Louise Burke, *Swami Vivekananda in the West: New Discoveries*, 6 vols., 3d ed. (Calcutta: Advaita Ashrama, 1983), 1: 71.

2. *The Complete Works of Swami Vivekananda*, 8 vols. (Calcutta: Advaita Ashrama, 1976), 2: 362-63. (Hereafter cited as *CW*, followed by the ed., vol., and pg. nos.)

3. Will Durant, *The Story of Civilization: Part I*, "Our Oriental Heritage" (New York: Simon and Schuster, 1954), 470.

4. See his book *Christianity and Other Religions*. A similar view has been propounded by S.J. Samartha and Raimundo Panikkar also in recent years.

5. Burke, *New Discoveries*, 1: 71.

6. *CW*, 1977, 1: 24.

7. *CW*, 1972, 4: 120-21.

8. *CW*, 1972, 4: 180.

9. *CW*, 1972, 4: 179-80.

10. *CW*, 1972, 4: 165.

11. *CW*, 1977, 1: 18.

12. *CW*, 1976, 2: 383.

13. *CW*, 1976, 2: 366.

14. *CW*, 1976, 2: 374.

Judaism and Vedanta

by Rabbi Asher Block

THE FOLLOWING STRIKING statement by Swami Vivekananda
(which he made in the course of one of his addresses in the West) may
serve us as the text and theme for this presentation:

> We must ask, what may be that force which causes this
> afflicted and suffering people, the Hindu, and the Jewish
> too—the two races from which have originated all the great
> religions of the world!—to survive, when other nations
> perish? The cause can only be their *spiritual force*.

Here we have a precious clue—from one of the giants of the Spirit—as
to what is at the root of the religious experience of mankind. If only we
could get a glimpse, an insight, into the nature of "spiritual force," we
would then be able to unravel, as it were, the whole secret and mystery of
human survival.

To begin with, let us look at the Jewish and Vedantic traditions in
their broadest perspective. Both, it happens, have an almost identical
formulation of the basic pattern of religion. In the classic Jewish text, *Pirke
Avot* (usually translated as "Ethics of the Fathers" but best rendered
literally as "Chapters on Religious Essentials"), a cardinal precept is: The
world stands upon three things—upon Torah or spiritual wisdom, upon
the worship of God, and upon deeds of love. This teaching is traced
directly to the revelation Moses received at Mount Sinai; and, indeed it is
quite clear that the Decalogue of Sinai encompasses these fundamental
elements: the truth of spirituality, worshipful relations to God, and ethical
relations to man.

We find an almost exact analogue of this structure in the three
principal yogas taught by Vedanta—the three great pathways that man
must follow in order to attain fulfillment in life: the path of jnana—
intellectual discrimination or wisdom; the path of bhakti—devotional
love of God; and the path of karma—ethical or selfless action in relation
of fellowman.

Even if Judaism and Vedanta had done nothing more than formulate these three pathways, it would have been a notable contribution. But
this alone is hardly an adequate guide. For people everywhere in all
religions have a way of getting bogged down in all these paths.

Take, for example, the path of wisdom, or knowledge of God. In so many religious circles, so much of interest and energy is focused upon what is merely academic: the study of texts, the elaboration of dogmas, the dissemination of creeds, and endless theological debates. Even though the subject matter be related to God, still such intellectualism is very dry and lifeless religion, for God is not in books, in preachments, or in arguments.

Sri Ramakrishna used the vivid parable of an almanac that predicts a heavy rainfall for the year. But take that almanac (said he) and squeeze it and squeeze it, and not a drop of water comes out. So it is with academic religion. Its God is only a word, a concept—not a reality, not a force in life. Human character is not changed thereby.

Now, many people, sensing this truth that creedalism and theology lack something vital, swing the pendulum in the opposite direction—to society and activity. And then we have what may be termed "social" religion. Here there is a great emphasis on doing good, on public welfare, and on social reform.

That of course is fine. But many who do not believe in God at all are also involved in these areas. Moreover, even with regard to the religiously oriented, as often as not they become overly ambitious and unduly prideful in their efforts, which is proof that genuine altruism is missing. Hence, though there is a *force* in such activities, there is no assurance that it is a *spiritual* or selfless force.

Thus we see that in terms of popular theology and morality, though they might have their utility, it is not likely that we shall find through them that spiritual force which Swami Vivekananda spoke of as the survival power of the great and ancient faiths.

And, as to the third area, that of worship—which most people would consider the heart of religion—here, too, we must be careful not to judge by appearances. Most conventional worship falls into the two categories of symbolism and ritualism. Though these may not be "academic" and "social" in the same obvious sense as before, they are often nonetheless disguised extensions of them.

Symbols, because of an aesthetic quality, usually call forth an emotional response. But what is the reality behind them? They are intended as representations of God, but if we have never seen or experienced God, what are we "representing" thereby? Here, too, as was the case above, many persons, suspecting an ultimate emptiness in mere symbols, will gravitate toward ritualism in their worship. Rituals have movement; rituals usually involve groups, and are associated with historical or social values.

Once again, however, there is no assurance that they are intrinsically related to God or that they will call forth results spiritual in character. In other words, they may only be subtle forms of social religion. Thus, if we are mercilessly honest with ourselves, we are pressed to the wall as to what is spiritual force. This is one of the grave problems of conventional religion: in each path there are serious diversions, and one is not led to the goal.

Because of these frequent shortcomings in conventional religion, earnest folk have historically been propelled toward mysticism—which, simply defined, is the taking of religion more seriously, in all its three substantive pathways of spiritual wisdom, devotion to God, and service to man. Within both Judaism and Vedanta these paths were, at various times, pursued with great diligence.

For instance—to cite Jewish history—in the days of the Second Temple there was the group known as the Essenes. Their stress seemed to be on social activity, on living a dedicated community life. During the Middle Ages, when the study of the *Kabbalah* was in the ascendancy, primary attention was upon knowledge of the unity of God. The most recent manifestation was the Hasidic movement started by Israel Baal-Shem Tov, and its motivating force was the devotional love of God.

First, let us consider knowledge of God. In this area, the Kabbalists asked some relevant and pointed questions. How shall we understand the basic instruction of Moses, when he declared: "Hear, O Israel, the Eternal is our God, the Eternal One"? Though this is central in Jewish prayer, few really think about it. Also, how shall we understand the Biblical teaching that "man was created in the image of God"? Our life is subject to manifoldness and to change, to birth and to death. How are we, or how can we be, related to God who is one and eternal?

The answer the *Kabbalah* gave was: "the image of God" obviously does not refer to man's body and mind, it refers only to the soul. Hence, for us earnestly to believe in God requires that we identify ourselves with our highest Self, with our inner immortal Spirit, and not with our mortal bodies or self-centered minds. We must strive to liberate ourselves from false attachments to these lower elements. And, with the help of God, we can. For (the Kabbalist added) this is what the opening of the Decalogue promises: "I am the Eternal thy God, who brings thee out of bondage!"

Here is a teaching which gets to the heart of Judaism, and pinpoints the ultimate goal of our lives. This is Torah—wisdom in its highest sense; this is practical knowledge of God, for it relates directly to our lives and character—to our purpose here on earth.

And this approach to Torah is surprisingly similar to the Vedantic approach to the Vedas. In Hinduism, too, there are different levels of insight and observance. Various parts of scriptures feature rituals, legend, or philosophy. Vedanta highlights the latter part of the Vedas—the Upanishads—which bids man rise above physical and mental limitations, and whose central theme (to quote the great commentator Shankara) is "the knowledge of Brahman (or God), the knowledge that destroys the bonds of ignorance, and leads to the supreme goal of freedom." See how parallel they are!

One of the significant advantages of being able to compare one ancient religion with another is that we have a verification of truth. But, much more important than that, we have a reinforcement of experience. In the last analysis, religion cannot stand on philosophy or theory alone—beautiful and logical as that might be—it must stand on the solid rock of actual living experience. When we examine experience, we find that results are often altogether different from what theory alone might indicate. In the one case, there is a static view of life; in the other, a dynamic adjustment to living.

In the application of this truth, two vibrant examples can be adduced: one in personal life, as when relating body to soul; the other in a cultural context, when seeking to integrate particulars with universals.

In the matter of dealing with the human soul, one might "logically" say that since the body and mind are lower elements, one should deliberately suppress them. Indeed, there have been religionists who tried to build a religious system on that very premise: "the flesh is evil," "man is a sinner," and so on. Hence, for some, asceticism and mortification became virtues; while for most, who could not abide by these, there were feelings of weakness and guilt. It is highly noteworthy that Vedanta and Judaism, in the mainstream of their history, did not sanction such negativism. Their basic approach is one of growth and (if we may use the psychological term) one of sublimation—for that is the law of life. Body is to mind, and mind is to spirit, as childhood is to adolescence and adolescence is to maturity. Childhood is not evil; it just has to be outgrown.

Likewise, it is interesting in this regard to examine the attitudes that people have toward universal and particular forms in religion. Many will say, for instance, that Buddhists and Christians are more "universal" than Hindus or Jews because they do not reside within a national or ethnic milieu. But here again, it is not a question of form, but of attachment to form.

Realistically, when Christians and Buddhists examine their own lives, do they find that by and large they are free of all national feeling? Hardly. The usual difference is that they are nationalists of *many* countries instead of only one.

Surely the religious loyalty of a person should far transcend any national or ethnic allegiance. But that applies equally to all individuals everywhere, regardless of the particular social or geographic environment in which they abide.

If religion, bearing the name of God, is deliberately "nationalized" or "racialized" or embroiled in politics, or diverted into a preoccupation with, let us say, wealth or power, diet or dress—that is a perversion and degradation of religion. On the other hand, when people like the Hindus or the Hebrews find themselves naturally in a certain environment and, for them, because of inner yearning, a city is not just a city, but becomes a Jerusalem or Benares; and a river is not just a river but becomes a sacred Ganges and a purifying Jordan; and a language is not just language, but Sanskrit and Ivrit, "holy tongues"; and civil servants are more than just that, they are brahmins, or priests and Levites; and constitutions are not just legal documents, but Torah and Veda; and food is *prasad*; and the table is a "holy altar"; and so on and on—that is something else altogether.

The basic experience of both Judaism and Vedanta over the centuries has been that the essential thing in religion is the control of one's mind and the purity of one's heart; and that in relation to that, work as work or outer situations as situations are a kind of double-edged sword, serving for good or for ill, depending on how we use them.

In Sanskrit, the word *karma*, when referring to ordinary work and reactions, implies a form of bondage, but *karma yoga* is a method of using dedicated effort as a means of emancipation. Likewise, there is a word in Hebrew, *avodah*, which means both "work" and "worship." On a low level, with impure motives, it spells compulsion and drudgery; but altruistically and with one-pointed consecration, it can lead us to God.

An additional vital matter, on which these two great ancient faiths can shed light, is the subject of teachers and their historic role of leadership. It is an established fact that all the major religions of the world have built their traditions around the lives of prophets—those inspired messengers of God who "mediated" the Divine to the human plane of their followers.

One practical aspect of this subject has long commanded wide interest and surely deserves our consideration. It is the question of relating means to ends. There are many, among traditionalists and modernists alike, who claim that one faith alone, one savior alone, will serve best to unite mankind. And it must be granted that, in theory, this sounds eminently logical. God is one, Truth is one; why should we not all have one way to reach God or Truth?

Well, there is one important response to that position. It is that (as we have seen earlier in matters of spiritual growth) actual religious experience is far more valuable than mere logic. Experience shows that individual temperaments differ, that cultural backgrounds differ, and that we cannot force all into the same mold. In fact, to attempt to do so is to invite trouble. In actual practice, the doctrine of an exclusive prophet or prophecy usually leads to a proud and superior attitude, and, historically, has often led to persecution.

It is most significant that the Hebraic and Hindu religions, which revere many prophets in their own traditions, did not engage in efforts to proselytize others. The assumption, based upon long practical experience, has been that though the goal is one, the roads leading to it are many.

The Bhagavad Gita affirms that in every age God appears in different divine forms to answer the needs of those times. Swami Vivekananda pointed out that "the Upanishads speak of no particular prophet, but they speak of various prophets and prophetesses." And he added, "The old Hebrews had something of that idea." Explicitly, the prophet Jeremiah expressed that truth when he declared to the people, in God's name: "Ever since the day that your fathers came forth out of the land of Egypt unto this day, I sent unto you all My servants the prophets—at times quite frequently."

One of the tremendous advantages of "multiple prophecy" is that there is no limit set to the spiritual expansion possible. As a matter of fact, it is intended to include all. Eventually we must learn to see God and to serve God in everyone. When an attendant once came running to Moses, and told him angrily that others were aspiring to prophecy, Moses replied, "Are you jealous on my account? Would that all the Lord's people might be prophets!"

This multiplicity of means *within* a tradition is then (by the same practical logic) made to apply to other traditions also. Thus, the prophet Micah preached: "Let every people walk each one in the name of its God, even as we shall walk in the name of the Lord our God." And the prophet Malachi, calling attention to the fact that among all peoples pure offerings are presented in God's name, asks very boldly: "Have we not all one divine parenthood? Hath not one God created us? Why do we deal faithlessly, one human against another?"

Correspondingly, the Vedantic position is expressed, in vivid imagery, as follows: "As different streams having their sources in different places, all mingle their water in the sea, so, O Lord, the different paths which men take through different tendencies, various though they appear, crooked or straight, all lead to Thee."

Swami Vivekananda uttered these words at the World Parliament of Religions held in Chicago a century ago. It is no exaggeration to say that much of the impetus behind the various efforts toward greater interreligious understanding that we have witnessed in our lifetime, dates back to that Parliament. To use the apt metaphor of the late Pope John, a new breeze has begun to blow, and windows long shut have been thrust open.

Advaita Vedanta and Christianity

by Thomas Keating, O.C.S.O.

THE WORDS "GOD" or "Godhead" are difficult terms to use in interreligious dialogue because of their historical resonances and the various ways that they are understood in different cultures and even in the same culture. I will use the term "ultimate Reality" to refer to "God" because, in the context of the growing interreligious dialogue between the major world religions, this term seems to correspond best with their most profound teachings and experience.

Faith is the surrender and response to the ultimate Reality before it is broken down into the various belief systems that the human family has received from its divine Source through natural means or supernatural revelation.

Vedanta emphasizes primarily the impersonal aspect of the ultimate Reality. Christianity emphasizes the personal aspect of the ultimate Reality. The ultimate Reality, of course, transcends both. There are no human concepts that can come close to describing the ultimate Reality which we so poignantly intuit and feel called to pursue.

On the basis of the growing mutual understanding among the great world religions, some profound questions are beginning to surface. One of these is, "Can one reach the experience of unity without passing through a personal experience of the ultimate Reality?"

It is a mistake to think that in the Christian contemplative path there is only the personal aspect of God. The nonpersonal, however, is not as well articulated as in Advaitic Vedanta which offers a developed exposition of the higher states of consciousness. This is why the Christian path has much to learn from the Advaitic tradition. But because the ultimate Reality is transcendent and immanent at one and the same time, there is no adequate way to express this unity in rational terms, at least not at this stage of interreligious dialogue. It becomes more and more obvious that the place where we will ultimately meet one another is the place of self-forgetfulness at the center of our own nothingness.

In the Christian spiritual journey the first phase consists in the development of a personal self. That may be an astonishing statement for people who are trying to get rid of their egos. Yet the fact remains, and indeed needs to be emphasized, that the first phase of the Christian path is not the destruction of one's self-identity, but the effort to obtain one! We have to have an ego not only to survive in this world in its present stage of evolution, but to be capable of healthy and enriching relationships with others and indeed with the ultimate Reality.

We cannot have a *polis*, that is, a community of interacting people, without verbal communication, liberation from our overidentification with our environment and cultural conditioning, and a growing capacity to postpone—and to sacrifice for higher purposes—the gratification of our instinctual needs and drives. Relationships help us to become fully human. The fact that the ultimate Reality comes to us as a person, fits the human condition precisely where it is right now on the ladder of evolution; it addresses head-on our need to become fully human and to respect our own and everyone else's personhood.

The great accomplishment of human evolution to date is full reflective self-consciousness. From the perspective of higher states of consciousness, the human family is right in the middle of the evolutionary process. It has evolved from the state of pre-self-consciousness, which it shares with the beasts, into the capacity for full personhood. Its destiny is to move into trans-self-conscious levels of unity with all reality.

At its present stage of evolution, the human family is crucified, so to speak, between heaven and earth. We cannot go up and we cannot return to the unself-consciousness of the beasts. Without the experience of union with the ultimate Reality, the state symbolized by the Garden of Eden, we find ourselves at the most vulnerable point in the entire history of the race. The beasts do not feel that they are separate from God. We, on the contrary, are acutely aware of it. As we become more aware of our alienation from the ultimate Reality, we are terrified to the roots of our being.

The egoic self builds up all kinds of alternatives to compensate for this painful sense of separation from God. There is a common understanding among the world religions that the human condition is incomplete, to put it mildly. Hence, human nature is bound to be in a state of unfulfillment. We are in a dualistic situation because we have a self that is distinct from every other object in the universe and from its Source. If the egoic self is not allowed to develop, we are heir to all the neurotic problems in the religious history of the human family: we act in a religious manner for the wrong reasons. Each of the world religions, in its own way, addresses this problem. There could be no greater contribution to the human family than the choice first to develop and then to surrender our egoic self and thus to enter into the flow of evolution toward higher states of consciousness.

The great possibility that full reflective self-consciousness opens up is the possibility of transcending it. But as we saw, we cannot transcend what we do not yet possess. This is why it is important in our time to take seriously the discoveries of psychology, especially the developmental psychologies that have pinpointed the way that an infant gradually emerges from identification with its mother, its environment, and its body, through the various stages of childhood, until it reaches the age of reason. This marvelous developmental process recapitulates the evolution of the whole human family. It is the capacity to affirm one's own identity over and against all the other objects in the universe. This is not a disaster. It is a triumph. It is what being human means. It is a mistake to set out for higher states of consciousness without submitting to the stages that have to be experienced first. It took humanity thousands of years to get to this point. We ought to take these stages seriously if we want to remain open to further possibilities of growth.

It is for this reason that in the Christian scheme of things, the personal love of Christ is central. It addresses the deep existential fear and insecurity based on the sense of being alone and alienated from oneself, others, and the ultimate Reality, in a potentially hostile universe.

Only love, experienced as the ultimate Reality or through other people, can bring a human being to life in the full sense of the term. When one has achieved an identity as a personal self, the next step is available. In the Christian experience this is the cultivation of union with Christ in one's inmost being, in one's ordinary activity, as well as through prayer and meditation. It is no longer ourselves, but Christ in the mystery of his glorified humanity living in us.

The chief distinction between Advaitic Vedanta and Christianity focuses around their respective understandings of Christ. This understanding might be seen as the difference between God giving himself to himself in human beings (Vedanta), or God throwing himself away and giving himself back to himself in human beings (Christianity). The historical Jesus Christ reveals the profundity of what corresponds to personhood in the ultimate Reality. At the same time, we must remember that the ultimate Reality is beyond personhood as we understand it, just as It is beyond nonpersonhood.

It seems to me that the followers of Advaitic Vedanta also begin the spiritual journey in a dualistic situation. Where else can one begin? This is the place where human beings actually find themselves when they awaken to full reflective self-consciousness. Although in Advaitic Vedanta there is a strong emphasis in the direction toward unity with the ultimate Reality, there certainly are relationships. If we have a relationship, we have a self. The important thing is to have a fully developed self. That is the gift that one gives in any relationship and which one ultimately surrenders to the ultimate Reality. But we have to have the gift in order to give it away. In the Christian path the personal love of Christ is the motivation for the full development of a healthy ego in the psychological sense of the term as well as for its surrender.

In the Christian and Hindu traditions, the guru has an analogous place. If I have understood the Hindu masters correctly, one cannot negotiate the spiritual journey without a master. The guru possesses the state of unity consciousness that the disciple is trying to reach. One's purpose is to identify with the wisdom that is embodied in one's teacher and to make it one's own. In the Hindu frame of reference, the wisdom of the guru is already the disciple's deepest self.

In the Christian frame of reference there is only one guru, one master: the Lord Jesus Christ. He is believed to be present in the Christian community, in the liturgical proclamation of the scriptures, in the Eucharist, and in the hearts of each of his disciples. Just as in the Hindu path, he too is believed to be present within us, guiding our interior states, and arranging all the external circumstances of our lives in order to bring us to the full development of our self-identity and to our total surrender to the Father.

This is the heart of Christianity. Christ did not endure his passion and death and his experience of abandonment by the Father merely to atone for our sins. To be a Christian in the full sense involves doing what he did, to share through suffering in the redemption of the human family. His teaching bears its ripe fruit only when his actual example is imitated.

Christ is inviting us to a higher state of union with God than personal union. Because of the night of sense, which is a purification of the emotional hang-ups that we bring with us from early childhood, and the night of spirit which purifies the roots of our spirit from unconscious motivation, one has entered into an abiding union and unity with Christ.

But what happens after that? In the Christian tradition there are examples of mystics who have reached the stage of union and have then returned to what seems to be another night of the spirit, this time not for their own development but for the sake of sharing in the kind of sufferings that the average unenlightened and unredeemed human being experiences.

We believe that Jesus Christ so identified with the human condition in his crucifixion that his suffering and death are the supreme revelation of the ultimate Reality. On the cross, Jesus Christ stands for the human condition in the full extent of its sinfulness and alienation from its Source in a person perfectly united with the ultimate Reality. "My God, my God, why have you forsaken me?" These words of Jesus on the cross might be paraphrased, "How can I, Father—your son—become sin?"

It is here that Christian practice enters its deepest and inmost center. The basic text for this state of final integration is, "The Father and I are one" (John 10:30). Christ and the Father are one reality. The experience of our guru, Jesus Christ, and the experience to which we are heading as Christians is the same: the experience of unity.

The purification accomplished in this third night corresponds with the highest wisdom of Advaita Vedanta, the consciousness of ultimate Reality giving Itself, not to us, because there is no more "us," but to Itself in us. This state of unity is difficult in the extreme to speak about, but it is a challenge that Christians need to explore. As the world religions gain understanding of each others' paths, they will perceive more clearly our human destiny of unity with the ultimate Reality, with each other, and with the cosmos. Someday we may find ourselves together in the place—or rather in the no-place—of perfect unity (eternal life).

The understanding of eternal life affirmed by St. Gregory of Nyssa is that we continue to penetrate the mystery of ultimate Reality for all eternity. This penetration includes the possibility of a Christian Advaitic experience and is articulated with eloquent simplicity in the Gospel of John. The prayer of Jesus related by John proclaims:

> The glory that thou hast given me I have given to them, that
> they may be one even as we are one. I in them and thou in me,
> that they may become perfectly one, so that the world may
> know that thou hast sent me and hast loved them even as thou
> hast loved me (John 17: 22-23).

Reading Vedanta at the End of the Twentieth Century

by Francis X. Clooney, S.J.

ONE OF THE great intellectual and spiritual events of the second half of the twentieth century in the "West" (i.e., Western Europe and North America) has been the astonishing advance in the publication, translation, and study of non-Western texts (and, in appropriate ways, of non-Western art, music, ritual, etc.), and the dissemination of this knowledge in universities, seminaries, research and spirituality centers, schools, local cultural and religious organizations, and more generally throughout popular culture. Although this event has occurred only gradually, in a thousand places, for a thousand reasons, by the work of thousands of individuals and institutions, the resultant increase in available knowledge has far surpassed what was known previously. It is so quantitatively significant that it now matters qualitatively too: we know more, and we know differently. The way in which the West understands itself and the rest of the world is being irreversibly changed, while the ideas, images, and texts from outside the West have themselves received new life.

The dramatic increase in our knowledge of Vedanta in the West is a stellar example of this quantitative and qualitative growth; we are witnessing a profound change in the way in which Vedanta can be learned and its truth apprehended. Let us consider what has been happening.

An increasing number of important Sanskrit and (more recently) vernacular language texts related to Vedanta are being edited and published—the great commentaries, but also many subcommentaries and independent treatises, including lengthy and difficult works such as Suresvara's *Vartikas* on the Brihadaranyaka and Taittiriya Upanishad *Bhasyas*, and even further commentaries on those *Vartikas*. There are now commonly available fine translations of the Upanishads, the Brahma Sutras, and the works of Shankara and many later Advaitins. Nor are other schools of Vedanta neglected. For instance, in the 1980s there began appearing fine new critical editions of Ramanuja's *Sri Bhasya* and related Vishishtadvaita works. Most of the Tamil and Sanskrit works of Vedanta Desika and Pillai Lokacharya have been printed or reprinted, and many of these have appeared in translation. There is also an increasing interest among scholars in the Tamil devotional works which are fundamental to Ramanuja's understanding of Vedanta. Similarly, we find an increasing range of good translations of the works of other Vedantins such as Madhva and Vallabha.

As we begin to use these newly available editions and translations, an expanding body of new historical and critical scholarship is available to help us put them in perspective. Yearly there appear numerous high-quality articles, monographs, and large-scale volumes, ranging in topic from inquiries into pre-Shankara (as well as even pre-Badarayana) Vedanta and comparative analyses of the theological methodology of Vedanta theologians, to sociological studies of the context of the various Vedanta traditions and historical studies of the so-called "neo-Vedanta" of the late nineteenth and early twentieth centuries.

On the more popular level, textbooks for use in colleges and secondary schools, and even some children's books, regularly discuss Indian systems of thought, particularly Vedanta. High-quality magazines make Vedanta known through straightforward articles and popular stories. While "Yajnavalkya," "Shankara," and "Ramanuja" are still far from being household names in the West, such texts do make it increasingly likely that such names will be recognized by people who are neither scholars nor academicians, nor even particularly interested in the "East."

We know more, and we know more concisely and clearly. Of course, we must not exaggerate the virtues of this abundant and high-quality information about Vedanta—as if the sheer weight of printed matter could make Vedanta ideals more real; the proliferation of texts and studies does not guarantee a surer grasp of the fundamental truths of the Vedanta, nor does the path to liberation become easier just because more has been written about it. It is only rarely that people become interested in Vedanta after surveying a bibliography or undertaking a systematic survey of the schools of Vedanta; most begin their Vedantic journey due to some fortuitous or providential event—such as coming across an interesting article in a newspaper, stumbling across a frayed paperback in a used bookstore, or meeting a person who radiates the ideals of Vedanta. For most people, the fact of the enormous range of available materials is discovered later, not earlier.

Such cautions duly acknowledged, those of us who seek a broader perspective on what is happening to the West and to Vedanta today must nevertheless recognize how important the increase in information about Vedanta is: the sheer quantity is adding up to qualitative change. For although "information about" is not "knowledge of," there is a deep connection between the "what" and "how" of knowing. In Vedanta, in particular, these connections are strong and explicit; the teachings of Vedanta have always been connected with principles which describe how those teachings are to be acquired, mastered, and followed through to completion. Even as we reaffirm that the goal of knowledge in Vedanta remains simple, unchanging, and liberative (be it the recognition of the identity of Self and Brahman, or the apprehension of the Lord who is the Self of the self, or still yet some other formulation of the Vedantic ideal) and even as we acknowledge that this truth is universally available (pertaining as it does to the fundamental reality of each person and of the world as a whole), we must nevertheless recognize the Vedantic insistence that this universal knowledge is available through the Upanishads and not directly from observation of ourselves or the world about us. When one has mastered the texts, one comes to see how it is that texts are no longer needed. But until that time, one must turn to texts if one seeks access to the truth of Vedanta; until that time what one reads and how one reads it makes a difference.

As the body of materials about Vedanta has grown, and as this information is refracted through a broader and more consciously noticed range of ancient and modern perspectives, the way(s) in which we can know Vedanta have changed. We ought not to shield Vedanta's liberative knowledge from the implications of these changes, and we need to say something about the broader patterns in the reception of Vedanta, and about how the abundance of good materials makes possible new patterns of education in Vedanta—and therefore something new in Vedanta itself.

The gradual disappearance (even in India) of the traditional oral milieu for the study of the Vedanta and the increasingly literate-printed, published-presence of Vedanta in the West makes that original milieu both more rare and less necessary. This in turn means that the Westerners who have taken some interest in Vedanta will also have the ability and responsibility to take the initiative in deciding how to pursue and deepen their primary intuitions. They will have to decide what to learn and how to learn it, including whether and how to take advantage of the primary and secondary materials mentioned above.

For instance, one must decide whether one is going to undertake this investigation alone, strictly relying on one's intuitions and guided by one's books, or whether it really is necessary to go in search of a teacher. One has to decide whether to learn Sanskrit—and even whether this decision is important or not. One has to decide whether to strive for a "pure Vedanta," or actively to seek to integrate Vedanta with religious and cultural values of Western origin. One has to estimate what kind of effect the study of Vedanta is to have on one's life-style, prior philosophical and religious commitments, etc. Since Vedanta can be studied in various ways and according to the traditions of various schools—and these in various novel combinations—despite the major commonalities of the schools that travel under the name of Vedanta, it is difficult for us today to say that there is "*a* Vedanta view" on each particular topic; so we must decide where we stand, which school's viewpoint we are going to follow, or whether we are going to "go it alone."

All of this tells us something about Vedanta itself. As the texts become available more broadly and in more variety, and as new options appear as to how one might learn from them, the path of Vedanta itself changes, Upanishadic knowledge is differently available to us, and there is a shift in the practice of Vedanta, and thus in its truth as this is communicated in practice. In the past the Upanishads were strictly safeguarded and orally transmitted texts, and it was possible to control the "audience" so that only a few competent men had access to the texts. Today there are too many translations and commentaries easily and widely available for such strictures to hold, and Vedanta is more "popular" than it has ever been before. Both the novice and advanced Vedantin have more freedom and more responsibility than ever before.

As we seek to read carefully, to ponder, meditate, and take into our hearts the truth of what we read, we must also cultivate the ability to make wise choices. Our decisions require a skillful passage through the contemporary marketplace of religious ideas, charted by a good bit of self-scrutiny, if we are to find what we are really looking for. One needs to be able to read the primary and secondary sources discerningly, and during one's reading to reflect with equal discrimination on oneself as reader: Am I reading the right books? Do I like the ancient authors more or less than the modern ones? Am I attracted by the truth of Vedanta, or by the way it was initially presented to me? Are the difficulties I face in understanding Vedanta merely temporary, or deeper? What culturally-bound and religiously-narrow ideas am I being disabused of—and what more must I let go of—if I am to get anywhere in this study?

The new resources entail new possibilities, and in some cases they make old positions seem less plausible: as when, for instance, modern linguistics makes it difficult to accept one or another traditional etymology of a difficult word; or when the historical and critical study of texts makes us skeptical about a traditional explanation of how one of the longer Upanishads is a single, unified whole; or when philological and literary studies make us disagree about which Upanishadic verses are the most important ones, and about whether it is really possible to identify any verses which can be marked as the most important ones.

As the multiplication and accumulation of such small decisions and differences combine with the input of other insights of readers influenced by the insights of Western culture and religion, we may be witnessing the creation of genuinely new readings of Vedanta texts which have no Indian precedent, and hence genuinely new expressions of Vedantic ideas; it may ultimately be possible to say that new schools of Vedanta are growing up outside of India. And the West itself, which can no longer entertain a noncommittal and mildly curious attitude toward Vedanta as an exotic import from somewhere else, must then come to terms with Vedanta as part of its own history and own identity.

And so on—until the truth of Vedanta is apprehended, however long that takes. If one learns properly, the complex possibilities I have outlined become exciting opportunities to apprehend Vedanta concretely in the midst of its new Western situation and, in the process, to achieve an understanding of ourselves as persons who were initially to be described in terms of that contemporary culture, and yet who in the course of learning gain freedom over against that cultural definition. Ultimately, at the end point of this process of reading and self-discovery, we will still have to pass beyond words, beyond texts, translations, and critical studies. At such a point it will not matter much whether one encountered Vedanta in Europe, America, or India.

Such a time will surely come for us as individuals and perhaps even as larger communities of seekers after truth. But now is not that time; we are still learning, and therefore are still readers who have to decide what to read and how to think about it, in the cultural milieu in which we find ourselves living. New information, new ways of learning, new insights and articulations, accommodated to the circumstances of the contemporary Western student of Vedanta: together these put us in contact with the "end" of the Vedanta, be it the cessation of the phenomenal self and the concomitant recognition of our identity with the Absolute, or a simple vision of a Lord who spoke the Upanishadic words of wisdom. As in ancient and modern India, Vedanta flourishes in the West of today, but in its own Western way; thoughtful, literate readers and writers of every background and interest are contributing to this new flourishing on this new soil, giving Vedanta new roots and branches, new names and forms.

Silence

by Pico Iyer

SILENCE MEANS ATTUNEMENT to the world; being in so high a
state of confidence and communion that the need for words quite
vanishes. Every one of us knows the sensation of going up, on retreat, to
a high place, and feeling oneself carried up to that state of exaltation so well
conveyed by Andrew Harvey, in his rendering of Rumi:

> For days I am no longer
> In the world. Nor am I
> Out of it. Not "here," not "there."
> Silence, light, air.

In such a place, in such a state, we start to recite the standard litanies:
that silence is sunshine, while company is clouds; that silence is rapture,
while company is doubt; that silence is golden, while company is brass. Yet
silence is not so easily won, and before we go prospecting for the gold in
those hills, we might well recall that fool's gold is all too common. And that
we have to pan for gold, to dig it out from other substances. "All profound
things and emotions of things are preceded and attended by Silence,"
wrote Herman Melville, one of the loftiest and most thunderous of souls.
Mounting to an ever more vocal cry of affirmation, he went on to proclaim
that "Silence is the general consecration of the universe. Silence is the
invisible laying on of the Divine Pontiff's hands upon the world. Silence
is the only Voice of our God." Yet for Melville, silence finally became
darkness, and hopelessness, and self-annihilation; for him it was the music
of oblivion. Devastated by the silence that greeted his heartfelt novels, he
passed into a public silence from which he did not emerge for more than
thirty years. Then, just before his death, he came forth with his final
utterance—the luminous tale of Billy Budd—and showed that silence is
only as worthy as what we can bring back from it, and what we can weave
of it into the clamor of the world.

We have to earn silence, then, to work for it; to make it not an absence
but a presence; not emptiness but repletion. Silence is something more
than just a pause; it is the enchanted space in which things open up and
surfaces fall away and we find ourselves in the midst of absolutes. In silence,
we often say, we can hear ourselves think; but what is truer to say is that

in silence we can hear ourselves not think, and so sink beneath our daily selves into a place deeper than mere thought allows. Silence is a way of clearing space and staying time; of opening out so that the horizon itself expands, and the air is transparent as glass, and "silence" truly seems an anagram for "license." In silence, we might better say, we can hear someone else think.

Or simply breathe. For silence is responsiveness, and in silence we can listen, and in listening to the self, the wind, the sea, we can hear something else, beating far behind. "As soon as you are alone, you are with God," wrote Thomas Merton, who was, as a Trappist, a connoisseur, a caretaker, of silences. It is no coincidence that places of worship are places of silence; if idleness is the devil's playground, silence may be the angels'. And it is only right that the Quakers all but worship silence, for it is the place where everyone can find his God, however he may express it. Silence is an ecumenical state, beyond the doctrines and divisions created by the mind, a place that anyone can recognize. If everyone has a spiritual story to tell in his life, everyone has a spiritual silence to preserve.

So it is that we might almost say that silence is the tribute that we pay to holiness; we slip off words when we enter a sacred space just as we might slip off shoes. A "moment of silence" is the highest honor we can pay to someone; it is the point where the mind stops, and something else takes over (words run out where feelings rush in). A "vow of silence" is the highest devotional act of a holy man. We hold our breaths, we hold our words; we suspend our usual selves, and let ourselves "fall silent"—and fall into the highest place of all.

It often seems that the world is getting noisier these days: in Japan, which may be a model of our future, cars and buses have voices, rooms and elevators speak. The answering machine talks to us, and for us, somewhere above the din of the TV; the Walkman preserves a public silence, but only so as to assure us that we need never—in the bathtub, on a mountaintop, even at our desks—be without the clangor of the world. White noise has become the aural equivalent of the clash of images, the nonstop blast of fragments that increasingly clutter our minds. As Ben Okri, the young Nigerian writer, notes, "When chaos is the god of an era, clamorous music is the deity's chief instrument."

There is—of course—a place for noise, as there is for daily selves. There is a place for roaring, for the shouting exultation of a baseball crowd, for hymns and spoken prayers, for orchestras and cries of pleasure. Silence, like all the best things, is best appreciated in its absence: if noise is the signature tune of the world, silence is the music of the other world, the closest thing we know to the harmony of the spheres. But the greatest charm of noise is when it ceases. In silence, suddenly, it seems as if all the windows of the world are thrown open, and everything is as clear as on a morning after rain. Silence, ideally, hums. It charges the air. In Tibet, where silence has a tragic cause, it is still quickened by the fluttering of prayer flags, the tolling of temple bells, the roar of wind across the plains, the memory of chant.

Silence, then, could be said to be the ultimate province of trust: it is the place where we trust ourselves to be alone; where we trust others to understand the things we do not say; where we trust a higher harmony to assert itself. We all know how treacherous are words, how often we use them to paper over embarrassment, or emptiness, or a fear of the larger spaces silence brings. "Words, words, words" commit us to positions we do not really believe, the imperatives of chatter; words are what we use for lies, false promises, and gossip. We babble with strangers; only with intimates can we be silent. We "make conversation" when we are at a loss; we unmake it when we are alone, or with those so close to us that we can afford to be alone with them.

In love, we are speechless; in awe, we say, words fail us.

Words fail us, then, when we least fail ourselves; they are like the carapace that the rocket sheds at takeoff. Silence, it often seems, is where our deepest self resides. But it might also be said—and this is why we cherish silence—that it is where even our deepest self evaporates. As Jamaica Kincaid, by no means the most mystical or affirmative of writers, put it, in a music born of silence, "Living in the silent voice, I am no longer 'I.' Living in the silent voice, I am at last at peace. Living in the silent voice, I am at last erased."

Practice

Facing the Restless Mind

by Swami Adiswarananda

THE MIND PLAYS a most crucial role in human life. An individual's real strength lies not in his muscle but in the tranquillity of his mind. Tranquillity is vital not only for his or her survival, but also for success and fulfillment in any walk of life. It is the source of his or her power, creativity, and self-confidence. It is as important for a saint or a mystic as it is for a scientist, an artist, an engineer, or a workman. The fourth chapter of the Bhagavad Gita tells us that the mind is our best friend when kept under control, and our worst enemy when we lose control over it. So the saying goes: "He who is the master of his mind is a sage, while he who is a slave to his mind is a fool."

But what is the mind? There are thinkers who have tried to explain the mind in such terms as a function of the brain, a product of heredity, a product of the environment, a by-product of the bodily processes, and so forth. These views only describe how the mind acts and reacts, but not why. They fail to explain a person's moral commitment, aesthetic sensibility, and spiritual aspiration. They leave out the most essential part of an individual—his soul, and reduce him to either a creature of circumstances or a stimulus-response mechanism. Vedanta considers these views to be incomplete and inadequate.

The seers of Vedanta gave a spiritual interpretation of man and his mind. Mind, according to them, is a positive entity that stands between the body and senses on the one hand, and the knowing self on the other. While the knowing self of an individual is the focus of the all-pervading universal Self, the mind serves as the ego-self. The mind is the leader of the sense-organs and pervades the entire body. Though closely connected with the body, the mind is independent of it.

The functions of the mind are four: deliberation, determination, I-consciousness, and memory. The mind is called our second body, or subtle body. The gross body is extension of the mind. The relation between the subtle body and the gross body is like that between a seed and a plant. Both mind and body are material by nature. The body is made of five gross elements—earth, air, water, ether, and fire, and the mind is made of the subtle forms of the same five elements. Being material by nature, these elements do not possess consciousness of their own. The body derives its consciousness from the mind, and the mind from the knowing self. The mind is not destroyed with the death of the body. The mind is the receptacle of the memories of past lives, and transmigrates from one birth to another. Each person is born with a particular mind that he or she brings from the past, and it is this mind that seeks expression through thoughts and actions in the present life.

Each person perceives the world through the prism of his own mind. His mind is his interpreter, guide, and constant companion. It receives sensory perceptions of sight, sound, touch, taste, and smell, interprets them according to its inbuilt conditionings, and then responds through its motor organs. Thus the world of an individual is in his or her mind. His birth and death, suffering and enjoyment, virtue and vice, bondage and liberation, are all experiences of the mind.

The mind has three levels of consciousness: subconscious, conscious, and superconscious. The conscious is that level from which a person makes decisions, choices, and value judgments. Beneath the conscious lies the subconscious, hidden and unperceived, exerting its influence on the conscious. The conscious is like the steering of an automobile, while the subconscious is like the propulsion. Above the conscious there is a third level, the superconscious, where individual consciousness comes in contact with the universal Consciousness. The subconscious is guided by instinct, the conscious by reason, and the superconscious by intuition. I-consciousness, or the ego, operates only on the conscious level. On the subconscious level it is unmanifest, while on the superconscious level it almost vanishes.

The mind is subject to three gunas, or the three modifications of matter: inertia (*tamas*), passion (*rajas*), and tranquillity (*sattva*). The preponderance of one over the other two at any time affects the moods of the mind. Tamas overpowers the mind with darkness, and rajas with agitation, while sattva gives the mind stability. In regard to the perception of reality, tamas causes nonperception and rajas distorted perception, while sattva brings clarity of perception. The mind of each individual represents a specific composition of the three gunas, and this composition determines the person's disposition, character, likes and dislikes. The guna composition becomes altered as one changes his or her way of living.

The mind rises and falls. Vedanta speaks of six subtle centers of consciousness located along the spinal column known as *chakras*, or lotuses. Their locations are: at the base of the spine, at the level of the organ of generation, at the navel, at the heart, at the throat, and in the space between the eyebrows.

The six centers are like six windows through which the mind perceives the outside universe. When the mind dwells in the three lower centers, it broods only on eating, sleeping, and gross sense enjoyments. When it rises to the fourth, it feels spiritual longing and makes spiritual effort. By rising higher, it eventually goes beyond the six centers and merges in the universal Consciousness.

The basic urge of the individual consciousness is toward unity with the universal Consciousness, and so the natural flow of the mind is cosmocentric. But because of the blocking of the ego, the flow becomes obstructed, falls back upon itself, and breaks into countless waves of negative emotions and urges, such as lust, anger, jealousy, and possessiveness. Unable to be cosmocentric, the mind becomes egocentric.

The mind is known for its proverbial restlessness. The sixth chapter of the Bhagavad Gita describes the mind by four epithets: "restless," "turbulent," "powerful," and "obstinate." A restless mind addicted to sense pleasures has been depicted in an ancient proverb as a "mad elephant." Shankaracharya describes it as a "huge tiger": "In the forest-tract of sense pleasures there prowls a huge tiger called the mind. Let good people who have a longing for liberation never go there."[1] Swami Vivekananda has compared the restless mind to a monkey that is not only drunk with the wine of desire, but is also simultaneously stung by the scorpion of jealousy and taken over by the demon of pride.

The restless mind is marked by several signs. It is dull, excited, or scattered, and never concentrated. Impulsive and hypersensitive, it has low frustration tolerance and is often guided by arbitrary whims and passing sentiments. Carried along by the waves of impulses, darkened by imaginations, unstable, fickle, and full of desires, it is constant prey to delusions and fancies. It swings from hyperactivity to depression, from self-pity to self-aggrandizement, from overoptimism to overpessimism. It is secretive and negative, divided and discontented. Harassed by its own anxieties and tensions, it drifts aimlessly and is unable to find rest.

A person with a restless mind does not act but only reacts, does not live life but merely copes with it. Mental restlessness manifests itself on the physical level as emotionally charged speech, restless body movement, sharp mood changes, uneven breath, restless movement of the eyes, and lack of concentration. From the point of view of the gunas, the restless mind is dominated either by inertia or passion, and from the point of view of the centers of consciousness, it dwells mostly in the three lower centers.

The mind is restless because it is weak. It is weak because it is impure, and it is impure because it has become a slave to the body and the senses. The weak mind is at the root of all suffering.

The five causes of suffering, according to Vedanta, are: (1) ignorance, which blocks the perception of the reality of oneness; (2) deluded ego, that projects its own world of fancies and desires; (3) deep attachment, which expresses itself as possessiveness; (4) strong aversion, which seeks the pleasurable and shuns the painful; and (5) clinging to life, which is the inability to change and grow.

Impurities of the mind are the subtle deposits of past indulgent living. They are not simply impure thoughts. Having been repeated over and over again, the impure thoughts have become persistent habits, striking roots into our body chemistry. Habits are always formed little by little. These habits are called *samskaras*. Samskaras cannot be overcome by mere intellectual reasoning and analysis. Time cannot erase them, change of place or diet cannot uproot them.

Some try to overcome restlessness by pampering the desires of the mind. But pampering eventually becomes suicidal. It is false psychology that says we can overcome our mind by yielding to its desires. Desires, like flames of fire, are insatiable. The more we add fuel to them, the more they burn, until in the end they destroy their very base, the mind. Unrestrained desires and unbridled gratification of libidinal urges only lead to disintegration and destruction.

Others try to overcome restlessness by punishing the mind. They resort to self-torture and mortification. But punishing only represses the urges and desires, driving them underground. Repression heightens the awareness of the desired object, causing fantasy and personality disorders. Still others try to escape restlessness of the mind by a change of environment. But soon they discover that they are being pursued by their restlessness. It is because wherever we go we carry our mind with us. The way to overcome the restless mind, according to the seers of Vedanta, is to face it.

Facing the mind has four aspects: self-acceptance, self-control, self-regulation, and moderation.

Self-Acceptance. Self-acceptance is the first aspect of facing the mind. This acceptance is not fatalistic and helpless passivity. Neither is it looking for scapegoats. Self-acceptance is acknowledging the fact that the problem of restlessness is our own creation, and we ourselves will have to overcome it. The solution to the problem will always elude our grasp so long as we deny this responsibility.

Lack of self-acceptance is at the root of all despair, self-pity, tension, and cynicism. A humorous story highlights the need for self-acceptance. A man suffering from a severe inferiority complex had been visiting a psychoanalyst for several years, with no result achieved. Finally one day, when the patient arrived for his session, the psychoanalyst told him: "Mr. Jones, I have good news for you. At last I've been able to make a breakthrough with your problem. You have no inferiority complex—you *are* inferior!" Self-acceptance teaches us that obstacles and imperfections are not to be avoided but acknowledged and overcome. A limitation or deficiency, when accepted with a positive attitude of mind, becomes a driving force for self-mastery. Benjamin Franklin said, "Those things that hurt, instruct."

Self-Control. The second aspect of facing the mind is self-control, which is control of the mind. According to Vedanta, the unruly mind never comes under control unless it is controlled consciously. Such control is never a windfall. It cannot be attained vicariously or miraculously or by mechanical or chemical means. The four paths of yoga outline four ways to achieve control of the mind: persuasion, purification, eradication, and subjugation.

The path of knowledge, or jnana yoga, upholds the way of persuasion. It relies heavily on reason. The virtues it prescribes for practicing control are: (1) discrimination between the realities and the unrealities of life; (2) detachment, which is freedom from the thirst for all sense pleasure; (3) restraining the outgoing propensities of the mind and the senses; (4) withdrawal of the mind; (5) fortitude; (6) self-settledness; (7) faith; and (8) longing for liberation. The intellect, the leader of all the faculties of the mind, is persuaded to reflect seriously on the harmful consequences of sense enjoyments, and then to give up such enjoyments voluntarily.

The path of devotion, or bhakti yoga, advocates the way of purification. The virtues prescribed for practicing control are: (1) purity of food, including whatever the mind draws in through the senses for enjoyment; (2) freedom from desire; (3) practice of devotion, and holy company; (4) truthfulness; (5) doing good to others; (6) straightforwardness; (7) nonviolence; (8) compassion; (9) charity; and (10) not yielding to despondency or excessive merriment. Bhakti yoga relies not so much on controlling the mind as on directing it toward the Divine. It maintains that the mind cannot give up the lower pleasures of life until it has tasted something higher.

The path of selfless action, or karma yoga, follows the way of eradicating the ego. The virtues prescribed for practicing control of the mind are: (1) giving up brooding over the results of action; (2) nonattachment; (3) eradication of the ego; and (4) dedication of the results of action to the Divine. According to karma yoga, all mental restlessness is due to the worldly ego and its attachments, involvements, and actions, and the only way to overcome restlessness is eradication of the ego. But the ego, hardened by repeated selfish actions, cannot be eradicated by any means other than performance of unselfish actions. Karma alone can rescue a person from the bondage of karma.

The path of meditation, or raja yoga, emphasizes the way of subjugation. It relies not so much on reason or devotion or eradication of the ego as on willpower. The virtues that it prescribes for practicing control are: (1) nonviolence; (2) truthfulness; (3) noncovetousness; (4) continence; (5) nonreceiving of undesirable gifts and favors; (6) external and internal cleanliness; (7) contentment; (8) austerity; (9) study of sacred texts; (10) self-surrender to the Divine; (11) control of posture and breath; and (12) withdrawal of the mind. According to raja yoga, reason is too weak to uproot the ingrained tendencies, devotion requires inborn faith in God, and ego eradication is a slow process. Only strong willpower can bring the wayward mind back to tranquillity. Raja yoga aims at controlling the subconscious with the help of conscious efforts. By control of posture and regulation of breath, along with the practice of the other prescribed virtues, the follower of raja yoga confronts the agitated mind and subdues it.

Self-control is achieved by following any of the four ways or a combination of them. Self-control is neither negative nor inhibitive. It is the technique of dealing with desires. Desires cannot be crushed or repressed. They cannot be fulfilled completely or postponed indefinitely. The only way is to reduce them to a healthy level. Self-control calls for withstanding the intensities of the gross impulses and urges, especially those of lust and greed.

Our body grows in health by bearing with physical intensities; so also our mind gains in strength by bearing with the intensities of its cravings and urges. The mind, like the body, needs exercise for its health and fitness. Unfortunately, we neglect this need of the mind. It is rightly said that the only mental exercise most people get is "jumping at conclusions, running down their friends, sidestepping responsibility, and pushing their luck!"

The logic for self-control is compelling. If a person is all muscle and metabolism, then he can never escape death. If he is nothing more than wild impulses and emotions, he can never get rest; and if he is all desires and dreams, he will ever remain unfulfilled. Vedanta asserts that our real nature is the pure Self and that we are not slaves of the body and mind, but their masters. Life is rebellion against the laws of material nature and not submission to them.

Self-Regulation. The third aspect of facing the mind is self-regulation. Self-regulation involves concentrating the mind on a single object and meditating on that object at a fixed center of consciousness. The object of concentration and meditation is called the Chosen Ideal. The Chosen Ideal may be the knowing self, which is the focus of the all-pervading universal Self, beyond all name, form, and attribute; or it may be the same knowing self with name, form, and attribute superimposed upon it.

No lasting serenity is ever possible without the practice of concentration on a fixed Chosen Ideal. The reason is that concentration cannot develop roots if the Chosen Ideal is changed frequently. Meditation culminates in absorption in the Chosen Ideal, which is the goal of all regulatory practice. In order to reach this absorption, each path of yoga suggests a number of supporting regulatory practices.

Jnana yoga prescribes hearing the great Vedic sayings and reflecting and meditating on their meaning. Bhakti yoga advises prayer, ritualistic worship, japa (repetition of a sacred word), and meditation. The follower of karma yoga adopts the supportive practices of either bhakti yoga or jnana yoga. Raja yoga advocates concentration and meditation.

The goal of concentration and meditation is to cultivate a single thought-wave. A restless mind is like a lake which is constantly being agitated by the winds of desires. As a result of this constant agitation, our true Self at the bottom of the lake cannot be perceived. When a single thought-wave is consciously cultivated by the repeated and uninterrupted practice of meditation, it develops into a huge wave which swallows up all the diverse thought-waves, and makes the mind transparent and calm. The concentrated mind is the mind that has taken this form of one single thought-wave.

Self-control and self-regulation represent respectively dispassion and practice—the two disciplines prescribed in the sixth chapter of the Bhagavad Gita for overcoming restlessness of the mind. The two must be followed simultaneously. Unless one practices control, one cannot succeed in regulation, and unless one regulates the mind, one cannot succeed in controlling it. Control without regulation never becomes lasting. Such egocentric control does not stand the test of stress. On the other hand, regulation without control is dangerous. An uncontrolled mind is impure, and an impure mind, when roused through concentration, becomes destructive. A Sanskrit proverb says: "To feed a cobra with milk without first taking out its poison fangs is only to increase its venom." Again, control and regulation are to be practiced repeatedly, in thought, word, and deed, for a long time, without break, and with devotion.

The psychology of repeated practice is to neutralize the deep-seated, distracting samskaras by developing counter-samskaras. Impure thought is countered by pure thought, impure imagination by pure imagination, uncontrolled speech by thoughtful speech, bad posture by good posture. A thought when repeated becomes a tendency, a tendency when repeated becomes a habit, and a habit when repeated becomes character. So Swami Vivekananda says: "Never say any man is hopeless, because he only represents a character, a bundle of habits, which can be checked by new and better ones. Character is repeated habits, and repeated habits alone can reform character."[2]

Moderation. The fourth aspect of facing the mind is moderation. The mind cannot be brought under control all of a sudden. Human nature cannot be hurried. Old habits die hard. They have deep roots and cannot be overcome all at once. A habit is formed bit by bit. So a counter-habit is to be developed bit by bit. If you drive a screw into a wall by a number of turns, you cannot simply pull it out. In order to remove it, you have to give the same number of turns in the opposite direction. The intensity of our effort to develop a counter-habit must be in keeping with the capacity of our minds to endure.

Effort when too weak and casual fails to change the habits, but when too intense and accelerated, can damage the mind itself. So the Bhagavad Gita advises moderation in all matters: "Yoga is not for him who eats too much nor for him who eats too little. It is not for him, O Arjuna, who sleeps too much nor for him who sleeps too little. For him who is temperate in his food and recreation, temperate in his exertion at work, temperate in sleep and waking, yoga puts an end to all sorrows. . . . Renouncing entirely all the desires born of the will, drawing back the senses from every direction by strength of mind, let a man little by little attain tranquillity with the help of the buddhi [discriminating faculty] armed with fortitude."[3]

No task is more urgent than gaining mastery over the mind by overcoming its restlessness. No sacrifice is too great to achieve this goal. No effort in this venture is ever lost or wasted. Success in self-mastery comes only to those who long for it, practice it, and persevere in their practice. Practice, however, is not talking, discussing, or debating but doing, and the secret of all doing is to do.

1. *Vivekachudamani* (Verse 176), tr. Swami Madhavananda (Calcutta: Advaita Ashrama, 1970), p. 68.

2. *Vivekananda: The Yogas and Other Works*, ed. Swami Nikhilananda (New York: Ramakrishna-Vivekananda Center, 1984), pp. 629-30.

3. *The Bhagavad Gita*, 6. 17-18 and 6. 24-25; tr. Swami Nikhilananda (New York: Ramakrishna-Vivekananda Center, 1944), pp. 166-67 and 168-69.

True Worship

by Swami Ashokananda

WORSHIP IS THE union of the individual soul with God. This union may be differently conceived, but it is the very essence of worship. Various means there are by which the union can be effected, and each of them is legitimate. But as it often happens with us humans, we forget the inner meaning and give ourselves over to the forms and consider *them* as worship. Thus performing certain rites, using certain articles, making certain offerings, repeating certain words and formulas, practicing certain postures of the body—all these signify to many the essence of worship. These by themselves are not worship. This is not to say that those practices are of no consequence. Every action has its effect. These also have theirs. But they do not amount to what constitutes the essence of worship.

Union with God presupposes the consciousness of God. God and man are not really separate entities. Whatever certain philosophies may say, unless there is a preexistent unity, there cannot be any union between God and man.

Man *is* God, only he is enshrouded by certain sheaths which have clouded his divine Self. When these sheaths are worn out, the divine effulgence bursts forth, and man becomes God. In any case, man feels united with God and he does not know where he ends and where God begins—the two become one. This is the culmination of worship. Whatever practice, thought, or action helps in wearing and tearing the veils that hide the divine Self, is worship.

Having ascertained the essential nature of worship, we have to remember that man as he is at present, is a weak being, full of errors, shortsighted, and often at the mercy of circumstances. He, therefore, cannot always determine what will help him in tearing his bondage. It is necessary, therefore, that he should have certain practices prescribed to him, which he may faithfully follow and which will by and by free him from the enveloping ignorance. In every religion there are such well-known methods. These methods have been tried by many spiritual aspirants and have been found quite reliable and efficacious. So for practical purposes, the practice of those methods can be called worship. Here, again, we should point out that an automatic practice is little helpful. Every practice must be made with sincerity and enthusiasm, and we must constantly watch if our practice is succeeding in lifting our consciousness above the normal level, freeing us from the bondage of desire, and taking us nearer to the presence of God.

Feeling the presence of God may be differently conceived by different persons. Those who follow the path of knowledge and discrimination will conceive it as the expansion of self, or rather as tearing the subjective bondages and realizing the higher Self. Those who follow the path of love and devotion will consider it as a gracious visitation on the part of the Lord. But in all cases there must be an awareness of the divine substance. And this awareness must grow from day to day till only God remains and nothing else. The practice that helps this realization is worship. . . .

Everyone must find the best form of worship for himself with the help of a true guru. . . . Very few persons have leisure enough to devote themselves to strenuous spiritual disciplines. Their bodies also are not fit. We are speaking of the average person. Devotion to God is best under these circumstances—devotion in the spirit of a servant or a child of God. Repeating the name of the Lord, meditating on him, worshiping him formally, visiting holy places and holy men—all these are helpful. But one should always think oneself as pure and perfect, the same as *Satchidananda*, that is, Existence-Knowledge-Bliss absolute, for the child of God is of the same stuff as the Father himself. . . .

Mere spiritual practice will not be effective enough for the average person unless he undertakes works for the purification of the mind. There is nothing so effective as the unselfish service of others. That purifies the heart quickly, frees us from our gross desires, and takes us nearer to God. Devotion accompanied by service of mankind in the spirit of worship—this, we think, is the best form of worship in the present age. But as we have pointed out, there must also be an element of spiritual knowledge in it—as when we consider ourselves as Satchidananda. This is essential. We must not consider ourselves as miserable sinners, forever bound, helpless, ignorant, and weak. We must look upon ourselves as free, illumined, perfect, and blissful, of the same essence as God.

✺

Control of the Subconscious Mind

by Swami Prabhavananda

WHAT IS THE subconscious mind? We all know something about the nature of the conscious mind. We think, feel, and act, and are conscious of our thoughts, feelings, and actions. And whatever we think, feel, and do—in short, all our experiences—are stored in the subconscious mind.

We can remember certain things we did. Why are we able to remember? Because what we did remains imbedded in the mind. Every thought, feeling, and action leaves an impression on the mind. Nothing is lost. The sum total of those impressions is what constitutes the character of an individual. We are the result of what we have thought, felt, and done. In turn, our accumulated tendencies determine and control our conscious thoughts, feelings, and actions. How we react to the objective universe is governed by our own individual character, which is the sum total of our past reactions. That is why individuals vary in their reactions to experience. The reaction varies according to the character of the individual.

But what about free will? Can we not choose the way we will react to given conditions and circumstances? Yes, we can choose; but the will is not absolutely *free* will. The will, by which I make choices, behaves in accordance with my character, that sum total of all my past deeds, thoughts, and feelings. And not only of this present life: the subconscious mind carries the record of many past lives.

Therefore we are what we have made ourselves. The subconscious mind carries the whole record of our past and present; it defines the character and the tendencies we are born with, and they in turn determine the way we react to present conditions. The subconscious, that part of the mind below the level of the conscious or surface mind, is a very influential factor in our present life.

We all realize the power of the influence exerted by the subconscious mind. Through experience, a certain growth takes place in the ideas held by the conscious mind. We develop a sense of good and evil. Certain new ideals and principles come into the conscious mind. We realize that we must live according to these new ideals and principles. We begin to know a better way of life. But we find ourselves helpless to live in that better way. This is an experience every one of us has had. We know, but we cannot do. A thief, for example, wants to reform himself; he does not wish to steal any more. Then he goes to a place where he sees that it would be very easy to steal without being caught. He knows better, but he steals. It is the same with any other bad habit. We have become slaves to our own subconscious minds.

Is there no way out of this? Yes. The so-called free will is controlled by one's character, so that the term "free will" is really a misnomer. There is, however, a certain freedom, which is not of the will or of the mind or of the intellect, but it is a freedom of the Spirit within us which says, "I cannot will, yet I *must* will." Although our minds and character say, "I cannot do it," the Spirit says, "You *must* do it." That is the freedom every individual possesses, and through that freedom of the Spirit each one of us may find salvation.

We recognize that there is something greater and higher which we have to achieve. Because of our habits and tendencies built up by past actions, we find it almost impossible—but not completely impossible. If it were completely impossible, then life would not be worth living. But, because of that freedom of the Spirit, though we may fail many times, we continue to struggle, and this struggle is life. Whether we know it or not, the real struggle is to overcome the subconscious mind, and to be free again.

How are we to achieve this? The only way to overcome the subconscious mind is to follow the psychology of religion. Simply to analyze ourselves and recognize this slavery does not help. We have to root out completely our impressions and transform our characters. This complete transformation and renewal of the mind is what is taught in the psychology of religion.

It is useless to try to overcome the past and be good in the future. This cannot work, because however we may try, our tendencies remain. The only way to erase all the past tendencies, or samskaras, is by a complete transformation of the mind. And what happens then? In the words of Vedanta philosophy, we realize the kingdom of the Self. In the words of the Bible, we realize the kingdom of heaven which is within us.

What is this true nature that we realize, this kingdom of God? It is perfection. Christ says: "Be ye perfect, even as the Father in heaven is perfect." Some theologians interpret this perfection which Christ speaks of as a relative perfection toward which we grow eternally, but never fully achieve. Christ did not mean that. He said definitely, "Be ye perfect." Not relatively perfect. Relative perfection is imperfection. Perfection, to be perfection, must be an absolute perfection, nothing less. And this perfection is to be attained as we empty ourselves of all the contents of consciousness.

The mind is like a lake of dirty water, lashed into waves. The reflection of the sun in that lake is not clear. But make the water of the lake clear and calm, and there is a perfect reflection of the sun. The sun, the light of God, shines within each of us, shines on the lake of the mind, but because of the imperfections of that mind, the light is imperfectly reflected.

What are those imperfections? They are the samskaras that we have created, which, in turn, create thoughts in us that lash the mind into waves, so that the sun within us, the light of God, cannot be properly reflected. We are not even conscious of that sun within. But the moment we are freed from our past tendencies, we are purified. The moment we attain the tranquillity of mind which Christ calls purity of heart, God can be seen. "Blessed are the pure in heart, for they shall see God." And not until we have seen God and have realized pure consciousness, can we say that the subconscious mind has been overcome.

What is really meant by the phrases, "making the mind tranquil" and "freeing the mind of all its contents"? Brahman, or God, is said to be *sat*—eternally existent. He *is*. He is also *chit*—consciousness itself. And He is *ananda*—happiness, or love, itself. Brahman is in some way reflected in our minds. We are always carrying Him within us, every moment of our lives. This existence is reflected in every one of us by the knowledge: *I am, I exist*. We are all conscious of that existence; none of us can imagine nonexistence. We must exist even to try to think of ourselves as not existing.

We exist, and we have knowledge of our existence, but this knowledge embraces only the contents of our minds, not of Reality. Only when we free ourselves from the contents of consciousness can we become aware of pure consciousness which is God, the infinite consciousness.

We not only think, we feel. What do we wish to feel? We wish to feel love and happiness. These are the two strong desires that exist in us, the desire for love and happiness. But they are only a reflection. When we still the waves that arise in the mind, we realize pure consciousness. Then we realize the *fulfillment* of the desire for love and happiness, which is infinite love and infinite happiness.

It seems so easy to say, "Free yourself from the contents of consciousness; be pure in heart, and you will reach God." But, owing to our different states of consciousness, we find that it is quite impossible to reach freedom, to reach God. In our waking state, our physical senses and limited minds can only become conscious of objects and things. We cannot reach pure consciousness, however we may try. Again, in dream we cannot realize pure consciousness. When we go into deep sleep, we become unconscious. But, although we seem to be freed of the content of consciousness, it is because there is only a veil of darkness which is covering our consciousness. So long as we live and move within the states of waking, dream, and dreamless sleep, it is not possible to reach the realization of pure consciousness. We cannot realize God.

In order to free ourselves from the contents of consciousness, we must reach a state beyond these three states of consciousness. This state is called in the Upanishads, *turiya*, the fourth. It is possible to reach that fourth state while living on earth. In this state of pure consciousness, we lose the contents of consciousness, we are freed from limitations, and we become one with infinite and pure consciousness.

But how is this to be achieved? As the goal is clear, so also the means to attain it are clear and simple. It is done by uniting our minds with pure consciousness through the practice of constant meditation. In this state there is a continual flow of thought towards God where nothing exists in the mind but he. This stage develops with practice.

Through ignorance many teachers have taught that the mind must be made blank in meditation. They think that since the mind must be emptied of all objects of consciousness and made blank, they will attain samadhi, transcendental consciousness. They do not stop to consider that when we go into deep sleep there is no content of consciousness in the mind, yet we do not attain samadhi.

What is the nature of samadhi, and what is the difference between it and deep sleep or becoming unconscious? A fool goes to sleep and he still comes out a fool, but if even a fool should go into samadhi, he would come out a wise man. He would come out an illumined soul.

Likewise, if you try to make the mind a blank in meditation, what happens? A fool you went in, or tried to go in; the same fool you came out—even a worse fool, for a person who tries to make the mind blank becomes lazy, *tamasic*. Laziness is not meditation. Meditation requires great strenuous effort to intensely concentrate the mind upon pure consciousness, or God. It does not matter what the conception or the ideal of the Godhead may be. There must be a positive ideal upon which to concentrate. We have to raise one strong wave of thought to the exclusion of the rest. Never try to make your mind blank—or you will remain a blank. But think of God, concentrate upon some conception of God, and you will become God!

This is what Vedanta means by meditation: a constant flow of thought toward that one ideal. In other words, we walk with God, we sleep with God, we eat with God, we live with God. We must struggle to maintain that constant flow of the mind toward God. When the mind is constantly united with God and is established in the constant remembrance of God, one achieves that state of meditation called *dhruba smriti*—the constant recollectedness of God.

To reach that stage we must acquire a certain mental purity by controlling the outgoing senses. We have to practice bringing the senses back from sense objects so that our attention may be fastened upon God.

Suppose you had the problem of cleaning a dirty ink bottle that is fastened to the table. You can't pick it up and empty the ink out. What will you do? You pour clean water in, and the ink and dirt spill out. You keep pouring in the clean water until all the ink and dirt have been washed out and the bottle contains nothing but clear water. In the same way, it is not possible to empty the mind by throwing out the contents of consciousness and making it blank; but what one *can* do is to keep pouring the clear water of the thought of God into the mind until the dirt spills out.

That is the experience of everyone in the beginning. At first we find ourselves worse than we ever thought we were. Such horrible thoughts and distractions arise when we try to meditate that we say, "Surely I was not as wicked as that before! Why should such wicked thoughts come into my mind just now when I try to meditate?"

That is a universal experience. In the beginning, it seems as if greater passions arise because as we pour clear water into the mind, the dirty ink flows out. The whole subconscious mind is disturbed. It is like the layer of mud at the bottom of a lake which, when stirred, muddies the whole lake for some time. We all pass through that stage of muddy water, muddy character.

It quite often happens that when a person starts to lead a spiritual life, his or her character apparently grows worse instead of better. All the worst things come to the surface. That is inevitable. Let them come up and then get rid of them. With patience and perseverance we have to go on pouring in the clear water of God. Distractions, evil thoughts, and wicked desires will arise in the mind. Struggle! Struggle to bring back the thought of God into the mind again and again. Practice constant recollection.

When Arjuna learned of this ideal, he said to his teacher, Sri Krishna, "You describe this yoga as a life of union with Brahman. But I do not see how this can be permanent. The mind is so very restless." Then Sri Krishna replied, "Yes, the mind is restless and difficult to subdue. But it can be brought under control by constant practice." Through practice and struggle controlling the mind becomes easy.

We cannot achieve this in a moment, nor in a day; but we must keep the ideal high; we must aim high and shoot high. We may fail many times; it doesn't matter, get up again, and continue to struggle. That is life! If there is no struggle in life, and if everything goes on smoothly, then either you are an illumined soul or you are an unawakened soul. But most of us are at neither end of the path.

As long as we are on the path, we must struggle. Life is struggle, struggle is life! My teacher, Swami Brahmananda, used to say, "Do or die!" Keep that in mind. Struggle—and you are sure to overcome.

Divine Love

Swami Satprakashananda

LOVE OF GOD is the very essence of spiritual life; without it religious practices are nothing but sheer physical and mental exercises. The sanctimonious observance of rites and ceremonies, or the worship of God for temporal interests, no matter how solemn, does not constitute spirituality.

The one purpose of all religious disciplines is to develop love of God within the heart of the aspirant. It is for this that he or she says prayers, chants hymns, studies scriptures, listens to sermons, makes offerings, observes fasts and vigils, and practices meditation. This love of God is the one supreme ideal of life as taught by all the great teachers of the world.

Even so, though we may know that God is the most lovable of all, the one inexhaustible source of all blessedness, goodness, beauty, and love, yet we do not feel that longing to know him. Even though we know that it is through love alone that we can be united with him, and attain eternal life, light, and joy, so dominated are we by our deep-rooted sense desires, our tenacious clinging to ephemeral objects, that we feel no yearning for him. To counteract these inveterate tendencies, to transform worldly attachment into spiritual urge, to create a Godward flow of thoughts and feelings, the spiritual aspirant must undergo certain disciplines, for it is only through the life of law that he can enter into the life of love.

Three distinct modes of worship constitute the practical methods for the cultivation of devotion to God, namely, physical, verbal, and mental. The physical, or external, mode of worship is performed by bowing down in reverence to God, by the observance of rites and ceremonies, the offering of flowers, lights, incense, etc., the practice of austerities, and personal service to the temple and the teacher. Verbal worship is observed by the saying of prayers, the chanting of hymns, the study of scriptures, and the repetition of a sacred name or formula, while the mental worship consists in the constant remembrance of God, the renunciation of attachment, self-resignation, contemplation, and so forth. Any or all of these modes of worship may be practiced by the aspirant, according to his own tendency, capacity, and situation in life. The practice of even one of these forms of worship, if followed with steadfast devotion, will generate love for God.

The repeated utterance of a sacred word or formula is a very simple method, yet nonetheless, most efficacious. No accessory is needed for its practice, which can be made audibly, semiaudibly, or mentally. Of the three methods, the mental is the most effective. It purifies the aspirant's mind to its very depths and enables him to hold his thoughts on God. In a sense, this constant repetition is a concentrated form of prayer. During prayer we think of God by numerous words and phrases, but as our spiritual sense deepens, and our feelings become intensified, a single word or phrase will convey all that God means to us. It becomes the focal point of all our ideas and sentiments regarding him. For example, to a Christian who has caught the inner spirit of Jesus Christ, the repetition of his name may do more to intensify his devotion to Christ than a whole scriptural text would.

Every word represents an idea, and, just as each thought has its own word symbol, so are there word symbols, or seed words, as they are called, to express mystical experiences. Through the constant repetition of a seed word spiritual awareness is germinated, and love of God grows within the heart of the devotee.

Thus, gradually, by the practice of these different methods of worship, the mind becomes purged of all dross and dirt, and its attachment to the transitory values of here and hereafter, and there grows a natural longing for God. The aspirant seeks God passionately for his own sake, until, like the needle of the compass which always points north, his mind centers upon God under all the varying conditions of life. He remembers God constantly. This constant God-recollectedness is called bhakti, devotion.

During the preparatory stages the aspirant's attitude toward God is very much stimulated by his thought, and by a feeling of awe and reverence rather than of love. The aspirant feels that God is the ruler of the universe; consequently, he or she is more conscious of His splendor and power than of His sweetness and beauty. He seeks God that he may be freed from all bondages, that in Him he may find real life, real light, real joy, knowing that none but He is worth seeking and loving as the supreme goal of life.

But, as love grows, the aspirant no longer indulges in such calculations. The might and majesty of God no longer concern him. To him God is all love, and love of God becomes the one motivating power of all his thoughts, feelings, and actions. Out of love of Him his hand works, his mind thinks, his heart feels. In short, he lives for God alone. The attitude of the loving devotee toward God is reflected in this prayer: "May my speech be engaged in the telling of thy glory; may my ears be engaged in listening to thy praise; may my hands be engaged in the performance of thy service; may my eyes see only that which is holy; may my head be ever bowed in reverence to the universe, thy abode, and may my mind be ever engaged in the remembrance of thy blessed feet."

Love and reverence are two different mental attitudes. So long as the worshiper thinks of the divinity as the almighty creator, or the stern ruler, or the dispassionate onlooker of the world order, he may have fear and reverence for God, but not love. He may even have the tendency to bow down before him, but only from a distance. He will not feel drawn toward Him; there will not be the urge to become united with Him, or to embrace Him as his own. But, with the growth of devotion there comes a sense of intimate relationship to God. The more intensely the votary contemplates God's love and grace, the deeper grows his devotion to Him. He looks upon God as his very own; he feels that "I am thine, thou art mine." This feeling gradually manifests itself in various devotional attitudes according to the aptitude and disposition of the aspirant.

The Hindu psychology of devotion classifies these attitudes under five principal headings. The first is *shanta*, the serene attitude, in which God is seen as the immutable Self, the calm witness of all mental and physical phenomena. The second is *dasya*, the attitude of service. This includes the attitudes of the protected toward the protector, the servant toward the master, and the child toward the parent. Third comes *sakhya*, friendship. In this attitude the devotee feels that he is a friend and companion of God, and his playmate. Next comes *vatsalya*, the attitude of a parent. The devotee looks upon God as his own child. Lastly comes *madhura*, the sweet attitude of the lover and the beloved.

It will be seen that in each succeeding attitude there is an increasing intimacy between the devotee and God. In each there is the reciprocity of love. In whatever way the devotee loves God, so does God love his devotee. Yet, even though God may play the role of master, father, mother, friend, or lover toward his devotees, he is actually our all in all, through all eternity, only we do not recognize him. There is no other father, or mother, or friend, or lover than he. All earthly relationships are temporary, and therefore unreal. So it is that the devotee prays: "Thou alone art my mother, thou alone art my father, thou alone art my friend, thou alone art my companion, thou alone art my wisdom and my treasure. Thou art my all in all, O God of gods."

The Hindu scriptures strongly advocate the association of the holy as an effective means to the cultivation of devotion to God. Love of God is not to be found in temples or churches or books, however sacred. Love of God exists within the heart of the devotee, and by associating with the lovers of God, by conversing with them, by serving them, and by observing their ways, one may imbibe their spirit of love. As a matter of fact, love of God is not kindled within us until we come in contact with those who carry that burning flame within them.

The grace of God usually comes through the grace of those who have already received it. Holiness is contagious. Robert Ingersoll once made the remark to Swami Vivekananda, "Had I been God I would have made health contagious instead of disease." "Little do we realize," replied the Swami, "that health is as contagious as disease, virtue as contagious as vice, and cheerfulness as contagious as moroseness." Moral and spiritual precepts, however sublime, may stimulate our thoughts and inspire us with noble feelings, but, unless we see them actually exemplified in the lives of great personalities, they do not implant themselves within us as the ideals of life and living.

Every human being is a potential lover of God. All our lives we have loved nothing but God, but our love has been misdirected. Through all our seeking after wealth, position, pleasure, friendship, love, and power there has been the search for God. It is the urge for the infinite, the eternal, the perfect that impels our seeking, and that is why our minds refuse to be satisfied with that which is limited and imperfect.

We have ever sought for the highest and the best. God alone is the highest and best. Your true being cannot respond to any other ideal than the attainment of the highest and best, and when you knowingly seek God as the goal of your life, when you are fully aware that you are living for something beyond which there is nothing more to gain, something which, once gained, you can never lose, something which removes all sufferings, weaknesses, and imperfections forever, then only can you exert all the energies of body and mind to that end. To nothing else can our whole being respond, because we know, in the heart of our hearts, that all achievements on the relative plane, no matter how glamorous, are short-lived and not dependable.

As the yearning for God grows, all thoughts and all feelings combine into one single stream flowing toward him. Thus, in the conscious search for God alone does the integration of personality become possible. No lesser object can integrate our entire being.

Just as each and every water course is constantly struggling to reach the ocean by straight or circuitous routes, even so each and every individual is wending his or her way Godward directly or indirectly, knowingly or unknowingly. It is the basic urge from which all his desires and strivings derive. In fact, it is the mainspring of his thoughts, feelings, and actions, though he is hardly aware of it. Impelled by this innate tendency to meet the highest and best, the saint worships, the philosopher contemplates, the patriot gives his life for his country, the mother rears the children, the miser amasses wealth, the robber steals.

The manifestations of the same pure force of divine love differ in various individuals because of dissimilarities in their mental and physical constitution, in the same way as radiant light expresses itself variously through diverse mediums, or clear water acquires various colors and tastes according to the nature of the soil through which it flows. Worldly desires are but love of God misdirected.

When a person seeks God consciously and in the right way, then spiritual life begins. So a great devotee of the Lord prays to him: "May I ever remember thee with that undying love which the unwise have for temporal things."

Fundamentally, there is no difference between sense attachment and devotion to God. The grossest sense desire can be transmuted into genuine love of God by turning it Godward. This is evidenced by the life of many a saint.

There are two distinct trends of love in the human heart. The one is to love, the other is to be loved. On the one hand, from your childhood you have been seeking someone to whom you can give all your love, whom you can make your heart's own. You have tried this with your parents, brothers, sisters, husband or wife, sons, daughters, friends, and even your pets, yet you have found none on whom your affection can wholly rest. Each one slips away from your loving hold somehow or other. Nobody seems to understand you. On the other hand, you have been looking for someone who will love you for love's sake, who will make you the sole occupant of his heart, but in this quest also you have been sorely disappointed. You do not find anyone who loves you as you want to be loved. Even your most intimate friends and relations fall short of your expectation. Always there is a gap between two meeting hearts, however close. Rare indeed is the beloved, rare indeed is the lover.

After many a long struggle man realizes at last that God alone is the supreme object of his love and God alone is his supreme lover, and that the two predominant tendencies of his heart can find their fulfillment only in him, who is Love, Lover, and Beloved in one. When such a feeling grows in the devotee's heart he cries out: "In this world, O Lord! in search of wealth I have found thee the greatest treasure. In this world, O Lord! in search of someone to love I have found thee the most lovable one. At thy blessed feet is the culmination of all knowledge; at thy blessed feet is the fulfillment of all desires; at thy blessed feet is the consummation of all love. Therefore, O Lord! I surrender myself to thee. Thou art my sole refuge, my goal, my abode, my sanctuary."

Basically, there are two perpetual streams of love in this world. The one is man's love for God, and the other is God's love for man. Running into different channels, they make numerous currents of love. It is man's love for God that assumes such varied forms as parental, filial, and conjugal love, as fraternity, patriotism, religious fervor, and as hankering after wealth, beauty, power, knowledge, fame, and so forth. And it is God's love for man that manifests itself as deep compassion for humanity, especially as saving grace, in the hearts of God-men and men of God. The great spiritual leaders and lovers of God are the confluences of the two streams. They are the mighty rivers of love flowing incessantly into the infinite ocean of love. They also form the channels through which flows God's love to humanity. By uniting with them through faith and devotion man receives God's grace, and within his heart there springs up a stream of love which flows toward God, until, like the small creeks which are united with the larger rivers, they reach the ocean.

Love of God is bliss itself. Even a modicum of it serves as a source of constant delight which does not depend on anything external, and which endures under all the conditions of life. As the love of God grows within, the devotee's entire being becomes vibrant with divine life, light, and sweetness. Fascinated and intoxicated with the nectar of divine love he lives in a state of ecstasy. He finds within himself a perennial spring of joy welling up from that fountainhead of all blessedness. One particle of that bliss makes the universe blissful; one touch of that beauty endows the face of nature with beauty; one drop of that love fills all hearts with love.

Thoroughly contented, he never looks back upon the transitory pleasures and treasures of the sense world. Man hankers after earthly or celestial glories and joys simply because he has no idea of the supreme bliss he can find within himself. Having once tasted the manna of divine love all thirst for enjoyments is quenched forever. He realizes once for all how trivial are the sense enjoyments of even the highest paradise, how futile and foolish it is to run after them instead of striving for the recovery of the eternity and blissfulness of the Self.

Love culminates in complete union with God. As it grows deeper, the devotee feels an ever-increasing longing for the realization of God. It becomes the sole concern of his life. His entire being centers upon this one idea. He feels God's presence nearer and nearer, until he comprehends Him as the supreme spirit shining within his heart as the very soul of his soul. While he still needs mental forms, attitudes, etc., to grasp the form-less spirit, he no longer contemplates on God in the external objects of forms and symbols, etc. Within his own heart he meditates on that particular form or aspect of the divinity which he has chosen as his Ideal, until, through continued practice, his mind becomes absorbed in the object of his meditation, and, by the light of knowledge which removes all darkness, he sees God revealed as his Chosen Ideal.

Yet it is by God's grace and love alone that he can be seen. Sri Krishna says: "With their minds fixed on me, with their senses directed to me, enlightening one another and always speaking of me, they find satisfaction and delight in me. To them, ever devoted, and worshiping me with love, I give the spiritual sight by which they attain me. Out of mere compassion for them, I, abiding in their hearts, destroy darkness born of ignorance by the luminous lamp of knowledge."

As love intensifies, the devotee's individual self becomes so completely unified with God that he realizes the divine being as his very Self, and as the Self in all beings. He lives in the full consciousness of the one Self immanent in the universe. Such a devotee completely surrenders his will to God. In the *Bhagavatam* it is said: "He who sees the divine Self in all beings and all beings in the divine Self is the best devotee of God. He who bears love to God, friendship to his devotees, kindness to the ignorant, and indifference to his foes, is of the second-best type, and he who faithfully worships God only in the image, and not in his devotees or others, is a novice."

Through devotion is also attained the knowledge of Brahman, the impersonal, absolute being. Sri Krishna declares: "By devotion he knows me in reality, what and who I am. Knowing me in reality he forthwith enters into me." Regarding this attainment of God-knowledge through devotion, Sri Ramakrishna says: "By constantly meditating on God the devotee loses his ego; he realizes that he is God and God is he."

Even so, the devotee may not lose his individuality. There are some who return after this highest attainment of samadhi, and, while enjoying the bliss of divine love, guide and teach humanity.

This state of transcendental devotion is reached by very few, but he who has attained it sees everything, within and without, permeated with divine consciousness and bliss.

Grace and Self-Effort

by Swami Prabhavananda

THE MOST IMPORTANT thing necessary for a spiritual aspirant is longing for God and the desire to seek and find him. There are many religions in the world, innumerable sects with their varied theories, beliefs, and doctrines, but these are helpful to us only in so far as they create in us the desire to realize God and show us the ways to reach him. They are of no avail if we simply believe in them and give an intellectual assent to their philosophical or theological doctrines. Creeds, theories, and beliefs alone cannot transform character; hence they cannot give us the stability of inner peace.

Sri Ramakrishna tells the following parable: A pundit hired a ferry-boat to take him across the river. He was the only passenger, so he began to talk to the ferryman. "Do you know the Samkhya or Patanjali philosophy?" he asked the man. "No sir, I don't," he replied. "Do you know Nyaya, Vaiseshika, or Vedanta, or any of the systems of thought?" "No sir, I don't! I am just a poor man who earns his living by ferrying this boat. I know nothing of all these things of which you speak." The pundit felt sorry for the man's ignorance, and in a somewhat superior manner he began to teach him some of the various doctrines. He was very proud of his learning, and was glad of the opportunity to air it. Suddenly, however, a storm arose, and the small boat became unmanageable; the waters became more and more turbulent, until finally the boatman asked his passenger: "Sir, can you swim?" "No, I cannot," the pundit said in alarm. "Well then, good-bye, sir! I am afraid your learning and knowledge of the scriptures will avail you little now in your hour of need if you cannot swim!"

In the same way, when we are battered by the storm and stress of life, our knowledge of theological doctrines is of no avail if we have not fortified ourselves by learning how to enter the kingdom of heaven, the haven of peace where God dwells. According to the Chandogya Upanishad:

> The Self within the heart is like a boundary which divides the world from That. Day and night cross not that boundary, nor old age, nor death; neither grief nor pleasure, neither good nor evil deeds. All evil shuns That. For That is free from impurity: by impurity can it never be touched. Wherefore he who has crossed that boundary, and has realized the Self, if he is blind, ceases to be blind; if he is wounded, ceases to be

wounded; if he is afflicted, ceases to be afflicted. When that boundary is crossed, night becomes day; for the world of Brahman is light itself.

Therefore, the only struggle must be to reach the light, the world of Brahman. Our sufferings and tribulations are direct and immediate experiences, and it is only the direct and immediate experience of the kingdom of God that can overcome the tribulations of the world.

"Erudition, well-articulated speech, wealth of words, and skill in expounding the scriptures—these things give pleasure to the learned, but they do not bring liberation," says Shankara. "A buried treasure is not uncovered by merely uttering the words 'come forth.' You must follow the right directions. You must dig and work hard to remove the stones and earth covering it, then only can you make it your own. In the same way, the pure truth of the Atman, buried under maya and the effects of maya, can be reached by meditation, contemplation, and other spiritual disciplines such as a knower of Brahman may prescribe—but never by subtle arguments."

Longing for God, longing for liberation from the tribulations of life, is the most important thing for the spiritual aspirant. Of course everyone wants to be free from suffering and misery; but, like some lower animals, our vision does not range beyond a few feet, so that we see only our immediate troubles and sufferings, and struggle to free ourselves from them only. Our vision is limited so that we do not try to get at the root, the source of all our tribulations. The root cause of all suffering is ignorance, and to free ourselves completely from all suffering is knowledge—knowledge of God, the one reality.

Sri Krishna says in the Bhagavad Gita:

> Among those who are purified by their good deeds, there are four kinds of men who worship me: the world-weary, the seeker for knowledge, the seeker for happiness, and the man of spiritual discrimination. The man of discrimination is the highest of these. He devotes himself to me always, and to no other. For I am very dear to that man, and he is dear to me.

It does not matter how the longing for God first arises, for Sri Krishna also says, "Certainly all these are noble." The important thing is that with whatever motive we begin spiritual life, if our only purpose and goal is God, we will find that all other thirsts and cravings leave us. Gradually, as our hearts become purified, intense longing for God arises, and that one desire becomes the one paramount thing in our lives. That is the one and perhaps the only condition needed to become a true spiritual aspirant.

How is this longing satisfied? How do we find God?

Those who have realized Him declare in no uncertain terms that it is only by his grace that God becomes known. I have known a few such blessed souls, the illumined ones, and they all unequivocally have asserted that it is through his grace and his grace alone that they realized God. Christ also tells us: "Ye have not chosen me but I have chosen you"; and the Upanishads say: "Whom the Self chooses, by him is He attained."

Yet again, these very great souls urge us to exert ourselves. They do not teach us to sit quietly and wait for grace. They insist that we ourselves strive strenuously to find God. Sri Krishna says, "What is man's will, and how shall he use it? Let him put forth its power to uncover the Atman, not hide the Atman: man's will is the only friend of the Atman: his will is also the Atman's enemy."

This seeming contradiction is resolved in one of the sayings of Sri Ramakrishna: "The breeze of God's grace is always blowing; set your sail to catch this breeze." This is further explained by the following saying: "A man may have the grace of his guru, he may have the grace of God and his devotees, but if he has not the grace of his own mind the others avail him nothing."

The grace of your own mind is needed to set the sail to catch the breeze of grace. God is not partial; neither is his grace conditional. He is like the magnet which draws the needle: when the needle is covered with dirt, it does not feel the attraction of the magnet. But wash away the dirt, and at once the needle feels the drawing power and becomes united with the magnet. One of the names of God in Sanskrit is Hari, which means "one who steals the heart." God is the one attraction in the universe, but in our ignorance, and because of the impurities of our hearts, we do not feel this attraction. Sri Ramakrishna used to say: "Weep! Weep for the Lord and let your tears wash away the impurities in your heart."

But again, this yearning of the heart for God does not come suddenly; that is why we need to exert ourselves. Those who practice spiritual disciplines and regularly pray and meditate will come directly to the experience of divine grace. It is a psychological experience, almost exactly like the magnet drawing the needle.

For example, you are trying to concentrate your mind on God with great regularity, yet the mind still remains restless. Through regular practice there grows yearning in your heart to see him, yet still you seem to be striking your mind against a stone wall. You see nothing but darkness. Then suddenly—whether from within or without—you feel another power drawing your mind inward, and you find yourself diving deeper and deeper within, in spite of yourself. You seem to be in another domain, the world of light, where no darkness enters. Many spiritual visions and ecstasies follow this experience; you come face to face with God. But whenever you are lifted up into this higher consciousness, it is your experience that God himself, by his grace, is lifting you up, attracting you unto himself and giving you ineffable joy and vision.

This, then, is a direct experience of God's grace, which comes only when your heart has become purified through the practice of spiritual disciplines.

Vyasa, the commentator on the yoga aphorisms, compared the mind to a river flowing in opposite directions. One current of the mind flows toward the world, and the other flows toward God, toward the attainment of liberation from the bondages of the world. First there must arise a struggle in our life, through the awakening of spiritual discrimination, to dam the rush of the downward current that flows toward the world and worldly enjoyments.

When we have been victorious in this struggle, we are completely drawn into the Godward current and experience the grace of God. And when we at last realize this grace, we enter forever into that kingdom which no storm or strife can ever reach.

⊛

Mantra Yoga

by Swami Shraddhananda

THE SPIRITUAL PRACTICE which enables one to be united with God with the help of a mantra, a holy name, can be broadly called mantra yoga.

What is a mantra? The word or words signifying God. Whether God is with form or without form, with attributes or without attributes, he can be indicated by a word formula. This formula is the mantra.

The mantra can be one word like *Narayana*. *Namo Narayanaya*—salutations to the Lord Narayana—is a two-word mantra. The mantra *Om namo Narayanaya* has three words.

Those who follow the path of Advaita, the nondualistic approach to God, also use mantras like *Om*, or *Om Tat Sat* (Om, That—the goal of your search—is pure existence).

Om is the most sacred word of the Vedas. It is considered to be one with Brahman—the highest Reality, personal or impersonal—and it is also the path to realize Brahman. Om is the Logos, the undifferentiated word from which all the manifested universe has been created. We read in the Bible: "In the beginning was the Word, and the Word was with God, and the Word was God." According to Swami Vivekananda:

> It is out of this holiest of all holy words, the mother of all names and forms, the eternal Om, that the whole universe . . . [was] created. . . . These three letters . . . A. U. M., pronounced in combination as Om, may well be the generalised symbol of all possible sounds. The letter A is the least differentiated of all sounds. . . . Again, all articulate sounds are produced in the space within the mouth beginning with the root of the tongue and ending in the lips—the throat sound is A, and M is the last lip sound, and the U exactly represents the rolling forward of the impulse which begins at the root of the tongue till it ends in the lips. If properly pronounced, this Om will represent the whole phenomenon of sound-production, and no other word can do this; . . . [Om] is indeed the first manifestation of divine wisdom, this Om is truly symbolic of God.[1]

The Upanishads mention some short sentences called *mahavakyas*, great sayings, which are treated by Advaita Vedantins as mantras. Some of these sayings are: *Aham Brahmasmi* (I am Brahman) and *Tat Tvam Asi* (Thou art That).

Buddhism also prescribes several mantras for spiritual seekers, such as *Buddham saranam gacchami*; *Dharmam saranam gacchami*; *Sangham saranam gacchami* (I take refuge in Buddha; I take refuge in Dharma; I take refuge in the Holy Order). These three sentences together form the three vows of refuge, the repetition and contemplation of which strengthen the spiritual life of the Buddhist seeker. In some traditions of Christianity and Islam the repetition of the divine name is practiced.

According to the ancient spiritual tradition of India, the mantra is not an arbitrary human composition, but is revealed to the pure-hearted seer. In Hinduism, meditation on God with the help of the mantra is widely prevalent. This is due to the very basic and central belief proclaimed in the Vedas and other scriptures that the *nama*—the name—is not different from the *nami*—the named.

Brahman is described as the Supreme Word—*Shabda-Brahman.* It is from this concept of Shabda-Brahman that the deep reverence for the holy name has sprung. The Taittiriya Upanishad declares: "Om—this word is Brahman," and "Om is all this."[2] This declaration is echoed in many of the sacred books of India.

A spiritually-minded Hindu cherishes the hope that, at the time of death, he or she may be able to remember the holy name of God. A person dying with the consciousness of the holy mantra commands admiration. In the eighth chapter of the Bhagavad Gita, the death of an ideal yogi is described as follows:

> Controlling all his senses, confining the mind within the heart, drawing the life force into the head and engaging in the practice of yoga and repeating Om, the syllable of Brahman, while meditating on the Lord—whosoever leaves the body in this way, attains the highest goal.[3]

A spiritual seeker goes on repeating the holy name, retaining great faith in its efficacy. This is the first step in mantra yoga. The principle mentioned earlier is that the mantra is one with the Ishta, the Chosen Ideal, which may be a divine incarnation or the Supreme Self. In the beginning, this is a difficult concept to understand. But it will be sufficient at the primary stage if the spiritual aspirant can practice *japa*, repetition of the mantra, remembering that the mantra is connected with the power of divine consciousness. The aspirant should think that the holy name is imparting spiritual vibrations in the body-mind-life system. This vibration is not like a material energy such as magnetism, heat, or electricity. It is generated by the power of the divine.

Gradually, the spiritual seeker merges the mantra vibration into the movement of *prana*,* the life force. He begins to experience the unification of the two movements. This leads to the higher experience that the movement of prana itself is mantra repetition. The japa has been transferred from the tongue or throat to the life principle operating in the body. Each pranic action becomes a vibration of the mantra.

As a result of this practice, a great harmony descends into the prana. What is achieved by the practice of *pranayama* in raja yoga, the yoga of concentration and meditation, is accomplished more completely in this stage of mantra yoga.

If the repetition of the mantra is directed to the five sense organs—eyes, ears, nostrils, tongue, skin—these organs become refined and the corresponding five sense perceptions—sight, hearing, smell, taste, touch—become purified. We know that sense objects constantly draw the mind outward causing distractions, agitations, and suffering. When the sense organs become more imbued with *sattva*—purity and calmness—this state of things changes. Then whatever we experience through our senses will no longer agitate the mind. We read in the Gita, "The self-controlled man moves among objects of lust and hatred, free from attraction and aversion. He attains tranquillity."[4]

The tranquillity indicated by that verse can be attained by the practice of mantra yoga. In a way, it is more effective than the efforts for direct control of the senses. If love of God or Self-knowledge be the ultimate aim of life, then the purification of body and senses is essential. This purification is easily obtained by mantra yoga.

Like the senses of perception, the senses of action also can be purified by the practice of mantra yoga. If japa is continued during our physical activities, like the movement of limbs, working, gardening, sweeping, etc., then the corresponding organs of action undergo an inner transformation. The spiritual aspirant gradually begins to feel a spiritual vibration

---

*Prana is the sum total of energy, from which all mental and physical actions are sustained. Prana manifests as motion, gravitation, and magnetism. It is the vital principle which sustains physical life, thought force, and bodily action. The force of prana within the body controls its vital functions: breathing, digesting, assimilating food, elimination, etc.—Ed.

in the movement of the organs. In one of the Bengali songs of the great eighteenth-century saint Ramprasad, we read:

> O my mind, you can worship Mother Kali in any way you please, as long as you repeat the mantra given by the guru day and night. Ramprasad declares with great delight that the Divine Mother is present in every activity. When you lie down, know that you are making obeisance to her. Meditate on Mother even while you are asleep. When you walk around the town, think that you are circumambulating the Divine Mother. All sounds that you hear are her mantras. . . . When you eat, think that you are offering an oblation to her.

The next step is to apply the mantra to the mental waves. Endless thoughts and emotions are constantly arising in the mind. It is indeed difficult to stop them. In the Bhagavad Gita, Arjuna mentions this problem to Sri Krishna, who replies, "Certainly, O Arjuna, the mind is restless and hard to control. But it can be subdued by constant practice and the exercise of detachment."[5]

The practice of mantra yoga in this context is to communicate the great power of the holy name with faith and love to the mental waves. In this practice there is not a bit of the toughness or aggressiveness that is required to challenge the mind directly. The distractions of the mind become naturally calm by the divine influence inherent in the mantra.

When the body, senses, prana, and mind become infused with sattva by the practice of mantra japa, it is time to purify all objects and phenomena outside of our individuality. This is possible and should be done. The endless sky above, according to our normal vision, is material. But when you look at the sky, and connect it with the divine through the inner repetition of the mantra, the material space will change its appearance. The goal of the mantra, namely divine consciousness, will be peeping from the sky, as it were. The sky will appear to be a shawl on the cosmic body of God. In a similar manner, the moon, the sun and stars above, the trees, shrubs, flowers, streams, forests, hills, deserts, and again, living beings on earth or in water, all of these endless segments of the universe can be purified by the mantra and be experienced as parts of the cosmic body of Satchidananda—Existence-Knowledge-Bliss absolute.

In the next stage of mantra yoga, the necessity of directing the mantra inside and outside to objects is transcended. Now, in our comprehension, the mantra has to be identified with the Ishta, the chosen ideal of God.

This comprehension should grow stronger and stronger along with the repetition of the mantra. The form of the Chosen Ideal or the impersonal idea of God should be present in the mind. As this practice ripens, the mantra and the Ishta, with or without form, will become more and more unified.

Mantra chaitanya, that is, the divine consciousness implied in the mantra, will then be awakened. No more will there be doubts that the mantra is one with God. The heart will be filled with joy and peace.

Slowly it will be felt that the mantra as Shabda-Brahman, Sound-Brahman, is emanating from the innermost center of the universe; the meditator's heart has become, as it were, one with the heart of the universe. Not only that, every object and event in the cosmos will be established and will function in the great reality which is the mantra.

In this stage of mantra yoga, the word is more and more revealed as consciousness. The mantra is felt to be the radiant light of consciousness. That light spreads out in the life principle and mind, flooding the heart with immeasurable peace. For a spiritual aspirant on the path of devotion, the form of the Ishta is experienced as the light of consciousness. The meditator's love for the Ishta becomes immensely intensified. In the path of *jnana*, knowledge, the mantra reveals the deepest reality of the Self, as clear as daylight. Mantra chaitanya, the divine consciousness of the mantra, and *Atma chaitanya*, the divine consciousness of the Atman, become one.

When the mantra is transformed as consciousness, the whole universe is experienced as consciousness grounded in mantra consciousness. The five *bhutas*—the basic elements that comprise this universe—and all that is made of them, are then nothing but the emanation of consciousness. The declarations of the Upanishads expressing Brahman or Atman as pervading everything such as, "All this is verily Brahman," and "Atman alone is all this" become living to the spiritual aspirant by means of mantra yoga.[6] Now there is no longer any repetition of the mantra in the usual sense of the term. The mantra is no longer a word or words, but one with Satchidananda, God as infinite existence, knowledge, and bliss.

The mantra, Shabda-Brahman, is continually revealing itself in its own glory. The culmination of this glory can be said to be the third or final stage. The body, mind, and prana are all expressions of the mantra chaitanya; so is this vast universe.

There is nothing else but the mantra as consciousness; consciousness far away, consciousness near, nearer, nearest. As if one colossal flood had inundated everything, all names and forms are drowned in one vast torrent of consciousness. In this stage, is it possible to perceive the dualities like great and small, gross and fine, outside and inside, preceding and succeeding, and so on? Only as long as the sublime experience of all-pervading consciousness has not come, can we use those terms associated with space and time. In consciousness there is neither space nor time. Space and time spring from consciousness. When consciousness is realized as the Supreme, both merge into consciousness.

Can we then describe this supreme glory of Shabda-Brahman in words? No, we cannot. We read in the Taittiriya Upanishad: "Whence words together with the mind turn away unable to reach, That is the supreme bliss of Brahman. He who knows this becomes free from all fear."[7]

Thus, at the ultimate level of Shabda-Brahman, words have become wordless, forms have become formless, all multiplicity has unified in consciousness stationed in that transcendent glory beyond mind and speech. The seeker has become mute, his mind extinguished.

Holding onto the Ishta mantra—the holy name received from the guru—with faith and love, experiencing the revelations of the mantra step by step, surely we can reach this ultimate goal of our spiritual life as declared by Vedanta.

1. *The Complete Works of Swami Vivekananda* (Calcutta: Advaita Ashrama,1973), 3: 57-58.
2. Taittiriya Upanishad 2. 7.
3. 8. 12-13.
4. Cf. Chapt. I, section 3.
5. 6. 35.
6. Chandogya Upanishad 3.14. 1. and 7. 25. 2.
7. 2. 9.

Prayer as a Spiritual Discipline

by Swami Bhajanananda

THERE IS HARDLY anyone who has not prayed at some time or other in his life. When a baby feels hungry or discomfort it cries. To its mother at least, it is an unarticulated prayer, and she runs to it and attends to its needs. In a way, every wish may be regarded as an unuttered prayer. In this sense even an atheist or a materialist prays; only in his case he prays to himself.

Prayers may be grouped into two main divisions: secular and spiritual. Secular prayers are for the fulfillment of worldly desires and needs. Life is full of uncertainties, and in the life of every person come times when he finds himself in the grip of forces which are beyond his control. Confronted with fear and despair, buffeted by sorrows and difficulties, millions of people turn to God in prayer.

There is no need to go deep into the question whether such prayers are answered and, if so, how it can be reconciled with the law of karma, for our purpose here is only to study the second type of prayer, namely, spiritual prayer—prayer practiced as a spiritual discipline.

The main purpose of spiritual prayer is to seek divine assistance in attaining moral purity and spiritual progress. A true devotee of God prays not for material things, which are after all transitory, but for spiritual enlightenment. Prayer represents the first stage in the aspirant's struggle for higher consciousness.

Even those who do not believe in a personal God or in the efficacy of prayer are advised to pray for others in order to free themselves from thoughts of hatred, jealousy, and selfishness which are inimical to their own spiritual progress. Prayer in this sense is only a way of purifying oneself by sending good thoughts to others. Since all individual minds are parts of a cosmic mind, this kind of prayerful thinking may help others. One may thus render service to others in silence—a form of mental karma yoga.

Another point to be kept in mind here is that, although spiritual prayer may also be petitionary, it is not so much the fulfillment of the petition that is important as the act of praying itself. The act of praying is in itself a technique of concentration. Through prayer the scattered powers of the will converge upon the object of prayer. The concentration thus achieved may not be total as in true contemplation or meditation, but it is a great help for its attainment. The fulfillment of a spiritual need such as purity or devotion may be the primary motivation to pray, but the act of praying serves as a technique of concentration and takes the aspirant nearer to God. A true spiritual aspirant prays not only for the fulfillment of his inner needs, but also because he knows that the very act of praying will take him closer to God. And, as he advances on the path of prayer, this aspect of concentration becomes more important than fulfillment of needs.

All the great religions of the world teach prayer. Among them Christianity gives the greatest importance to it. Christ himself prayed long hours and taught his followers to "watch and pray." His apostle St. Paul's exhortation to "pray without ceasing" is famous. Origen, a great third-century Christian theologian of Alexandria, says that to pray for earthly things is disobedience to God. St. Augustine points out that the purpose of prayer is not to instruct God, but to elevate man, to bring man round to what he ought to desire—desire for God. Prayer for St. Thomas Aquinas is concerned only with man's faith and contemplation of God's love. Meister Eckhart regards each prayer as a part of the eternal foresight of God. To St. Teresa of Avila prayer is the only door to those mystical graces that the Lord bestows upon the soul.

In Hinduism prayer once dominated the life of the people during the Vedic period. But later on worship, meditation, and self-inquiry almost completely replaced it. Though the common people still prayed, prayer as a spiritual discipline was seldom stressed by the great teachers. It may be said that in modern times Sri Ramakrishna has revived it. In the *Gospel of Sri Ramakrishna* one finds the Master recommending prayer on several occasions. Once a devotee asked him, "Then what is the way, sir?" Sri Ramakrishna answered, "Prayer and the company of holy men." After explaining the benefits of holy company, the Master continued, "There is another way: earnestly praying to God. God is our very own. We should say to Him: 'O God, what is Thy nature? Reveal Thyself to me. Thou must reveal Thyself to me; for why else hast Thou created me?'" Another day M, the author of the book, told him, "God gives to some full spiritual consciousness, and others He keeps in ignorance." Immediately the Master corrected him: "No, that is not so. One should pray to God with a longing heart. God certainly listens to prayer if it is sincere.

There is no doubt about it."[1] What Sri Ramakrishna meant was that through sincere prayer everyone could overcome his inherent limitations and gain spiritual experience by God's grace.

Sri Ramakrishna's divine consort Sri Sarada Devi also emphasizes the importance of prayer very much in her teachings. Among the direct disciples of Sri Ramakrishna, Swami Brahmananda and Swami Shivananda teach constant prayer to God as an important spiritual practice.[2]

A unique feature of Hinduism is that it offers to humanity two great highways, or *margas*, to liberation: the path of knowledge, *jnana marga*, and the path of devotion, *bhakti marga*. From time immemorial these two seemingly contradictory paths have coexisted within its fold, giving to it great dynamism and adaptability.

These two highways represent two fundamentally different orientations of the human soul to the ultimate Reality. In jnana marga the ultimate Reality is regarded as impersonal and without attributes, whereas in the path of bhakti, it is regarded as personal with or without a human form. Secondly, jnana marga emphasizes self-effort while bhakti marga is the path of divine grace. Thirdly, the path of jnana is subject-oriented; it is an inquiry into the true nature of Reality as the subject. The path of bhakti is object-oriented; it is an attempt to realize the true nature of God as the highest object and establish a true relationship with him. The path of bhakti involves what Martin Buber calls an "I and Thou" relationship between the soul and God. The path of jnana involves an "I-That" relationship, as the Advaitic interpretation of *tat tvam asi* clearly shows; but even this relationship is illusory, and what jnana marga establishes is not a relationship, but the real nature of the transcendent Self.

The "I-Thou" relationship can be expressed in three ways: prayer, worship, and meditation. These are the three most important disciplines of the path of bhakti and represent three successive stages in it.

In Hinduism, *prarthana*, the Sanskrit word for prayer, always means petitionary prayer and has been given only limited importance. It means asking God for help to free oneself from the hold of the senses and turn away from the darkness of ignorance to the light of truth. It is the first stage in the struggle for higher consciousness in which the aspirant, realizing his limitations, opens his heart to divine power and light. It is in effect a movement from God to the soul.

Worship is offering something to God—it may be a material object or one's own body, mind, and soul. The Vedic *yajna* or sacrifice meant "sacrificing things for the sake of the Deity." Worship shifts the focus of man's activities from the ego to the divine and detaches the soul from external objects. It is primarily a movement from the soul to God.

As a result of these two movements, the soul draws closer to God. This act of approaching God is what *dhyana* or meditation means. The Vedantic term for meditation is *upasana* which literally means "sitting near"—sitting near God.

So then, prayer, worship, and meditation represent three degrees of the development of intimacy between the soul and God. One begins spiritual life by asking God for favors, then starts offering things to him, and finally succeeds in going nearer to him. These three steps also represent three stages in the progressive transformation of the aspirant's consciousness. When Christ in the Sermon on the Mount speaks about asking, seeking, and knocking at the door, he is referring to these three stages—prayer, worship, and meditation respectively.

In the history of Vedic Hinduism we can clearly see the development of these three attitudes or steps. The Vedas are divided into four parts: Mantra, Brahmana, Aranyaka, and Upanishad, which according to modern scholars were composed at four successive periods. The Mantra portion mostly contains hymns and prayers. The Brahmana portion deals with rituals and rites of worship. The Aranyakas mostly discuss various types of meditation. The Upanishads also contain meditations, but they are chiefly a record of the direct experiences of the sages.

With the decline of Vedic culture, the Mantra portion lost its hold on the people, and prayer gradually lost its importance as a spiritual discipline. The Gayatri is practically the only prayer that now remains of what was once an important and widespread spiritual practice in ancient India. Vedic rituals were replaced by new rituals. The meditations of the Aranyakas were forgotten, and new types of meditation on various deities and the yoga of Patanjali took their place. Gradually concentration became the most important test and form of spiritual practice. Even the Bhakti schools could not escape the influence of contemplation.

If Hinduism neglected prayer, Christianity raised it above all other disciplines. During the Middle Ages, Christian spirituality recognized three disciplines: meditation (*meditatio*), prayer (*oratio*), and contemplation (*contemplatio*). Christian meditation corresponds, not to what is called dhyana in Hinduism (which is nowadays translated as "meditation"), but to *manana* or reflection which follows reading. Prayer during the early centuries did not have any definite method, and each individual was free to pray in his own way. This kind of prayer later on came to be called affective prayer (which corresponds to prarthana in Hinduism) and, when simplified and reduced to a single formula or a "silent interior gaze," came to be called "prayer of simplicity" or "prayer of the heart" (which corresponds to dhyana in Hinduism). Contemplation was regarded more as an experience resulting from meditation and prayer than as a discipline. It meant an intimate knowledge of God which was God's free and loving gift to the soul. In this sense it corresponds to samadhi of Hinduism.

However, owing to the influence of the great Spanish mystics of the sixteenth century and the French mystics of the seventeenth century, all spiritual disciplines came to be included under the blanket term "prayer," a distinction being made between "vocal prayer" (meaning the chanting of hymns in choir and private recitations) and "mental prayer." Mental prayer came to be divided into two: active prayer and passive prayer, also called infused prayer. Of these, active prayer is a state in which prayer is done with self-effort, and consists of three progressive stages or degrees: meditation (or discursive prayer), affective prayer, and prayer of simplicity.

Passive or infused prayer is contemplation. It is a state of transcendence free from self-effort in which the soul experiences union with God, which according to St. Teresa consists of four stages or degrees. By including all these different disciplines under one common term "prayer," what is really implied is that a prayerful attitude, an attitude of submission to God, is maintained throughout one's spiritual life. It is important to keep in mind that it is only affective prayer, meaning a free and informal personal prayer to God, that corresponds to the prarthana of Hinduism. For the remaining types of Christian "prayer," Hinduism uses different technical terms like manana, dhyana, samadhi, etc.

In Christian spirituality there are two definitions of prayer which have come down from very ancient times. One is that of Clement of Alexandria: "Prayer is a conversation with God." The other is that of John Damascene and Evagrius of Pontus: "Prayer is the raising of the soul to God." It is the first definition that corresponds to the Hindu concept of prarthana. (The second definition is more general and can be applied to all the different forms of Christian "prayer," but specially to Christian mysticism.)

Prarthana or prayer is "speaking to God." It represents the first attempt of the ordinary human soul to approach God. Just as our meeting with our fellowmen takes the form of a dialogue, so also the first meeting of the soul with God takes the form of an inner dialogue. It is the first effort of the soul to express its spiritual aspiration, for that is the only way the infant soul can orientate itself to the supreme Reality.

Just as a child speaks about its needs to its parents or a student seeks guidance from a teacher or a servant places his problems before his master, so does the soul speak frankly to the Lord about its difficulties, needs, and wishes. It is by expressing its needs that the child goes closer to its parents and understands its relationship to them. In the same way, prayer takes the soul closer to God and reveals its relationship with him. It is this "speaking" to God and dependence on his grace that distinguish prayer from other disciplines.

Though God is unseen, prayer is not a monologue. It is a mystic interior exchange with the unseen divine Partner going on through the medium of faith. A true devotee does not feel that God is unknown or does not respond. His burning faith makes God a living presence. It is this continual exercise of faith that makes prayer a spiritual discipline.

The next question is, how to pray?

Talks with those whom we love are always personal and informal. The interior conversation with God, or prayer, too must be intensely personal, natural, spontaneous. Each individual must be free to pray in his or her own way. Let him begin praying in any way that is possible for him. Prayer itself will guide him about how to proceed further, and will perfect his prayer.

Nevertheless, all people do not have equal capacity to pray, and may not be clear about what to pray for. Even those who habitually pray may not always be in a mood to pray. To help such people, formal prayers have been composed by illumined seers. In Hinduism the most famous and popular of these formal prayers are the Gayatri and the Abhyaroha Mantra: "Lead me from the unreal to the real, from darkness to light, and from death to immortality."[3] One may make use of these prayers now and then as guidelines, but true prayer is something welling up from the depths of one's heart naturally according to the soul's extreme needs.

Prayer can be done in two ways: externally and internally. In external prayer one stands or sits before an image or picture of the Lord, preferably in a temple or one's own private shrine, and gazing at the image pours forth one's heart in a fervent appeal. In internal prayer one sits with closed eyes, visualizes the Lord's image in the heart, and appeals to him mentally.

Some people seem to think that prayer would reduce them to the position of a beggar, which is beneath their dignity. Ignorance and egoism lie at the root of such thinking. In begging there is no relationship between the beggar and the begged. But spiritual prayer is addressed not to a total stranger, but to a Being who is the Soul of one's soul, the Ruler of the universe, one's eternal and inseparable Beloved. When a child expresses his needs, his parents do not think it to be begging; they only give him what really belongs to him. Similarly, prayer is only a way of preparing ourselves to receive what is really ours by divine right. When a student approaches a teacher for instruction, it is not considered begging. Prayer is only seeking guidance from the eternal guru, the teacher of all teachers.

Another wrong notion about prayer is that it is only a form of aspiration. But, as St. Teresa has pointed out, "It is one thing to desire the grace of devotion, and quite another thing to ask God for it." Aspiration becomes effective only when converted into a spiritual discipline. This can be done in several ways, and among these prayer is one of the simplest. Prayer is not mere aspiration; it is the soul's dialogue with God.

Another notion, though not wrong, is that prayer is only a lower form of spiritual practice meant for beginners. This is indeed true, for prayer may be regarded as the kindergarten of spiritual life. But when it comes to spiritual life, most people are mere babies and need a kindergarten. In these days yoga and meditation are becoming very popular, and millions of people in the East and the West are practicing them. But not many people seem to understand that dhyana or true meditation is a fairly advanced stage of concentration. A large number of people seem to spend their whole life trying to meditate. For many, meditation itself acts as a trap preventing them from moving forward.

Attempting higher degrees of concentration without fulfilling the primary conditions is one of the main causes for failure in spiritual life. Unreal things cannot change one's life. It is always good to remember that a simple prayer which an aspirant can do, which is real to him, can transform his life far more than a higher spiritual technique which is unreal to him because it is beyond his capacity.

"This divine maya of Mine is difficult to overcome; those who take refuge in Me alone cross over this illusion," says Sri Krishna.[4] Spiritual power is necessary in order to overcome the obstacles and gain spiritual experience. Just as physical strength comes from the food provided by the physical universe, and knowledge comes from ideas originating in the mental universe, so also spiritual power comes from God. At the unseen touch of the golden rays of God's grace the lotus of the heart bursts into bloom.

The main purpose of prayer is to seek divine power. Says Sri Ramakrishna, "Through prayer all individual souls can be united to the Supreme Soul. Every house has a connection for gas, and gas can be obtained from the main storage-tank of the Gas Company. Apply to the Company, and it will arrange for your supply of gas. Then your house will be lighted."[5] There is an inner resistance in all of us to the free flow of divine power. This resistance is offered by the ego. Sri Ramakrishna used to say, "Rain water does not collect on a mound." Prayer reduces the inner resistance and opens the heart to grace.

True meditation is a state of relaxation, calmness. The mind becomes relaxed and calm only when it feels security and is detached from desires. Life is full of uncertainties and difficulties, and modern conditions of living have increased mankind's anxiety and feeling of insecurity. The best way to overcome fear and insecurity is to constantly pray to the supreme Lord, the controller of the destinies of all beings. Even those who practice japa and meditation have to pass through dark periods when they feel forlorn and hopeless. During such arid periods prayer gives great support to the soul. Says St. John of the Cross, "In all our necessities, trials, and afflictions, there is no better nor safer remedy than prayer, and hope that God will provide for us in his own way."

Meditation is the conscious, self-directed focusing of a continuous stream of thoughts on a mental object. This becomes possible only if the mind (or, to be more precise, the *will*) is free from the hold of external objects and desires. This withdrawal of the mind or the will is called *pratyahara*. One way to do this is repeated practice. But especially during the early stages of spiritual life most aspirants find this too difficult. Intense prayer, however, quickly accomplishes it. Prayer is the bhakta's— the devotee's—way of practicing pratyahara.

Every person is capable of a certain degree of concentration on external objects or even on mental images, provided he likes them. The main difficulty is in concentrating the mind at a higher center of consciousness. For this two conditions are to be fulfilled. The higher spiritual center should be developed and made active to some extent. And then the will and mental energies must be given a higher turn. Prayer accomplishes both these tasks. Prayer is the best way to stimulate the heart center. After a day's distracting work you feel that your mental energies have become scattered in different parts of the body, and it is difficult for you to meditate. When this happens, try intense prayer. You will find prayer quickly gathers up the energies at the heart center and you feel a new access of strength. Prayer not only detaches the will but focuses it upward. If the mind is not lifted to a higher center through prayer, the spiritual aspirant who tries to meditate very often runs the risk of concentrating on lower thoughts.

Another danger is, if the mind is not lifted up, it may sink into *tamas*, inertia, and be overpowered by sleep. That is why meditation very often ends up in sleep. The best way to avoid drowsiness during meditation is to pray. Prayer and sleep can never go together. Prayer keeps the mind alert.

Prayer thus gives a sense of security to the soul, detaches the will from desires and objects, activates the higher centers, gives a higher direction to thoughts, keeps the mind alert, and above all, clears the way for the inflow of divine power. As the aspirant goes on praying intensely, he finds that gradually prayer merges imperceptibly into dhyana, or true meditation.

One may begin with a petitionary prayer using many words. But as prayer gains in intensity and depth, words drop away by themselves, leaving only a silent aspiration in the heart. Then the inner Image becomes still and the mind flows in silence toward it. Prayer has transformed itself naturally and spontaneously into meditation. This is the ultimate goal of prayer.

Prayer, we have pointed out, is the simplest first step on the path of bhakti, or devotion. But if it is to become an effective and powerful tool, it must fulfill certain conditions. The first condition is, of course, a prayerful temperament. All people do not have an inclination or capacity to pray. Those who find it difficult to pray may try other spiritual techniques.

The test of a prayerful temperament is spontaneity. True prayer bubbles up from the bottom of the heart spontaneously. But it is also true that through practice one gradually acquires or strengthens the capacity to pray.

The prayerful temperament must be supported by strong faith—faith in the existence of God, that God listens and responds to prayer. This faith must be so strong that there is no room for negative or contrary thoughts. If we pray for something but are deeply convinced that we are not going to get it, we only obstruct the working of God's grace. Prayer becomes effective only when the faith that supports it is total. The prayerful man must practice the sixfold surrender to God taught in one of the devotional scriptures of India: "Thinking of what is auspicious and favorable, not thinking of what is unfavorable or inauspicious, faith in God's saving power, always preferring God's protection, self-surrender, and feeling of helplessness."[6]

Along with faith there must be reduction of egoism, and a spirit of self-surrender. *Karpanya*, or a feeling of helplessness, is a great aid in practicing self-surrender and prayer. In fact, it is out of sheer helplessness that many people pray to God. A person who is cocksure of everything need not pray. Sri Ramakrishna used to say that as long as there is a storekeeper looking after the storeroom, the master of the house does not go there. Speaking about self-surrender, Swami Vivekananda himself teaches in the *Inspired Talks*, "God helps those who do *not* help themselves."[7]

A devotee of God uses every experience of sorrow, suffering, and difficulty as an incentive to pray to God. Karpanya is, however, not a weakness. It only means that the devotee refuses to depend on matter but depends only on Spirit. Strong in the strength of God, he is not afraid even of death.

This does not mean that we should pray only when difficulties come. Prayer becomes effective as a spiritual discipline only when there is continuity and intensity in it. A true aspirant prays only for God-vision. His need is internal and does not depend on external things. So he prays continually. When difficulties come his way, he is ready to face them. Similarly, he prays with intense aspiration. Prayer without intensity has little power. Only a spiritual hero can keep up this kind of intense prayer for a long time—for several years if necessary.

The human soul is surrounded on all sides by the boundless ocean of divine power and light. And yet how few people make use of it! It is not even necessary to pray to a deity. It is enough if one opens one's heart to the divine power and light through a strong prayerful wish, which we may call "autosuggestive prayer." Many of the Vedic prayers still in use are not directed to any particular deity. They are mostly of the nature of autosuggestions.

Finally, it should be remembered that Hinduism does not thrust prayer upon everybody. For those who do not feel the need for it and for those who feel a constitutional dislike for it, Hinduism has opened other paths—self-inquiry, meditation, etc.

However, it is also true that, protected and supported by divine grace, the man of prayer moves faster on the spiritual path than the person who depends solely on his own limited resources. While some toil all their lives rowing their boats against the waves, others unfurl their sails and let the wind of divine grace carry them across the ocean of transmigratory existence.

1. M, *The Gospel of Sri Ramakrishna*, trans. Swami Nikhilananda (Madras: Sri Ramakrishna Math, 1974), pp. 21-22 and 196.

2. Cf. *The Eternal Companion* (Madras: Sri Ramakrishna Math, 1971), pp. 166, 183, 255; *For Seekers of God*, trans. Swami Vividishananda and Swami Gambhirananda (Calcutta: Advaita Ashrama, 1975), pp. 1-2, 66, 151, and *passim*.

3. Brhadaranyaka Upanishad I. 3. 28.

4. Bhagavad Gita 7. 14.

5. *The Gospel of Sri Ramakrishna*, p. 139.

6. *Ahirbudhnya Samhita* 37. 28.

7. *The Complete Works of Swami Vivekananda* (Calcutta: Advaita Ashrama, 1972), 7: 91.

The Practice of Self-Affirmation

by Swami Vedarupananda

THE OUTSTANDING TEACHING of the Vedanta philosophy is that you are the Atman, the Spirit. Your being is not limited to a small physical body, or an individual mind. You are a divine spirit-soul. As such, you have all the divine qualities within your very nature. You are infinite, immortal, all-powerful, all-knowing, and all-wise. You are complete, joyful, and abide in the peace that passeth all understanding. The spirit-soul is not something you have to become. You are that this very moment. All you have to do is acknowledge it.

On hearing this truth, a person has an intuitive affirmative response. At the same time, we know that we do not *feel* our divine nature. This is due to the fact that we are suffering from a sort of metaphysical amnesia. We have forgotten our true nature, and have built our lives on a whole new foundation of false beliefs. One such false belief is that you are a body. Another is that you are a mind. In order to regain our lost self, we have to deny these false beliefs and assert and affirm the truth.

In ancient times, the practice of self-affirmation was called jnana yoga. If our basic problem is self-forgetfulness, the jnanis argued, then the simplest form of spiritual practice is simply to remind ourselves of our true nature. The jnanis taught a particular kind of meditation called *nididhyasana*. This is not the same as yogic meditation, but consists in affirming the truth. You do not have to become the Atman, the sages tell us. You do not have to *become* infinite and immortal. All you have to do is acknowledge it, affirm it, assert it. The more you affirm the truth, the more convinced you will become. In time you will fully assimilate it and realize it.

The practice of self-affirmation is based on a principle: "As you think, so will you become." It may sound incredible that by holding a thought in mind we become that which we are thinking about; but there is nothing magical about it. By the law of mental impressions, every thought leaves an impression that forms our character. By the law of correspondence, every thought generates corresponding feelings, speech, and action. By the law of attraction, we draw to ourselves all the helps we need for this practice. If a person holds the thought of success in mind, he will become successful. Similarly, if you think of yourself as a divine immortal soul, you will become that too.

The legendary King Janaka is a model in this regard. Janaka once approached the sage Ashtavakra and asked: "How can knowledge be acquired? How can liberation be attained?" Ashtavakra answered: "If you think you are free, then free you will become. If you think that you are bound, then bound you will remain. This famous saying is true: As a person thinks, so does he become." Hearing this, Janaka immediately realized his mistake and began to repeatedly affirm his true nature.

You can read about Janaka in the *Ashtavakra Samhita*, one of the classic texts of the Vedanta philosophy. Janaka's first reply on gaining right knowledge is an expression of amazement: "O I am spotless, tranquil, pure consciousness, and beyond nature. All this time I have been duped by illusion." This is a beautiful affirmation. You see what is meant by an affirmation: a clear, definite statement of fact. To affirm anything is to assert positively that it is so. After gaining right knowledge, Janaka constantly affirmed his identity with the Atman. Thus he remained living in happiness, joy, and peace. We can do the same. We need only to repeat the great statements of truth that affirm our true nature.

Someone may object here that Janaka was not doing any form of spiritual practice, that he had actually realized his true nature and was just singing his natural song. A skeptic might object to the use of affirmations, saying that they are mere words, and that just repeating empty words can't make any transformative change in your life. This is a naive belief. Certainly, the ancient philosophers never underestimated the power of words and the thoughts that they represent. In the first place, there is no such thing as mere words or empty words. Anyone who has studied the Indian philosophy of language knows that words have tremendous transformative power. Words and groups of words (sentences) form our basic beliefs. The whole world is created out of words. By holding in mind the right and true words, we can gradually achieve Self-realization.

In order to begin using affirmations in spiritual practice, you have to make a collection of those that you can use. There are two ways to do this. One way is to study the sacred scriptures of the world and cull out those affirmations that express the highest truth. In the textbooks of Vedanta, for instance, there are many inspiring verses. What you are looking for are short, declarative sentences such as the following from the *Avadhuta Gita*: "The essence and whole of the Vedanta is this knowledge, this supreme knowledge, that I am by nature the formless, absolute Self." Such a statement is an excellent affirmation to be used during the day.

Another way to collect affirmations is to formulate them for yourself. If the ancient verses don't have an immediate, emotional appeal, then make up your own. Scriptural verses have a ring of authority, but yours may have more personal significance. This formulation of your own affirmation would be taboo in the context of mantra meditation. But the affirmation is not a mantra. It is the idea that is important here and not the mystic sound.

The affirmation is not like a suit of clothes that can be tried on and worn occasionally. You have to repeat the affirmation again and again for it to be effective. One of the best times to repeat the affirmation is in the morning. Sit down as if for meditation; then repeat the affirmation slowly to yourself. Focus on the meaning, not on the sound. Rote repetition doesn't work here. Self-affirmation is not the same as japa.

The affirmation is not a mantra that has to be repeated with regular, rhythmic sound. The mystic vibration of the mantra brings its own result even if you don't know the meaning. The affirmation is different. It is like a reminder of something forgotten. The important thing is the meaning. Let it sink into your unconscious. As you repeat the affirmation, try to feel your divinity and long for freedom. The more you can identify yourself with the Self, the more you will recall your true nature.

After repeating the affirmation in the morning, you will feel the effect throughout the day. It is comparable to hiking to the top of a mountain and looking down on the town below. Later on, when you are in the marketplace, on a busy street corner perhaps, you will remember your view from the mountain above. Standing on the corner of a busy street, caught up in the hustle and bustle of the noon rush hour, you will recall your great thought, "I am the witness," and immediately tensions will relax, and you will get a new perspective.

During the day it is important that you repeat your affirmation whenever you can. The mind is naturally forgetful. It is like a chronic amnesia patient. Trying to get such a person to do something for you is difficult. You have to keep reminding him. He means well, but he forgets. You have to remind him. Put a little card on his desk or something.

In the evening, before you go to sleep, it is a great relief to practice affirming your true Self, the Atman. At the end of the day, you may feel incomplete and unfulfilled. Perhaps you have had a hard day, and there is still a long list of things to do. At this time, what a relief it is to recall, "I am already perfect. I am already complete and fulfilled just as I am."

The story of the King of Smritinagar shows the transformative power of self-affirmation:

Once upon a time, in ancient India, in the city of Smritinagar, which in Sanskrit means the City of Lost Memory, there lived a king who ruled wisely and well. One day he decided to go out hunting alone. He mounted his horse and rode out of the city limits, through the royal forest, and unknowingly crossed the border of his kingdom into a neighboring land.

As the king rode through the forest, a snake slithered across the trail. Seeing the snake, the king's horse shied back, reared up, and threw the king from the saddle. The king flew through the air, fell to the ground, hit his head, and was knocked unconscious. He lay there for two hours. When he revived, he got up and looked around. He didn't know where he was or who he was. He was suffering from amnesia.

In his confusion, the king noticed that he was dressed as a hunter. "Maybe I am a game warden of this forest," he thought. That night, he built a rough shelter. The next day he built a more sturdy hut and began to live in the forest.

Time passed. The hunter-king made a comfortable living for himself. During the day he would patrol the forest. In the evening, he would cook his supper by the fire. But when he fell asleep, he was troubled by a strange dream. He dreamt of a palace with many rooms filled with treasure and saw courtiers, princes, princesses, and a queen, all attending on the king who was himself. But then he woke to find himself a mere huntsman.

Time passed. One day a merchant came through the forest and stopped to visit. As they were talking, the hunter-king related his strange dream. "I see you want to become a king," said the merchant. "That is a common desire we all share. Take my advice and first become a merchant like myself. Buy, sell, trade, and make deals—pretty soon you'll be rich, and wherever you go you can live like a king." So saying, the merchant departed.

"That's good advice," thought the hunter-king. And the next day he went into town and bought some cloth to sell in the market. He bought and sold and traded all day; but at the end of the day he went bankrupt. The king realized he wasn't cut out to be a merchant and sadly returned to the forest.

Time passed. One day a soldier passed by that way. While they were having tea, the hunter-king related his strange dream. "Yes sir," said the soldier. "I see you want to become a king. My advice is simple. First become a soldier like myself. Serve the army well, and you will be promoted. When you become a general, you can go to war and conquer a kingdom." So saying, the soldier departed.

"That's good advice," thought the hunter-king, and the next day he went into the village to the army recruiting office. But when the sergeant saw him, he shook his head. "You are too old and fat to serve in the army," he said. The hunter-king sadly departed and returned to the forest.

Time passed. One day a holy man came by that way. He immediately recognized the lost King of Smritinagar and rushed up to him. "Where have you been, Your Majesty?" he said. "The entire kingdom is in confusion seeking your return."

"What do you mean?" said the hunter-king who was baffled by the strange words of the holy man. "But, by the way," said the king. "I do have a strange dream every night."

When he related his dream, the holy man understood what had happened. He devised a plan to get the king back. "Let me give you some advice, my son," he said. "I will tell you how you can make your dream come true. Go and hire a white horse and a silver saddle and some horsemen to ride along with you. Ride east into the neighboring kingdom of Smritinagar and proclaim yourself king."

"But," said the hunter-king, "that is ridiculous. Merely saying I am a king won't make me a king."

"No, my child," said the holy man, "but I will, by my grace, give you the power of hypnotic speech whereby whatever you say people will believe." Now the hunter-king was a pious man, and he believed the saint, and he kneeled down and received the blessing of hypnotic speech.

The next day the hunter-king went into the village, hired a white horse and silver saddle and a contingent of men to ride with him. He rode in the direction of the Kingdom of Smritinagar. As he crossed the border, he saw a patrol of mounted soldiers approaching. In great trepidation and a timorous voice, the hunter-king said: "I am the lost King of Smritinagar." To his amazement, the patrol of soldiers dismounted and bowed before him. The blessing of the holy man was powerful indeed!

As the hunter-king came to the city limits, peasants streamed out. "I am the lost King of Smritinagar," he proclaimed. And again he found that all welcomed him with great joy and bowed before him. His self-confidence grew. Riding through the streets, he proclaimed to the right and the left, "I am the lost King of Smritinagar!" The more he affirmed his royal nature, the more his joy deepened. As he rode, the charm of hypnotic speech began working on himself. His happiness increased.

As he rode along, the houses and streets seemed even more familiar. He had a strong sense of déjà vu. And when the great white walls of the palace rose before him, his memory cleared, and he rode boldly through the gates.

❁

A Stone in Water

by Swami Viprananda

FATHER JEAN PIERRE de Caussade, the eighteenth-century French Jesuit, once wrote to a nun concerning her anxieties, fears, and distractions of mind: "Allow them to drop as a stone drops into water." With this simple metaphor Caussade has beautifully described an indispensable part of all spiritual paths: detachment, or "letting go." The metaphor he used is particularly appropriate for two reasons. First, it suggests a finality to the act—once the stone is dropped, it is gone, not to be recovered. Second, it suggests that the stone is relatively unimportant. Similarly, detachment gives the mind the freedom to let things drop once and for all and allows us to see that what is being dropped is not as important as we had thought.

Much of what we consider necessary and stubbornly cling to in life does not seem so important when judged from a higher point of view. Can we imagine going on a vacation and trying to load all our household goods, garden tools, and clothing into the car? What a burden that would be! We take with us only what we think necessary. Our needs for a vacation are different from our needs at home. But this is exactly what we often do in a psychological sense in our journey through life. We carry with us excess baggage in the form of attachments and aversions, which makes our journey burdensome and wearying. We bear the load of desire for the objects of our attachments as well as of disappointment and pain at their loss. It is no wonder that we often feel so weighed down and despondent—we have become self-centered. The long-term effects of this view of life are a sense of meaninglessness and feelings of emptiness, loneliness, and despair. The Bhagavad Gita describes how a person under the sway of attachment loses his discrimination and is lost:

> Thinking of objects, attachment to them is formed in a man. From attachment longing, and from longing anger grows. From anger comes delusion, and from delusion loss of memory. From loss of memory comes the ruin of discrimination, and from the ruin of discrimination he perishes.

What is the difference between simple desire and attachment, and why is the latter so harmful? Let us take an illustration from everyday life. Suppose we want to eat an ice cream cone. This is a simple and harmless desire. But what if we *have* to have an ice cream cone or will otherwise feel upset or miserable? This then is an attachment, and it is harmful in that our freedom of thought and action is lost, and we become bound. We are no longer the masters of our minds or actions. Not only does such an outlook deprive us of peace, it also distorts our sense of reality since we experience the world in terms of our attachments. For instance, if we are greedy, we see the world primarily in terms of acquisition. This distortion of reality includes ourselves as well, since our self-image becomes defined by these very attachments.

Detachment, on the other hand, is a means of achieving freedom of thought and action, and of experiencing peace and fulfillment. It is always accompanied and supported by another spiritual discipline, discrimination, which is the ability to discern the real from the unreal, truth from untruth, the transient from the eternal.

As our discrimination deepens and our detachment becomes stronger, our outlook and actions begin to change. Our clinging to the world is gradually lessened, and we awaken to the infinite human and spiritual potential that lies within us. This shift in outlook is an important step in our spiritual development, as it constitutes a turning from self-centeredness to God-centeredness, from selfishness to selflessness.

A story of two monks illustrates the difference between attachment and detachment. Once two monks were wandering through the countryside. One day they happened to come to a river and were about to wade across it when a beautiful, young woman approached them and said, "I must cross the river, but there is no ferryboat and the water is much too deep for me. Please carry me across." One of the monks immediately agreed. Taking her in his arms, he carried her to the other shore and set her down, while the second monk also waded across. The two monks then resumed their journey. After they had gone some distance, the second monk said to the first monk, "You are a monk. You should not have carried that woman across the river." The first monk replied, "I carried her across the river and set her down, but I see that you are still carrying her."

Detachment has been extolled by all religions. Buddha declared, "For that which clingeth to another thing there is a fall: but unto that which clingeth not no fall can come. Where no fall cometh, there is rest." Jesus said, "He that loveth his life shall lose it, but he that loseth his life for my sake shall find it." Swami Vivekananda said in his *Karma Yoga*, "Without non-attachment there cannot be any kind of Yoga. Non-attachment is the basis of all the Yogas."

Sri Ramakrishna advised his disciples and devotees to live in the world in a spirit of detachment. He used the analogy of a maidservant who lives in her employer's house in the city and performs all her duties as if it were her own home, even calling the children "my Hari" or "my Ram." But all the while she is aware that her real home and family are in the village far away.

I know of no better example of detachment amidst the trials and tribulations of life than that of Sri Sarada Devi, the Holy Mother and spiritual consort of Sri Ramakrishna. She was truly "in the world but not of it." She performed her duties, mixing with all, and accepted life as it came to her, but was never attached to the world or bound by it. Because of her detachment, she had the capacity to discern the underlying spiritual reality in all persons and at the same time value the uniqueness of every individual. As a result, her love was both universal and intensely personal and intimate. In a world in which attachment and self-centeredness are the norm and even considered necessary, her life shines as a perfect example of the glory of detachment from self and attachment to God.

The stone is dropped into the water and is gone, and we go on our way. We do not mourn its loss, for we know that in life separation is inevitable and that we cannot stop here; we must go on. A hawk with a piece of meat in its beak was chased by a flock of crows. In whatever direction it flew the crows pursued it, until at last the hawk, weary of being tormented, dropped the piece of meat into the river below. At once the crows left, and the hawk found peace.

Letting go means freeing ourselves from the bonds that tie us to the world and bring us so much suffering. It means emptying ourselves of self so that we may be filled with God, the source of all peace.

The Art of Building Shrines

by Brahmachari Veda Chaitanya

ABOUT TEN YEARS ago I had the privilege of making a shrine for the Vivekananda House in South Pasadena where Swami Vivekananda lived for several weeks in 1900. I had recently helped restore the house to its original condition, just as it might have been when Swamiji actually lived there, and the whole time I was working on the house, I felt greatly inspired just knowing that such a noble and heroic soul had lived there. Later, as I was making the shrine which was to be installed in the room which served as Swamiji's bedroom, my mind was filled with thoughts of him and his stay in California. I could picture him sitting at the breakfast table in the morning, smoking his pipe in the garden, or absorbed in deep meditation in his room. It was a very special period for me and one in which my mind naturally tended toward higher thoughts while I worked.

Since I carry out various types of maintenance chores at the monastery where I live, I was often given jobs not nearly as inspiring to work on. As it turned out, my very next assignment was a stand for an old pump motor in one of our storage sheds. I had completed the basic structure and was working on the final finish of the stand. Very likely I was paying more attention than necessary to the aesthetics of the job and may have gone a little overboard in sanding and finishing a structure which would very soon be splattered with grease and gasoline. Having just completed the shrine project, however, I was blissfully unmindful of my unwarranted attention to detail and beauty.

One of the brothers happened to see me putting the final touches on the stand and jokingly asked, "Are you making another shrine?" His words, though casually uttered, caught me totally off guard. Something clicked inside my head, and I immediately realized that, without my knowledge, the same attention to detail, the same concentration of mind, and the same devotional feelings that had been my constant companions throughout the shrine project had managed to infiltrate the seemingly trivial job I was working on. So, despite the fact that the stand I was making was to bear not a picture of Swami Vivekananda but rather an old pump motor, I at once saw that I *had* been building another shrine, though unconsciously, and replied (incredulous that he had to ask), "Yes, as a matter of fact, that's *exactly* what I'm doing!" And from that moment on, I have tried to maintain the same attitude in all my work, to feel that whatever I was making was a shrine to the Lord.

The experience that I had that day was a particularly valuable one for me. I began to understand the great importance of attitude in spiritual life. I saw that with the help of a healthy imagination and a smattering of devotion, all action can be converted into acts of worship. All activities can be spiritualized until the line of demarcation between sacred and secular, spiritual practice and worldly duties, begins to gradually melt away. We can wash the dishes with the same care that we take when polishing the sacred vessels used in worship; we can spread the tablecloth and set the table for the evening meal with the same reverence that we feel when arranging the altar cloth in the shrine room; we can serve our family and friends with the same devotion that we would feel when serving the Lord.

The critical element is our attitude. We need not sand and stain the stand for a motor with the same zeal that we would the shrine, but we should try to maintain the same state of mind and the feeling that we are performing our work as an offering to God.

We find this same idea beautifully expressed in the Bhagavad Gita: "Whatever you do, whatever you eat, whatever you offer, whatever you give away, whatever austerities you perform, do all of them as an offering unto Me." The spiritual aspirant who adopts this attitude is limited only by his imagination with regard to spiritualizing his everyday activities. There is a wonderful song by the great mystic poet of Bengal, Ramprasad, which reveals the heights to which the devotee can aspire along this path:

> O my mind, worship Mother Kali in any way you like;
> Repeat her name both day and night.
> When you lie down for rest, feel you are bowing at her feet;
> While you sleep, feel you are meditating on her;
> And when you eat, think you are making oblations to Mother.
> Whatever sounds you hear, know them all to be Mother's mantra;
> For Kali is the embodiment of all the letters of the alphabet.
> Ramprasad says with joy: "Mother dwells in all things;
> When I walk about town, I am circumambulating Mother herself."

What do we gain by adopting such an attitude? The fruits of this practice are many and enduring. By keeping our minds fixed on our spiritual ideal at all times, we become forgetful of self. Our actions become purged of selfish motive, and the heart becomes purified. We no longer feel that strong sense of attachment to work which only leads to greater misery and bondage.

When we look upon action as an offering, we can freely give it up. Since our work takes on a new importance for us, we naturally perform our duties with greater attention and efficiency. Knowing that we have done the best job we can, we are not disturbed by the praise or blame of the world, especially since our motive for action is no longer a self-centered one but a God-centered one.

We also find that much of the drudgery which normally accompanies work begins to disappear the more we think of it as worship, until even the most menial task becomes a source of joy. At that point we no longer look upon any activity as "secular" or "worldly." All our actions become opportunities for spiritual growth because the mind remains fixed on God or the spiritual ideal throughout. By cultivating the attitude that all action is an offering to the Divine, we can ultimately make our whole lives an offering to God. By mastering this art of "building shrines" we can, in the course of time, make that final offering of the lower self into the higher Self, the soul into God, and so attain the final aim of human life.

The Meaning of Ritual Worship

by Pravrajika Varadaprana

WORSHIP BRINGS A feeling of stillness to the soul, a sense of unity with God. These moments of communion create a longing in the soul to reach complete union with the Supreme Being.

The purpose of worship, as practiced in the various religious traditions, is communion with God. The methods used may vary according to the tradition, but the end result is the same.

These methods of worship may include such diverse practices as prayer, meditation, sacred music, rituals, and loving service to man as God. In Vedanta, any or all of these methods may be incorporated into one's spiritual life.

One of the underlying principles of Vedanta is that the soul is divine, one with God. But the covering of ignorance must first be removed before we can be aware of this divinity. Any way in which we can lessen this ignorance of our true nature is a legitimate path to God. As Vedantists, we attempt to lead a life based on the ideal of seeing the divinity in all living beings and the oneness of all existence.

One of the most important paths to God is prayer. A Hasidic mystic, Or Ha Emet, described prayer in the following terms: "A person should be so absorbed in prayer that he is no longer aware of his own self. There is nothing for him but the flow of life. All his thoughts are with God. He who still knows how intensely he is praying has not yet overcome the bonds of self."

Meditation is a direct method of impressing on the mind the divine nature of the soul, by contemplating the one Reality which exists within us and all around us. This practice gradually purifies the mind, lessening the veil of ignorance—the sense of ego which separates us from God. The object of meditation may be either a personal loving form of God, or a more abstract concept of God.

In the Russian Orthodox tradition, Theophan the Recluse also speaks of God as dwelling within: "You seek the Lord? Seek, but only within yourself. He is not far from anyone. The Lord is near all those who truly call on him. Find a place in your heart, and speak there with the Lord. It is the Lord's reception room." We find a striking similarity here with the words of Sri Ramakrishna: "The heart of the devotee is the drawingroom of God. He dwells in all beings, no doubt, but he especially manifests himself in the heart of the devotee."

Ritual is another method by which we can commune with God. Through symbols we can more easily grasp subtle and abstract ideas. The Christian mass, the lighting of the menorah, bowing to Mecca with prayers five times a day, the chanting of the Tibetan monks, and the ceremonies of the Native Americans are all meaningful ways of worshiping the divine.

Just a simple ritual such as lighting a candle and waving incense before a picture or image with concentration and devotion can be a magical moment of communion with the divine. The picture, symbol, or image represents the living presence of God to the worshiper. Any offering made wholeheartedly to the purest of the pure helps to purify one's mind, and lifts it above the sense of ego and material desires.

Sri Krishna says in the ninth chapter of the Bhagavad Gita: "Whatever man gives me in true devotion: a fruit or water, a leaf or flower: I will accept it. That gift is love, his heart's dedication." We know that the Lord of all creation has no needs or wants, but for our sake he accepts our offerings.

The ritual worship, or *puja*, performed in many of the Ramakrishna Mission centers was adapted from the ancient Tantric tradition of worship. It is a highly scientific and psychologically satisfying form of worship, but it requires some explanation for the observer to fully appreciate it.

The puja incorporates aspects of all the four yogas: devotion, meditation, action, and knowledge. It also satisfies the worshiper's artistic sense of beauty of form and movement. The mind of the worshiper is occupied every moment, which forces the mind to concentrate. In puja the Lord is treated as the honored guest to whom every amenity is offered. This brings to the worshiper a sense of closeness to the Lord.

One of its opening prayers sets the tone for the puja: "As man with his eyes open sees the sky before him, so the seers of truth see always the Supreme Reality, God, the all-pervading existence." The worshiper tries to feel that the God who is dwelling in the heart is one with the God he or she is worshiping on the altar. The same God is in all the surroundings, the articles of worship, and the offerings that are to be made.

The puja can be roughly divided into four main sections. First comes the purification and sanctification of the worshiper, the surroundings, and all the articles of worship. This is done with the help of mantras, *mudras*—position of the hands—and *yantras*—geometric symbols drawn with water, that represent aspects of the divine.

The second section consists of a meditation on the impersonal aspect of God. All the elements which make up the body and the universe are mentally dissolved into the source from which they came. The worshiper thinks of the spiritual energy coiled up at the base of the spine and mentally raises it to the highest center of spiritual consciousness in the head. The worshiper prays for illumination, and tries to feel oneness with the Supreme Spirit.

The worshiper now feels completely purified and ready to worship God with a new and spiritualized body. This is an important part of the worship, because as the Tantras point out, a person must first become divine before he or she can worship divinity.

In the third section of the puja, the Deity is worshiped mentally within the heart center. Through appropriate mantras and mudras, the Deity is invoked in the heart and various parts of the body.

Mental worship begins by offering the lotus of the heart as a throne upon which the Lord is seated. Ambrosia is offered to bathe his feet, and the nectar of immortality for his bath. He is clothed in space. The subtle essence of the earth is offered as fragrance; the mind is offered in the form of flowers. The vital energy is offered as incense, and the essence of fire for his light. An ocean of nectar is offered as food, and the sound of Om as the ringing of a bell. The essence of air is offered to fan him; the restless mind is offered as a dance before him.

At the conclusion of this meditation, the Deity is worshiped in his formless aspect in the water of a conch shell. Some holy water from the conch shell is then sprinkled all around; on the worshiper, the altar, vessels, and flowers, giving the worshiper another opportunity to feel the one divinity present everywhere.

The worshiper is now ready to proceed with the external worship. After bathing the picture or image, the worshiper meditates on the Lord, holding a flower at the heart level in the meditation mudra. With a mantra, the living presence of the Lord is breathed from the heart into the flower and then offered to the Deity on the altar. Thus throughout the external worship the worshiper keeps a connection between the Lord within, and the same Lord who is being worshiped on the altar.

The worship continues with the offering of various articles such as water to wash his feet, flowers, bath water, perfume, incense, light, and food. In more elaborate worships, the presence of God is first worshiped in each item before it is offered, completing the feeling of unity.

Puja is performed not only for the worshiper, but on behalf of all those present and for the good of the world. After worship it is customary to distribute the sanctified food, the *prasad*, to those present as tokens of grace from the Lord.

Worship can extend to everything we do in life. It is comparatively easy to think of God at the time of prayer, meditation, or worship, with eyes closed. The challenge is to keep a remembrance of the divine throughout the day with eyes open. The insights and inner feelings that we have gained through our worship and meditation need to be kept alive as much as possible during the day. The love we experience for God during our worship, we can try to transfer to all our associates, who are the children of God.

We often get distracted and forget the main goal we have set out to achieve. However, with constant diligence the mind is gradually purified, and it becomes easier for us to think of God more frequently. When the mind is purified, free from ego and desire, God's grace is experienced, and then it will become possible for us to worship God everywhere, at all times.

In the meantime we can try to perform every action as an offering to the Lord, who is present everywhere. At our place of work, we can offer the results of our actions to God. In our home, we can keep the house clean and shining for God who dwells there. Most important is for us to see God in all our associates, and to serve them in the spirit of serving God. We can invent our own techniques, whatever works best for us, in an effort to make every moment of our lives a worship of God.

✵

Contentment in a Discontented World

by Pravrajika Brahmaprana

STRESS, FRUSTRATION, EMPTINESS. Grief, loneliness, and despair. Those of us who have experienced any one of these know what a devastating effect it can have upon our lives. We lose our balance, our friends, our career, our spouse, our family. At such times our entire being sends out an SOS. Then we ask, "What went wrong?" "Why me?"

Contentment is something we all treasure. But real contentment is the treasure of very few.

A burning discontentment with *who* and *what* we are is the painful blessing most of us need before we hunger for inner peace. It has been said, "Contentment comes not by the fulfillment of what we want, but with the realization of what we already have."

Spiritual life begins when we learn the futility of unfolding our divinity outside of ourselves. The person who rushes through meals, dashes to the office, and toils all week for a paycheck is in search of the same fulfillment as the yogi seated in meditation, trying to forget the world and to find God within. Both are struggling to unfold their divinity. One struggles to find fulfillment outside of himself or herself—in impermanent material objects or fleeting pleasures; and the other within—in the Self, or Atman, the eternal Spirit within all. One ends in conflict; the other in contentment.

Contentment does not depend upon externals; it changes with our mental attitude. John Milton wrote:

> The mind is its own place, and in itself
> Can make a heaven of Hell, a hell of Heaven.

Vedanta says: We cannot change the world, we can only change ourselves. The world is like a dog's curly tail. No matter how hard we try to straighten it, it will always curl up again. We can only straighten ourselves.

To find contentment, we must go to its source—the Atman, the blissful Self. One who attains knowledge of the Atman is freed from the tyranny of the world.

Since we *are* the Atman, we must struggle to realize that—to manifest that consciousness in our everyday life. In this effort, our physical, intellectual, and emotional lives become spiritualized and one-pointed. All of our duties, relationships, and goals become avenues leading to one Goal. Then our life becomes integrated and harmonious. In such an environment, contentment flourishes.

We know this. Why then is contentment so elusive?

After a crisis, every part of our being suffers the aftershock, and cries out for care and attention. But until we are able to administer first aid and proper nourishment to our body, mind, and soul, we are not yet on the road to recovery. We cannot successfully heal our selves nor find true contentment.

In an early 1980's *Reader's Digest* article, a woman shared the secret of *her* recovery from a devastating bereavement. Her daily prescription for contentment provided such a healthy plan for a balanced spiritual life and seemed so in tune with Vedantic principles that I still remember it today: (1) Do something for yourself; (2) Do something for someone else; (3) Do something you don't want to do; (4) Do a physical exercise; (5) Do a mental exercise; (6) Count your blessings.

(1) Do something for yourself: In the Bhagavad Gita, Sri Krishna says:

> The uncontrolled mind
> Does not guess that the Atman is present;
> How can it meditate?
> Without meditation, where is peace?
> Without peace, where is happiness?

Meditation acquaints us with our minds. Through the repeated practice of meditation we learn the art of making friends with the mind.

An uncontrolled mind is like a drunken monkey stung by a bee. "Truly the wind is no wilder," Sri Krishna commented in the Gita. Through the practice of meditation, a spiritual aspirant learns how to watch over the "monkey" mind until, embarrassed by its antics, it becomes subdued and controlled. A calm mind is a reliable friend. With that friend we can commune with God. Swami Brahmananda, a disciple of Sri Ramakrishna, once said:

> Remember Him when you eat, when you sit, when you lie down; remember Him whatever you do. By such repeated practice you will find that when you go to meditate, it will be easy to remember God and become absorbed in Him. As your mind becomes absorbed in meditation, a fountain of joy will spring up within you.

(2) Do something for someone else: Once in India a young man complained to Swami Vivekananda that he had practiced much meditation, but had achieved no peace of mind. "My boy," said the Swami in a voice full of sympathy, "if you take my word, you will first have to open the door of your room and look around instead of closing your eyes. There are hundreds of poor and helpless people in the neighborhood of your house; them you will have to serve to the best of your ability."

Sometimes people mistake spiritual life for a selfish escape. Christ taught, "Love thy neighbor as thy self." "Yes," Vedanta says, "we must love our neighbor, because he or she *is* our very Self."

The same Atman dwells in all living beings. To see God in all living beings—not just in ourselves—creates true contentment. The first step toward attaining unity with all is to show loving-kindness toward others. If we can make it our daily practice to do even *one* thing for someone else, it is bound to bring us some measure of peace. We will begin to experience joy through the happiness we give others. And the more we do for others, the greater will be our peace.

(3) Do something you don't want to do: Procrastination is a stumbling block to our mental peace. At times we feel stymied in undertaking even simple tasks. Why should we let this troublemaker disturb our contentment, when a little self-introspection can free us from the burden?

Procrastination sometimes stems from unnecessary mental clutter—whether an unkept promise, a job undone, a hurt inflicted, or a wrong committed. Unfinished chores subconsciously nag at us, distract us, and diminish our incentive until we learn to face them and finish them. Then only do we feel free and confident to tackle more important tasks.

Daily self-analysis can bring these disturbing unfinished actions to our attention. We can then strive to rectify them. By keeping our word, finishing what we start, and correcting our mistakes, a psychological load is lifted from the mind, and we feel a greater sense of peace. A good housekeeper cleans house regularly. So also the dust and debris of the mind must be routinely swept away. Otherwise, we lose the capacity to think clearly and act calmly.

(4) Do a physical exercise: The body is the temple of God. If it is to serve our spiritual needs, we must give it proper attention by feeding, clothing, and exercising it. It should be a strong vessel "with muscles of iron and nerves of steel," Swami Vivekananda advocated, "gigantic wills

which nothing can resist, which can penetrate into the mysteries and the secrets of the universe, and will accomplish their purpose in any fashion even if it means going down to the bottom of the ocean and meeting death face to face." With a strong body we can calmly withstand the ups and downs of everyday life. This is essential for peace of mind.

The body should be maintained in such a way that the aspirant may forget it at the time of meditation. "Yoga is not for the man who overeats," Sri Krishna warned:

> or for him who fasts excessively. It is not for him who sleeps too much, or for the keeper of exaggerated vigils. Let a man be moderate in his eating and his recreation, moderately active, moderate in sleep and in wakefulness. He will find that yoga takes away all his unhappiness.

(5) Do a mental exercise: Sri Ramakrishna used to say: "Never squander the energies of your mind." Swami Brahmananda explained, "This means remember God constantly. The worldly man is very careful not to squander his money, but he gives little heed to how he squanders his mind."

Even with a steady mind, it is not possible to remain absorbed in meditation throughout the day. Therefore, Vedanta advocates scriptural study to keep the mind tuned to a higher level. Sri Ramakrishna used to say: "The object of study is to find the means of knowing God and realizing Him." He used to ridicule a mere "bread-winning" education as useless compared to knowledge of God.

Scriptural study feeds the mind with nourishing thoughts which provide the aspirant with a spiritual undercurrent throughout the day. Even amidst the stress and turmoil of the workplace, our minds will continue to feed off the strength of these thoughts, and remain centered and calm. At the time of meditation, they will then help to gather the forces of the mind into an unbroken thought of God.

Throughout our spiritual life, careful study of the lives and teachings of the great masters brings conviction; with conviction comes calmness of mind.

(6) Count your blessings: Behind this platitude is a deep philosophical truth. We are what we think. If we dwell on the negative aspects of life, our minds shrink and we develop a puny, petty ego—always

quarreling and complaining. But if we strive to cultivate a constructive attitude toward ourselves and others, we take the first step toward self-improvement. By emphasizing the positive, we expand ourselves and manifest our higher nature.

"Be content with externals," Swami Brahmananda told his disciples, "but practice divine discontentment." By focusing on our spiritual goal in life—something larger than ourselves—trivial disturbances or irritations lose their importance. By reminding ourselves of what is important, the little things in life can never take possession of us. When this attitude is daily maintained, we develop such a power of mind that even tragedies cannot throw us off balance. This is the ultimate test of contentment.

It is said, "Every wall can be a door." Any burden can be lifted if we have the determination and skill to learn spiritual jujitsu. Then worries and sorrows become the springboard for the soul to soar, and its wings to fly. Nothing can inhibit our freedom.

As we learn to face life's tragedies, we develop compassion for ourselves. This is the greatest peace work, because then we understand what it is to feel compassion for others.

Compassion is the last word in spiritual life. No matter what or whom we encounter, we are fearless. By covering every thing and every one with God, we experience the unity of existence. Who is there to fear whom? All is God. Sri Sarada Devi, the Holy Mother, gave this as her final message:

> I tell you one thing—if you want peace of mind, do not find fault with others. Rather see your own faults. Learn to make the world your own. No one is a stranger, my child; the whole world is your own.

Our search for contentment ends here.

A Meditation:
God Dwells In the Depth of Your Heart

by Swami Satprakashananda

THINK THAT THE atmosphere around you is wholesome, pure, and serene. Think that you are inhaling from the atmosphere something purifying and uplifting. Think that as you inhale the air, your body is being purified through and through. All its impurities, all its weaknesses are being wiped out. All weariness and excitement have left the body. It feels lighter than usual. Your nerves are soothed. You feel refreshed and regenerated.

Think that the body has become perfectly calm and steady. It no longer offers any resistance to the quietness of the mind. Think that the mind is getting purer as it turns to God, the light of all lights. It becomes more and more quiet at the same time, because all its restlessness is due to the impurities adhering to it.

How is the mind purified? Its impurities arise from ignorance. Darkness prevailing within the mind causes all its weaknesses. The only cure for darkness is light. When you let the light of the Supreme Spirit enter into your mind, then it becomes purified. Being purified, it becomes pacified. No pacification of the mind is possible without its purification. The more you think of God, the purer you become, the more your thoughts become concentrated on him.

How will you meditate on him? He is all-pervading. He is in all forms. He is also beyond forms. He inhabits the entire universe. He is also beyond the universe. He holds time and space in his bosom. He is also timeless and spaceless. How will you hold the Supreme Being within your mind, who is the all-powerful, all-knowing Creator and Preserver of the universe, whom thoughts cannot reach, whom speech cannot express? How will you meditate on the Supreme Being?

It is true that the supreme Lord is present everywhere, that he is formless, featureless, beyond time, beyond space. But he is also manifest within your heart as your innermost Self. Right here in the depth of the heart his light is constantly shining. In order to realize him you will not have to go anywhere. Nowhere can you find him but in your heart. It is in the depth of your heart that you can know him directly, most intimately.

Vain is your search in the mountain cave, on the beautiful landscape, in the snowy peaks, in the expanse of the deep blue waters, in the flowering meadows, in the starry heaven. Nowhere can you reach him. Everywhere you can see his manifestation, but not him. His very manifestations hide him from you. The supreme Lord, who manifests and sustains the universe, has hidden himself by his own glory, as it were. We see only his manifestation.

Turn your thoughts inward, into the inmost depth of your being. There he is shining as your very Self, as the Soul of your soul. Deep within your heart there is a luminous space, the seat of your intellect, your right knowledge. Visualize the luminous space within your heart. Here is the very center of your personality. Here is the very basis of your being. Meditate on that luminous space, as the region of your self-awareness, as the abode of your spiritual self.

It is the light of the conscious Spirit shining within the heart that rules over the mind and body, that controls all the senses. It is the light of the conscious Spirit that enables the eyes to see, the ears to hear, the hands to work, the legs to move, the mouth to speak. In deep sleep, when the radiance of consciousness recedes from the body and the sense-organs, the senses cease to operate, and the body becomes inert. This light of consciousness emanates from your spiritual Self dwelling within the heart. This light is the source of all your knowledge and love, all your goodness and greatness.

Visualize that light of consciousness within your heart and meditate on your innermost Self, the changeless Spirit that witnesses all the changes of the body and the mind. It shines with constant effulgence that never flickers, that never gets dim. In waking, in dream, and in deep sleep it is ever the same.

Visualize the luminous space within your heart and intensely meditate on your spiritual Self, until you identify yourself with that, until you feel that you are not the physical body but the radiant Spirit.

You were young some years ago. You think you have grown in size. But it is the body that grows, that decays, that has birth and death. Ageless, birthless, deathless, without decay is the luminous Self. Unchanging, it appears to change, being identified with the changing conditions of the body. Unchanging, it appears to change, being identified with the changing conditions of the mind. The same light expressing itself differently through different mediums undergoes no change. Forget that you are the body, that you are a psychophysical being. Realize yourself as pure Spirit.

Meditate on the luminous Self shining in the depth of your heart. As you identify yourself with this, you no longer find yourself confined within the mind or the body. You transcend all limitations. Behind each and every wave there is one ocean. If you look beyond the wave form that seems to separate it from the ocean, you recognize its oneness with the ocean.

The spiritual Self shining within your heart is not limited by it. This is essentially one with the same Supreme Spirit that manifests the universe. It is egoism that creates a seeming difference between the individual consciousness and the universal consciousness. You are not the finite form that the wave has assumed. You are the very substance of which the wave is formed. You are of the essence of consciousness. Forget the limiting form. Realize your essential unity with the supreme Consciousness.

The moment you withdraw from the body, the senses, and the mind, and realize yourself as the pure Spirit that has no circumference, you find yourself united with the Supreme Being, unbounded by space, unbounded by time. In this realm there is no past, no present, no future. It is Absolute Consciousness, which is perfection itself, bliss itself, one infinite existence beyond all limitation. It is an ocean of bliss where there is no trace of darkness, where death is unknown, where there is light and light alone.

You are in the supreme Godhead. You are of That. You are in That. You live in him, you move in him, you have your being in him. But still you do not perceive yourself as you really are. Just as blind persons living and moving in the full blaze of the midday sun know nothing of the splendor of sunlight; similarly we live and move in him, yet because of our spiritual blindness we are unaware of him. Let the veil of darkness drop from our eyes. Let us realize our essential unity with the Supreme Self, which is purity itself, life itself, light itself, bliss itself.

Om, Shanti, Shanti, Shanti.

Peace, Peace, Peace unto all.

Dryness and Dark Night

by Gerald Heard

ONCE ANYONE REALIZES that real growth of the spirit can be made, he becomes interested in method. He sees that he need no longer leave his life to accident, nor drift and look to amusement to give living whatever meaning it may have: he sees that he must set about intentional living, he must undertake training, he must coordinate all his activities and his whole way of life along the path which has appeared and toward the goal at which that path aims.

This insight, or foresight, raises a number of questions. How is he to set about his new task? How much of his past life, which was based upon deliberate distraction and amusement, can remain? When anyone changes over from a way of living in which it was taken for granted that however you lived, the fundamental fact was that life meant nothing and went nowhere, to a way of living in which the meaning of life is apprehended and the place of the individual in that scheme has been discovered, then there must be very considerable modification of the things that are done as well as of the thoughts that are thought.

Right livelihood, the fifth step in the Eightfold Path to liberation and enlightenment, is something more than abstention from certain debarred occupations and professions such as armament manufacturing or white slave trafficking. It is even something more than abstaining from gambling in stocks and bonds or from being absorbed in the advertising business.

It is getting rid of everything which may distract one's attention from the one end and purpose of living. Many things which are obviously of no particular harm to anyone else have to be put out of the way, not because they are harmful in themselves, but because they take up too much time and attention when all the time one has, and all the attention which one can command, is required for the one main purpose which now makes meaning of every moment.

Most people think that as long as what they do harms no one else and is not unhealthy for them, there is no reason why they should not enjoy themselves whatever way they please. This familiar standard of morality cannot, however, satisfy those who have found the meaning of life. For them every moment is precious, and every ounce of attention is husbanded to bring them as soon as may be to their goal.

But once that is clear to them, and once they have resolved that only so they can live, they have to ask, How best may I get to my end? Most of us find that the discovery that life has a meaning, a meaning as urgent as it is vast, breaks on us with a shock of surprise and also delight. "So after all that we see about us, the pointless lives of most individuals, the blind clash of classes, the hideous anarchy of the nations, life has a meaning, it goes somewhere, we can go with it."

That is the huge wave of relief. The accepted nightmare which drives people to addictions, to possessiveness, to pride and violence and despair, is false. Then comes also the wave of counter-concern. If that is true, then there is not a moment to be wasted. Already one has wasted so much. "Work while ye have the light; the night cometh when no man may work." It is urgent not to waste a moment more of the all-too-few hours of daylight. So there is a double pressure urging us to use every second. There is the attraction of the goal and there is the rapidly passing opportunity of working on the means to the goal.

This sense of stress and attraction undoubtedly sometimes makes beginners suffer from anxiety and a kind of febrile haste. This may be one of the causes of disappointment and that giving-out of interest which is generally called "dryness." There is much need here, it is obvious, for good teaching and wise guiding. Even if we start young, which is uncommon in the West, we are by nature an impatient lot and all human beings, whether of the East or the West, seem to have this factor in common that their lives are run on what we may call an "alternating" rather than on a "continuous" current. With the best will in the world and with the wisest training, it does not seem possible for them to avoid a certain, and perhaps a necessary, fluctuation.

Now this it is which is so difficult for the ardent and anxious beginner to endure, and it is here therefore that it is very interesting to try and compare the findings both of the masters of the West and also of the East, as to how far this ebb and flow is necessary, and how far the fluctuations—like those of unemployment—may be "flattened out" as the economists say, so as to save the booms and slumps.

The obvious question here is whether the slumps—as in employment—might not be saved, by "backpedaling" when the booms are on. Psychologists have taught for a long while those of their patients who have a tendency to too big a fluctuation, and so are honored with the fine frenzied title of manic-depressive types, to check the moment of elation and so save themselves from the moment of depression. But, beyond this very natural and practical advice, may we not learn more?

Quite obviously there are a number of rules for the spiritual life which apply to all of us whether we are stolid or excitable. There is a lower limit of observance and practice which, if we go under it, we shall be simply slothful and not making any real effect on the will and the character.

After all, we are like people in a ship which has a leak and which is making for the shore. We must work at a certain pace at the pumps or the water will gain on us, rising in the hold, and we shall founder before we can be safely beached. But there is also a higher limit, a limit above which strain comes on. To use the same simile again: there comes a time when the crew may wear itself out in pumping and so have to abandon their labor before the shore is reached. The leak cannot be wholly stopped, what we have to do (at least we beginners) is to keep the water level down, to keep on pumping out more or at least as much as is coming in.

Now our question is, Where do those limits lie? To take another simile, this time from Alpine climbing. The young when they go out with an experienced guide are always surprised at the slow and almost loitering pace at which he starts. They cannot endure this dilatoriness. They swing off ahead but when the sun is up and the higher slopes are reached, he passes them for they have to sit down exhausted in order to get back their strength. His set pace is a thought-out balance between fatigue and the distance to be covered and the time for covering that distance.

It is significant that all Alpine distances are given not in kilometers but in hours and minutes—it is a well-thought-out race, however slow it looks, a race between the time before the sun will set and the energy at the climber's disposal. Some violent fluctuations would therefore seem to be due to lack of foresight on our part. After all, risks are nearly always taken and accidents nearly always happen because we will not look ahead. Instead we suddenly see an oncoming difficulty and try to get out of it without sufficient time in which to make the necessary change.

But there are deeper rules of fluctuation and of ebb and flow which do not seem due to our present mistakes and carelessness. Nor under our present control. In learning a language, a golf swing, the piano, in every skill where knowledge has to combine with knack and blend into skill, there seems a wave motion, an ebb and flow. There is a period of rapid surface-mind learning and then a disappointing ebb when even that which was thought to have been mastered disappears.

It seems possible that during this disappointing time some deeper process is going on, what may perhaps be called a period of storage and profound modification and, again it may be, no new knowledge or knack could safely be taken in unless first of all the first load had been safely stowed and room and relation found for it in the ways and means, the methods and functions of the body-mind. We are probably far more full up than we know, and a new knowledge and power must always mean a modification of old ones. But still again beyond this recognition of gaps, and waits, and periods when we seem to "lose way" as sailors say and "hang fire," there are deeper dips.

What of those states which the western saints and contemplatives call the "dark nights of the soul"? Here a number of difficulties confront the researcher. First there is the difficulty of the words themselves. Do all the writers mean the same thing when they use this same title? It seems difficult to think that they do. For example, a textual authority on western mysticism such as Dr. W.R. Inge gives . . . as examples of the dark night, passages from Ruysbroek and the *Theologia Germanica*—two sources near one another in date and place.

But the Ruysbroek passage where he talks of an autumn of maturing fruits after the lush springing of summer seems to refer to dryness and a fruitful dryness at that, a rich reflection after a high experience, and not to deep despairs and utter emptiness. Ruysbroek mentions physical losses and hardships as being part of his "autumn." The desolation of the night seems in other cases so profound that they would be quite unaware if they were given all the health in the world or lost their closest relations.

The *Theologia Germanica* says the soul is sent to hell, and medievalists did not use that term lightly. The loss of the Presence—*that* alone counts and to regain *that* is the one hope. In these latter cases, then, there does not seem a storage, an autumn harvesting going on. Rather, it would seem we might say, the very barn itself is being harvested, cut down, and taken to pieces. Here we seem past the acquiring of virtues and the abandonment of vices and specific weaknesses. It is the very Self itself which is being challenged and attacked.

Eckhart, who does not seem to say much about the dark night as a specific term—perhaps because he welcomed it—yet teaches a path which certainly with most good people would lead to acute distress. He says that there are three things which keep us from God and, it would seem, three stages whereby we may and do return to him. The first is by loosing ourselves from our specific sins, the second is by loosening ourselves from all sense of self, and the third by loosening ourselves from time.

Many a Westerner, when he reads even those introductory lines of Emerson's,

> The strong gods pine for my abode,
> And pine in vain the sacred Seven;
> But thou, meek lover of the good!
> Find me, and turn thy back on heaven.

feels a certain chill. And certainly Christianity has never been comfortable with what its teachers called oriental nihilism, though, it is all the more important to note, all the master saints of Christendom as they climb beyond a certain height seem to view the same prospect which so daunts those on the lower levels.

Perhaps such high matters should not concern beginners. Perhaps all we on our level have to fear is quite common laziness, the wish for comfort and excitement, the impatience with the slow assimilation, the lack of advance because we will not let fall much that makes, by its weight and back-pull, our advance necessarily slower than it need be, would we abandon more.

Still the problem remains as one of interest to all students of humanity. How much of our difficulties, even the difficulties of the advanced, is due to ignorance, which greater knowledge could remove, and how much is due to the necessities of the case?

An entomologist was particularly anxious to hatch out successfully a valuable moth which had been found in its cocoon stage. The moment came when it began to emerge. It was watched with delighted care. But just when the dangerous emergency seemed safely over, one of the beautiful wings, which made so largely the value of the specimen, remained caught in the husk of the cocoon. In vain the moth seemed to struggle to get free, and at last it seemed quite clear to the anxious watcher that the insect's strength was failing and that it must die in the vain struggle. As it lay helpless and exhausted on its side, trapped and inert, the watcher snipped with sterilized scissors the stiffened edge of the cocoon.

The wing was released. The insect crawled out free. But it could not fly; the specimen was ruined. The wing remained curled and shriveled. That final struggle to the limits of life and strength seems to have been necessary. The circulation was not driven into the delicate veins of the wing and so it could not expand. The agonizing effort was not merely to get free but to grow whole, not merely to get out into the new world of winged flight but to have, full of power and energy, the fully unfolded wings, without which the new and larger life was vain and a mockery.

So it may be with our struggles. We may be made, not merely to win the larger life, but, through the agony of effort, to attain the powers and capacities and the quality of consciousness to function fully and rightly in that life.

A Psychologist Looks at Vedanta

by U-Shaka Craig with Ann Myren

MY NAME IS U-Shaka Craig, and I am an African-American. At the time I came to Vedanta, I was searching for my own roots.

I had left a job at a multinational corporation and gave full time to pursuing a deeper understanding of spirituality. This period lasted about a year and a half. I studied and practiced the ancient Egyptian religion as well as the more traditional African religions and began to see that there were parallels among the religions and universality not only in Vedanta but in other religions. As a result of my inquiry into the practices and philosophies of various religions, my interest became more intense, and I especially wanted to know how I could become a realized soul. Vedanta offered me a means of self-realization. But I needed practical guidelines. The four yogas, the discipline of meditation and practical instruction became my guidelines and the way to realization for me. I found these practices helped me to become established in Vedanta. What I really wanted to do was manifest these Vedantic teachings in everyday life by empowering myself and helping others.

There was another very important dimension to my attraction to Vedanta besides ideas and guidelines. When I first went to the temple in Hollywood, I was struck by the ambiance and was able to connect with that energy although I did not always understand what was going on. Whatever it was, it was unique and fascinating. I became closer to my Indian friend Mehta, and we talked about many of the Vedantic ideas. Through this interaction I was able to understand more and eventually felt extremely comfortable and began to integrate these principles into my life. I was pulled in.

In 1973 while still in my self-examination period, I moved to Berkeley. Here I changed my name. I had been thinking of finding a name to represent a strong image or model that would help me develop a sense of myself as a courageous man, capable of enduring hardship and mastering my environment. I took myself to the U.C. library, and went searching for the books on Africa. I found them and one literally fell on my head. I picked this book up, opened it, and found the story of a great African warrior, Shaka. Ah, here was my heroic image. I became U-Shaka, adding the "U" to Shaka to show reverence and humility and desire for self-mastery.

At this time I was practicing Vedanta on my own. One day I had an especially deep spiritual experience. Although I felt wonderful from this experience there was another side to it. I began to have very bad dreams, really bizarre, and I became somewhat concerned. I had heard about the Vedanta Society in Berkeley, so I went there and met Swami Swahananda. As a teacher he helped me to understand what I was going through. He explained to me that the mind is a clear pool beneath many layers of mind-stuff from previous lives. The swami helped me with his guidance and support, and eventually the bad stuff subsided. So I was able to continue to focus on developing a union between the lower and higher self.

Personally, Vedanta has give me, an African-American, so many important things, such as a feeling of congruence and universality—that we all belong to one humankind and that there is a spiritual path for everyone. I also feel related to the civilization of the Indus Valley. There is some evidence that ancient Africans took their culture there. I feel that I have tapped into an ancient tradition.

Being African-American, I am very conscious of racism. Vedanta has put me in touch with inner strength, perseverance, and courage. The sense of the Self, the Atman, has helped me to cultivate these qualities. Also meditation lets me go inside to find peace and solace when it gets too rough outside. Through meditation I am able to make the connection between the inner and outer worlds.

I have had two careers in which Vedanta has helped me. First, I worked with Vietnam War veterans for some time. Many of them suffered from post-traumatic syndrome. Much of their agony was transferred to me in our counseling sessions which caused me a lot of stress resulting in terrifying war dreams. Detachment was particularly important here to help me deal with these very strong emotions which evoked the horror of the war in a very real way.

The second career in which Vedanta has helped me is as a practicing psychologist. I am just finishing my doctorate and have been an intern therapist for several months. Frequently during a counseling session a client will mention an old but lapsed connection to a church. If it is possible and appropriate, I encourage that person to reestablish that connection, and go back to prayer or other spiritual practices. I try to show the continuity in life from "small person" to Spirit. I want those clients who are interested in this approach to understand that there must be a balance among the three aspects of life, physical, mental, and spiritual.

We active, spiritual people should let our light shine out. We should become models, not just be there, without saying anything. Spiritual qualities filter through. People come to recognize that we can maintain balance in chaos, and they will want to emulate those qualities. We must play an active role. People are suffering.

At one time I thought that money was the solution to life's problems, but it's knowledge. If we have the knowledge of an existence without destructive behavior, then we can help others move away from destructive behavior. Vedanta leads away from destructive behavior toward improved behavior and better self-esteem. This is a difficult concept to grasp. To talk about the self includes the spiritual soul. Basically we say, "We are God." We connect with the higher Self. We're not little worms. Vedanta gives greatness to the individual.

We should do more to help society to progress. This does not mean that we have to move away from Vedanta. We could, perhaps, become involved with the youth. We have something to share here, to give. We could develop programs to teach meditation, values, philosophy, or perhaps have meditation workshops. We might even try to have programs of direct help such as providing meals. *

About the future: Vedanta can ripple out like water in a pool when a pebble is tossed into it. We can affect city, country, and world because of our ideals and who we are. Being able to do that, exposing the ideas of Vedanta would expand the base. That way we can talk about a goal for common people in a common world. That's where we want to go with universal principles, harmony, and peace.

Three basic principles should "ripple out." First, the teaching that we are to love others and the Self—go within and love that divinity, that Atman, that Spirit. By doing that we cannot help loving people around us. Second, the practice of meditation should "ripple out" so that people can be at peace with themselves. This is valuable, practical training. And finally, the idea that we are one—our connection to each other—that humanity is one should "ripple out." If the bedrock principles of Vedanta are taken seriously, Vedanta will have an impact on the growth of the individual, family, state, country, and world.

---

* Many of the Vedanta Societies are involved in some form of social service; several are involved in food distribution to the homeless.—Ed.

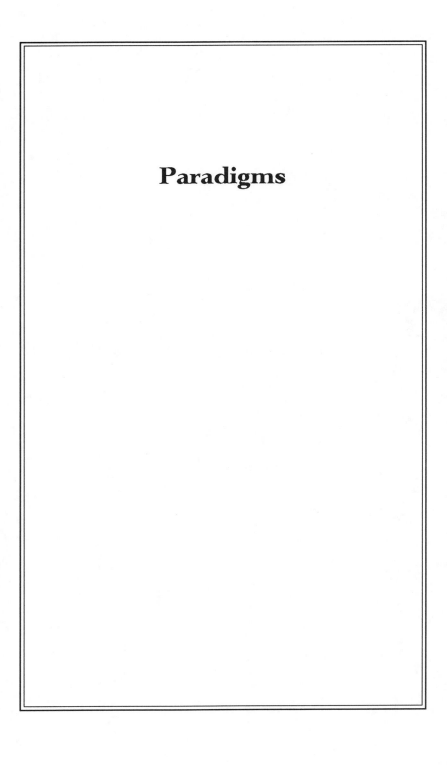

Paradigms

The Avatar

by Swami Prabhavananda

The universe, according to the theory of the Hindus, is moving in cycles of wave forms. It rises, reaches its zenith, then falls and remains in the hollow, as it were, for some time, once more to rise, and so on, in wave after wave and fall after fall. What is true of the universe is true of every part of it. The march of human affairs is like that. . . . This motion is always going on. In the religious world the same movement exists. In every nation's spiritual life, there is a fall as well as a rise. The nation goes down, and everything seems to go to pieces. Then, again, it gains strength, rises; a huge wave comes, sometimes a tidal wave—and always on the topmost crest of the wave is a shining soul, the Messenger. Creator and created by turns, he is the impetus that makes the wave rise, the nation rise: at the same time, he is created by the same forces which make the wave, acting and interacting by turns. He puts forth his tremendous power upon society; and society makes him what he is. These are the great world-thinkers. These are the Prophets of the world, the Messengers of life, the Incarnations of God.

With these words, Swami Vivekananda traces the pattern of the history of mankind and points out its relationship to the advent of a divine incarnation or avatar.

What is an avatar and what is his function? The literal meaning of this Sanskrit word is "descent of God." The Hindu view is that whenever the spirit of religion is forgotten, God comes down, as it were. He incarnates in human form to show mankind how to ascend toward Godhead. Sri Krishna states this mission in the Bhagavad Gita:

> When goodness grows weak,
> When evil increases,
> I make myself a body.
> In every age I come back
> To deliver the holy,
> To destroy the sin of the sinner,
> To establish righteousness.

As scientists discover the universally and eternally existing laws of nature, similarly divine incarnations discover the eternal and universal spiritual truths. Truth is always the same. It is not the property of a particular age, and no sect has a monopoly on it. The same truth that was revealed to Christ has been revealed to the seers of the Upanishads, to Krishna, and to Buddha. There were many such discoverers before Buddha and Christ and there will be in ages to come. Gautama himself proclaimed that many Buddhas were born before him.

The avatar has a double function. First of all, he fulfills the needs of his particular age. In our present era, for instance, when scientific advancement has made distant countries with different cultures, ideologies, and religions practically next-door neighbors, Sri Ramakrishna emphasized the ideal of harmony.

Secondly, and most important, the avatar reestablishes the spirit of the one eternal religion. For this reason his teaching has a universal and timeless meaning as well as a special message for his age. Buddha, for example, came at a time when religion in India had degenerated into mere ritualism. A powerful priestcraft preached that only those who memorized and chanted the Vedas properly could gain salvation. The priests proclaimed themselves the only qualified knowers of the scriptures and extorted material returns for their intercession for the ignorant laymen. Buddha was born to remind humanity of the truth that divinity exists in every being and that this divinity is to be unfolded through his own struggles. Again, when the truth of God became forgotten, and the Pharisees and Sadducees abounded, Christ came and taught: "Ye shall know the truth and the truth shall make you free."

What is this knowledge of the truth which the world teachers tell us is the purpose of human life? It is not the knowledge of external objects. It is not intellectual assent. This knowledge of the truth transcends the senses and the mind. It is a realization of our union with God, of which we are not aware in our ordinary limited consciousness. All the divine incarnations insist that we must have this realization of God for ourselves. Christ taught: "Be ye perfect even as the Father which is in heaven is perfect." Sri Ramakrishna said: "Know the One, and you will know the all. Ciphers placed after the figure one gets the value of hundreds and thousands, but they become valueless if you wipe out that figure. The many have value only because of the One. First the One and then the many. First God, and then the creatures and the world."

Why must we realize this truth of God for ourselves? As an illness cannot be cured if someone else takes the medicine for us, similarly our ignorance of our divinity is a direct and immediate experience which can be removed solely by the direct and immediate knowledge of God.

Only when our sight opens to this transcendental experience do we overcome all bondages and suffering and realize the "peace that passeth understanding."

We find the concept of the avatar in the philosophy of Christianity as well as Hinduism. As students of Western philosophy will know, the Christian doctrine of the avatar evolved from the Greek theory of Logos, which was an attempt to bridge the gulf between the known and the unknown. In brief, Platonism represented the Logos as transcendent and the visible universe as an imperfect shadow of it. According to the Stoics, the Logos is the principle of eternal reason, conceived as immanent in the universe.

Philo, an Alexandrian Jew who was a contemporary of Jesus, reconciled Stoicism with Platonism. He insisted on the existence of a supreme self-existent Deity and sometimes represented the Logos as identical with it. Sometimes he spoke of the Logos as the highest mediator between God and the world, the firstborn son of God or operative Reason. The Logos was therefore immanent as well as transcendent.

St. John was strongly influenced by Philo in his conception of the Logos and gave it expression in the opening lines of the fourth Gospel: "In the beginning was the Word, and the Word was with God, and the Word was God." In the Vedas we find an almost identical passage: "In the beginning was Prajapati [Brahman]; with whom was the Word; the Word is Brahman."

There is an important difference between the Christian and Hindu concepts of Logos. The Christian belief is that the Word was made flesh only in Jesus, whereas according to the Hindu view, the Word, which is Brahman and therefore transcendent as well as immanent, is made flesh in every creature. Then what is the difference between an ordinary human being and a divine incarnation? The difference lies in the expression. In the ordinary person the divinity is hidden, whereas in the avatar it is manifest. Moreover, the unenlightened person is forced to be born again and again by past karmas, the tendencies and habits formed in previous lives. The divine incarnation, on the other hand, *chooses* to be born to reestablish the spirit of religion.

There are two theories concerning the avatar's awareness of his divine mission. According to the first, he is always conscious that he is one with God. His apparent human weaknesses, struggles, and moments of doubt are merely assumed in order to show humanity how they can be overcome and perfection achieved. And according to the second theory, although in a way the avatar is the master of his maya, when he clothes himself in human form he takes upon himself the maya as well. As such, his human side also is real. Whichever theory is accepted, the human aspect of the avatar makes it possible for man to worship God in a human way.

A unique characteristic of the avatar is his great manifestation of power. An illumined soul also is aware of his own divinity and can show others the way to God-realization. But only an avatar can give that realization by his look, his touch, or his mere wish. When Christ said, "Be thou whole," that perfection in Godhead was instantaneously brought to pass.

In our age, Swami Vivekananda came to Sri Ramakrishna and asked him, "Sir, have you seen God?"

Sri Ramakrishna answered, "Yes."

"Can you show him to me?"

Vivekananda was given a touch, and his divine sight opened. At one time whoever touched Sri Ramakrishna had the vision of God. And the vision which these divine incarnations give means a complete transformation of mind and life.

There is a special force and conviction behind the words of such world teachers. Christ preached "as one having authority, and not as the scribes." But again, the words of these avatars fall short of their lives and life experiences, and therefore they often transmit the truth of God in silence.

It is difficult to recognize an avatar, and he is worshiped for what he is only by a few individuals during his lifetime. The multitudes, who were superficially attracted to Christ for his miracles, soon left him, and only a handful of disciples remained. But the momentum of the religious force he released increased after his death until Christianity became a major religion. In the same way, it took several hundred years after Gautama's death before Buddhism became established and swept Asia. The power that the divine incarnations bring needs time to unfold.

Every religion insists on prayer, meditation, and devotion to God. But how can we conceive of the infinite, absolute Reality? Even to define God is to limit him. Yet again, we are taught by every major religion that the worship and adoration of an avatar is one of the paths by which God is realized. In the Bhagavad Gita, Sri Krishna said, "Worship me." Buddha, who preached such apparently abstract truths, told his disciples,

"Meditate on me." Christ taught, "Follow me." Sri Ramakrishna said, "Think of me."

Among certain intellectuals the idea is prevalent that since the Godhead is impersonal and formless, any "anthropomorphic" conception must be rejected. But what do they know of the Absolute beyond the spelling of the word? We can only conceive of that which is finite and limited, yet we must begin with some idea or conception of God. It is said that we can take up any object or symbol—a rock, a tree, an image—and if we worship it as divine we will find God through it, because his presence is everywhere. But for most people it is easiest to find God where he is most manifest, and his greatest manifestation is in a divine incarnation. Any conception of God we may have is surpassed by the divine play on earth of these avatars.

How should an avatar be worshiped? It is not enough to regard him as a historical personality or an exemplifier of religion. He *is* God incarnate and must be adored as such. Great emphasis is laid on one-pointed devotion to the Chosen Ideal. This is not fanaticism. A fanatic recognizes only the avatar he has accepted, whereas a true devotee sees his own Chosen Ideal in all other aspects of Godhead, remembering that it is the one God who in different ages incarnates in human form. In fact, the devotee ultimately sees his Chosen Ideal in every creature. Wherever the eyes of the shepherdesses fell they saw their Krishna manifest.

Moreover, the devotee should try to feel that in his particular Chosen Ideal—whether Christ, Buddha, Krishna, or Ramakrishna—are contained the three aspects of the one Godhead: Father or Brahman, the all-pervading Spirit; Son or the manifestation as the avatar; and Holy Ghost or Atman, the indwelling Spirit. Through worship of one of these aspects of the Trinity the others become revealed. And so Christ proclaimed, "He who hath seen me hath seen the Father."

By meditating on any one of the avatars, divine love arises in the heart of the worshiper. As devotion becomes intensified through the practice of concentration on the Chosen Ideal or identification with him, the devotee begins to imbibe the divine attributes. Constant recollectedness and absorption follow. Finally, the divine sight opens, and the absolute Godhead becomes a concrete reality. Sri Ramakrishna has likened the Godhead to a field extending to the horizon and beyond. Our vision of it is obstructed by a wall in front of us. The avatar is like an opening in that wall. Through him we can see into the infinite meadow.

Sri Ramakrishna

by Swami Lokeswarananda

SRI RAMAKRISHNA DID not perform miracles: he himself was a miracle. His life, alien to common, everyday experience, was a puzzle to many.

If Ramakrishna's life inspired reverence and awe, it also aroused doubt, and even disparagement. People asked if Ramakrishna was the latest incarnation of God. On the other hand, even his chief disciple, Swami Vivekananda, wondered during their first meetings whether Ramakrishna was mad.

Ten years after Ramakrishna's death, the philosopher Max Müller introduced him to the Western world as "not only a high-souled man, a real *Mahatman*, but a man of original thought." Later, the French writer Romain Rolland presented him to the West as "the consummation of two thousand years of the spiritual life of three hundred million people." And Mahatma Gandhi described the story of Ramakrishna's life as "a story of religion in practice," observing further that "his life enables us to see God face to face."

Yet it is not an easy life to understand. The goddess Kali, Ramakrishna's chosen ideal who is no other than Time herself, alone knew who he was. * Though many years have passed, Sri Ramakrishna remains an enigma, provoking diverse reactions and interpretations.

The debate continues, and perhaps it will continue for a long time to come. A characteristic of great souls such as Ramakrishna is that they always remain controversial. Many of Buddha's and Christ's teachings are still debated, and divisions among their followers continue to multiply.

The difficulty is that people try to understand them through their own little intellects. That is not possible. These great souls belong to another world, the world of spirituality. If you are not familiar with that world, you will never understand them. To use Ramakrishna's analogy: "How can an eggplant seller determine the value of a diamond?"

Another difficulty in the case of Ramakrishna's predecessors is a lack of reliable records. In this respect Ramakrishna is fortunate: he is not known by hearsay; everything about him is authenticated. Ramakrishna's disciple M. kept a diary, known today as *The Gospel of Sri Ramakrishna*, which presented Ramakrishna's message to humanity. In this diary M.

---

*The word "Kali" comes from the word *kala,* "time." Both Kali and time are all-consuming and all-devouring. Kali is frequently called the "Mistress of Time."—Ed.

meticulously recorded Ramakrishna's everyday life.

Ramakrishna was the first man widely proclaimed as an avatar to be photographed. Caught by the camera in the bliss of samadhi, spiritual ecstasy, the photograph serves as a call to taste the ultimate religious experience.

Samadhi, the highest spiritual state, and an everyday experience for Ramakrishna, was baffling to some. Ramakrishna was critically examined by Dr. Mahendra Sarkar, an agnostic, who was the founder of the Indian Association for the Cultivation of Science, and a scientist of eminence. Dr. Sarkar, an M.D. and a medical practitioner, found Ramakrishna a normal person—lovable, intelligent, and extremely witty. Dr. Sarkar spent so much time listening to Ramakrishna that his practice suffered, but he did not mind. Ramakrishna's words captivated him.

Unquestionably, Ramakrishna was the antithesis of most of his contemporaries, who were desperately trying to copy their British masters. At a time when a little bit of English education was the password to employment, Ramakrishna refused to have anything to do with it. The only English words he knew (and sometimes used) were "very good, thank you." He had perhaps picked them up from the conversations he had heard between English-educated Indians who loved to spice their native dialect with English words.

He also had no interest in Sanskrit education, for he noticed that the motive behind such education was the same as the motive behind English education—earning money. The education he wanted was that education which would give him knowledge of the highest Truth which he termed God.

Nineteenth-century rural Bengal was ravaged by malaria, famine, and a host of other problems, but by and large its people were simple and friendly to one another. The cinema was unknown, but there were varieties of entertainment provided by religious festivals, which came in close succession throughout the year. Ramakrishna always looked forward to them. He enjoyed them and also found much to learn from them.

When Ramakrishna was young, he often skipped his village school to attend these popular plays, where under the cover of mythology, the highest spiritual truths were often presented. The characters in those plays were such as one often meets in real life: representatives of good and evil, their inevitable clashes, and the ultimate victory of good. Ramakrishna had a remarkable memory, and learned most of the plays by heart, particularly the songs that were included in them.

Ramakrishna was a keen observer of everything, including human character. Nothing passed in the village from which he did not draw a lesson. Because he was discerning, he saw through things easily, and he had strong common sense. Humanity and nature were the sources of his education.

A versatile artist, Ramakrishna sang, danced, and told stories with superb artistry and could act the roles of various characters in the same play. He made images of deities like a professional. Even professionals sometimes sought his help to place eyes in the images they had carved—the most difficult part in the art of image making.

As a boy Ramakrishna was totally guileless; he was much sought after by young and old alike, and commanded the respect of his elders, inside his family as well as outside. If there was ever a disagreement about what was right and what was wrong, invariably Ramakrishna's view prevailed.

Some of the villagers believed the young Ramakrishna was divine. One old man, well-versed in the scriptures, formally worshiped him saying, "Lord, a time will come when many will recognize you as an avatar. I will not live to see that. I only pray that you will ever look with compassion upon this unworthy servant of yours." This, however, did not turn Ramakrishna's head. He continued to be the simple, playful child that he was.

When the time came for Ramakrishna's sacred thread ceremony, a great dispute arose in the family over who should be the first person to give alms to the boy since the almsgiver is an important figure in the ritual. This ceremony is central in the life of a brahmin boy.

The custom was that only a brahmin could give the first alms, for it marks the formal recognition of the boy as a brahmin by the entire brahmin community. But Ramakrishna would have none of this. As a nine-year-old boy, he had promised a woman from the blacksmith caste, the midwife at his birth, that he would take his first begged food from her. He must do this, he said, because he had given her his word. The entire family and even the neighbors pointed out that this was never done. But the boy was adamant. His argument was that a brahmin must keep his word; if he did not, the sacred thread would be a mockery. And his argument clinched the issue.

As a boy Ramakrishna was highly sensitive to any reference to God or any natural phenomenon of great beauty. His first spiritual experience came when he saw a flight of white cranes silhouetted against a bank of dark monsoon clouds. The sight so thrilled him that he lost consciousness. On another occasion, he was called upon to act the role of the god Shiva in a play. When he appeared before the audience, he was so overwhelmed with the feeling that he was Shiva that he could not speak, and he lost external consciousness. He stood motionless looking like Shiva himself, and many in the audience were deeply moved.

Another time, he was going to a temple with an elderly woman who asked him to sing some devotional songs. Soon after he began to sing, he became choked with emotion and was lost in ecstatic contemplation of the Divine Mother.

At the age of sixteen, Ramakrishna came to Calcutta and stayed with his eldest brother, Ramkumar, who ran a Sanskrit school and wanted his brother to have a Sanskrit education. But Ramakrishna's mind was elsewhere. He made it clear that he was not interested in that kind of education; he was only interested in learning about God. Ramkumar did not insist, for he knew it was useless. He was, however, happy to notice that Ramakrishna loved to worship deities in the different houses of the neighborhood, and that everybody who came to know him loved him.

Soon after this, Ramkumar moved to Dakshineswar to serve as the chief priest at the Kali temple there. Ramakrishna followed him, rather reluctantly, and became his assistant. His job was to decorate the image; this work was closest to his heart since he was an artist *par excellence*. He not only made Kali look exquisite, she looked alive under the touch of his artistic fingers.

Ramkumar was becoming old and sick, so after some time Ramakrishna assumed the position of the chief priest at the Kali temple. He began worshiping Kali with great enthusiasm and meticulous care.

But soon Ramakrishna began to ask himself if Kali were a mere piece of stone. Why didn't she respond to his prayers? There was no sign that she was a living being and was pleased with his worship. Then he began to wonder if there was anything lacking in himself. Perhaps he was not earnest enough to make Mother Kali reveal herself to him. She had revealed herself to the saint-poet Ramprasad and to other devotees; perhaps, he thought, they loved her more and their yearning was deeper. Sometimes in the midst of his worship, Ramakrishna would cry aloud, "Mother, why are you so partial? I know I'm ignorant, a fool. Is that why you neglect me?" As evening approached, he would rub his face on the ground till it bled. He would say, "Mother, another day is gone and yet you did not reveal yourself to me. What is this life for?" Seeing him, bystanders thought he had lost his mother, or had gone mad.

One day as he was performing his worship, he began to weep, saying, "I can't bear to live without seeing you. I must end my life." His eyes fell on the sword hanging on the wall. Seizing the sword, he was about to strike himself when he saw a light emanating from Kali and advancing toward him. As it came closer, it grew in volume. He was soon enveloped by it; he fell down and lost consciousness.

After that, the relationship between Ramakrishna and Kali was as intimate as between a petulant child and an indulgent mother. Ramakrishna would demand from Mother Kali that she reveal herself to him in all her many aspects. If she did not seem to immediately oblige, he would cry until she yielded. People thought he was mad. He was—mad for God. He often forgot to eat or bathe; he rarely slept. Had his nephew Hriday not attended to his needs, Ramakrishna very likely would have died.

The relationship between Kali and Ramakrishna has no parallel in religious history. Kali was Ramakrishna's mother, guardian, friend, and playmate. He would not do anything without first asking her. To Ramakrishna, Kali was the only reality. She filled his world.

Where most mystics are satisfied with experiencing one aspect of God, Ramakrishna wanted to practice the spiritual disciplines of other religions also. In the years that followed, Ramakrishna practiced almost every faith and spiritual discipline known to religion. But, invariably, before embarking on a new experiment, he first obtained Kali's consent. He would ask, "Mother, show me how other people worship you."

One interesting feature of Ramakrishna's spiritual practices was that whenever he wanted to follow a spiritual path, a teacher would appear— as if out of nowhere—in order to help him. Totapuri, the Advaitin monk who initiated him into nondualistic spiritual practices and into monastic life, came this way. In fact, Ramakrishna had not even planned on practicing nondualism, but Totapuri offered to teach him Advaita Vedanta. Ramakrishna said he would have to ask his "Mother." Kali told him that she had arranged for Totapuri to come so that Ramakrishna could learn nondualism from him. If nondualism is a difficult concept to grasp, it is more difficult to practice. Ramakrishna, however, mastered it within a few days, much to Totapuri's amazement.

After following the different paths of Hinduism, Ramakrishna practiced the spiritual disciplines of Islam. For a Hindu to practice Islam is unprecedented, if not unthinkable. Nevertheless, Ramakrishna took initiation from a Muslim spiritual teacher, and during this period did not even enter the courtyard of the Kali temple. He wore his clothing like a Muslim, repeated the name of Allah, and said the daily prayers of Islam. Kali must have approved of all this, because Ramakrishna only did his Mother's bidding. Ramakrishna followed this spiritual path until he attained the highest realization.

Some years later, while visiting a devotee's house, Ramakrishna's eyes fell upon a painting of the child Jesus seated on the Virgin Mary's lap. He looked at the painting for a long time, and as he gazed at it, a ray of light emanated from the picture and entered his body. Immediately all of Ramakrishna's Hindu ideas and tendencies were pushed to the back of his mind, and he was filled with love for Jesus. He had visions in which he saw Christian priests burning incense, and Christian devotees praying in churches. For three days he did not enter the Kali temple; he was completely absorbed in devotion to Christ. On the third day, he saw a tall godlike man of fair complexion walking toward him. The tall stranger was wearing foreign garments; a voice from within told Ramakrishna that this man was none other than Jesus. Approaching Ramakrishna, Jesus embraced him and entered into his body. Ramakrishna went into deep samadhi. The two became one.

Ramakrishna's spiritual experiences convinced him that all religions were essentially teaching one common truth: perfection—perfection in the spiritual sense. As Jesus said, "Be ye therefore perfect, even as your Father which is in heaven is perfect." This is the essence of religion: everything else is peripheral. If there is a dispute between one religion and another, it is over nonessentials. Nonessentials vary from religion to religion because of different tastes and temperaments, and because of different social and cultural contexts. We must ignore them, and go to the essentials. In essence, all religions are one.

Ramakrishna's realizations showed him that there was in fact one single Being, but that single Being appeared to be many because of the diverse names and forms superimposed on it. The saint and the sinner were one and the same. The same divinity was present in them, but did not show itself equally. In the saint the divinity was shining, but in the sinner it was concealed. Given love and encouragement, however, the sinner's divinity would begin to reveal itself. Gold is always gold, even if it is covered with dirt.

Ramakrishna did not preach any creed or dogma. Nor did he reject any. His sole concern was that men and women achieve their full potential in terms of moral and spiritual growth. As far as spiritual growth is concerned, mankind is as limitless as God. Not only that, mankind's love and compassion are also limitless. We have the potential of feeling one with everyone and everything. If there is pain anywhere, we can feel that pain as our own. If others are happy, we too are happy.

Sri Ramakrishna respected every religious belief and practice. He never argued with anybody. He respected every point of view, no matter how primitive. He tried to point out how rich and varied religious perceptions were. It was wrong to think that there was only one path leading to God.

Since he had traversed them, he knew that each of the many paths to God is good and valid. He encouraged all people to follow the path that he or she had chosen, and not to stop midway. They must continue until they reached the end without believing that their path was the only path.

As long as the goal is the same, the path one chooses does not matter. It is like choosing food according to one's taste. Christians, Hindus, Buddhists, and Muslims will all eventually reach the same goal. There should be no quarrels about the way; Ramakrishna wanted to see everyone follow his or her own path, suited to his or her own temperament, to reach the goal. Each religion has produced great saints and sages; this is the proof of its validity. He upheld not one particular religion, but each and every religion.

Ramakrishna was as much a Christian, a Muslim, or a Buddhist, as a Hindu. He taught Hinduism to Hindus, Islam to Muslims, and Christianity to Christians. He was the sum total of all religions. When a Hindu spoke to Ramakrishna, the person felt that Ramakrishna was his ideal; Muslims and Christians felt the same. He was the embodiment of the beginning as well as the end of religion; he taught the essence of religion.

Ramakrishna lived in and with God. God alone was real to him. Ramakrishna's experience was that God was everywhere, in everything, and in every being. Ramakrishna felt that the Supreme Being was *his* being.

Religion is a process of growth; God is the ultimate goal of this process. This is why Ramakrishna said that the goal of life was God-realization. To know God is to be God. You see him inside yourself and you see him outside also. You see him everywhere and in everything. You see nothing but God.

The world is divine, so is humanity. Ramakrishna realized this, and this was his message. Ramakrishna was his own message.

Sarada Devi: The Holy Mother

by Swami Nikhilananda

HOLY MOTHER, IN a unique way, fulfilled the duties of wife, mother, and nun. There have been before in the world the ideal wife, the ideal mother, and the ideal nun, but a combination of the three in one person is rare indeed. Holy Mother was wedded to Sri Ramakrishna at the age of five, lived with him as long as he lived, and ministered to his physical needs in the best tradition of a Hindu wife. She was his companion in spiritual life. She demonstrated that wifely devotion and love are possible without demanding physical satisfaction from one's mate. In spite of her marriage she remained a nun, pure in body and mind, and in uninterrupted communion with God. Though she had no children of the flesh, she had many of the spirit. Like an earthly mother she looked after her disciples' physical comfort. But unlike an earthly mother she was totally unattached in her love and expected no return from it. Truly Sister Nivedita declared that Holy Mother was Sri Ramakrishna's last word on the ideal of Indian womanhood. But why of Indian womanhood alone? She can very well represent the universal ideal of womanhood.

Holy Mother's immaculate purity, her unceasing meditation and prayer, her all-embracing compassion and utter selflessness, endowed her with the delicacy and tenderness of a maiden, a subtle grace and quiet dignity, and withal guilelessness and simplicity.

Her innate motherliness put visitors at ease. To a person coming to her for the first time, she conveyed the feeling that she had been eagerly waiting for him. Holy Mother always inspired reverence but never a feeling of remoteness. . . .

Sri Ramakrishna used to speak of two kinds of illumined persons. One consists of ordinary human beings who through the practice of spiritual disciplines attain the knowledge of Brahman and merge in the Supreme Spirit. They are no longer concerned with the activities of the transitory phenomenal world. The others are God-men, born perfect, who have a special message for humanity. After the realization of their true nature, they remain at the phenomenal level, working for the spiritual regeneration of their fellow creatures. God becomes manifest through God-men. The Infinite sings its melody through their finite minds and bodies. Hence the sport of God as man, the *naralila*, is so appealing. Reason cannot unravel this mystery, but the heart may enjoy it.

It is extremely difficult for ordinary men to recognize God when he is embodied as man. An apparent victim of hunger and thirst, pain and pleasure, hope and despair, sickness and fear, he weeps, laughs, and suffers without really losing awareness of his divine nature. In the God-man humanity blends with divinity. When living at the phenomenal level the God-man is alert about human affairs, possesses practical knowledge and realism, and observes the conventions of society. Side by side with divine ecstasies, he cultivates humility, magnanimity, ethical sensitivity, love, the spirit of service, modesty, and other similar traits in order to set a model for others. He also shows how one living in the world can rise above it and enjoy inner peace in the midst of life's turmoil and worry.

The life of Holy Mother is a demonstration of these facts. Though an embodiment of divinity, she identified herself of her own accord with the lives of her relatives, the people of her village, and her devotees. She rejoiced at the happiness of others and wept at their suffering. Purposely she often suppressed her true nature, because, as she said, "The excessive manifestation of divinity creates fear in the minds of devotees; they cannot feel intimate." Once a disciple spoke of her being the Divine Mother, and she said, "You always harp on that one theme. I say that I am your mother, and that does not satisfy you." Her language was simple and natural, and her conduct spontaneous and unostentatious. She never lost these characteristics, even while giving initiation or spiritual instruction. In her conduct she was always alert, remembering that in the future people would regard her as an ideal to follow. . . .

Her brothers regarded her as their affectionate big sister, her nieces and nephews as their indulgent aunt, and her disciples as their mother. Many ladies, after visiting her, said that she was just like one of them. Yet she said to a disciple that, even in the midst of all her activities, by a mere wish she could remember her divine nature in a flash, and realize the world to be the playground of maya. If she was constantly conscious of her true self, how could she fulfill her mission?

How humble she was! Once when she was ill an ordinary priest was called in to perform some special worship for her recovery. After the ceremony she took the dust of his feet. When someone told her of his having a loose character, she remarked, "That may be. One must show respect for the brahminical garb. The Master was not born to break traditions."

Often she said to her disciples that she constantly prayed for the total effacement of her ego. And yet she once said openly: "I am the Primordial Power, the Mother of the Universe. I have assumed this body out of compassion for the world. I have been born in every epoch in the past; I shall be born, too, in the future."

She respected the traditions and norms of society. One notices here a difference between Holy Mother and Buddha and Shankara. Buddha repudiated the gods, religious rituals, the scriptures, and the caste system as obstacles to attaining the freedom of nirvana. Shankara accepted all these as preparatory disciplines for the knowledge of Brahman, which he said could be attained only by monks who renounced the world and went beyond rituals, worship, and social convention. Holy Mother, however, though practicing true renunciation, remained a householder and till the end of her life respected the gods, rituals, and social proprieties. She performed religious rites and showed veneration even to a minor deity such as the village goddess Simhavahini. Someone said to her, "Mother, why do you do that? Everything happens by your will alone." The Mother replied, "If you vow to worship gods and goddesses at the time of illness, you can be cured by their grace. Besides, everyone should get his due." Before she started on a trip she consulted the almanac for the auspicious day, according to the Hindu belief. She enjoyed listening to the reading of Hindu religious books.

Generally Holy Mother obeyed caste rules; but she often made exceptions in the case of her disciples, especially about food restrictions. In her opinion devotees of God belonged to a single caste, a spiritual family. About other social matters she used her discrimination and common sense and did not wantonly violate social standards. In most respects Holy Mother lived as a Hindu widow of the brahmin caste, though Sri Ramakrishna had assured her that he was not really dead.

An orthodox Hindu widow is not permitted to remarry and thus leads the austere life of a nun. This austerity is all the more rigorous in the case of a brahmin widow. She avoids such food, clothes, and ornaments that may stimulate her physical desires. Thus she is permitted to eat a full vegetarian meal at midday, but takes only fruit and milk at night. She cannot eat certain foods, such as onions or garlic. A widow in Bengal uses a white sari without a border, cuts her hair short, and gives up all ornaments. Through these strict disciplines imposed on widows, the Hindu lawgivers constantly reminded them of the ideal of chastity, which is deeply ingrained in the Indian mind. They wanted widows to be living examples of simplicity, renunciation, purity, nonattachment, and the spirit of unselfish service. . . .

Holy Mother observed some of these rules. Like a Hindu widow, she was a vegetarian, but again, unlike a Hindu widow, she did not cut her hair, wore gold bracelets, put on a sari with a narrow red border, and ate a light supper at night. On many occasions she did not observe the pollution of food by touch, especially when some of her nonbrahmin women disciples touched her plate. She regarded all her disciples as her own children. . . . For some young widows who were her disciples she relaxed the strict rules about food, saying to one of them, "What good will it do to torture the soul?" To another she said, "If the soul's craving for food is not satisfied, one commits an offense."

Holy Mother condemned the morbid passion for purity, especially regarding pollution by touch, that people show in the name of religious orthodoxy. But she never encouraged or condoned carelessness, and she disapproved of vanity.

Holy Mother was practical and realistic about mundane affairs. She learned to be so from Sri Ramakrishna at Kamarpukur after her marriage, and later at Dakshineswar. For example, she scolded some of her disciples for going on foot to Jayrambati from Koalpara on a stormy night and said, "This kind of rashness is not right." . . .

One day Swami Vivekananda dismissed a servant for stealing money. The servant went to Holy Mother at the Udbodhan and said to her with tears in his eyes, "Mother, I am very poor and cannot manage my expenses with my small salary. I have a big family. That is why I acted that way." In the afternoon Swami Premananda came to her house, and the Mother said to him, "Look here, Baburam, this man is very poor. Being harassed by want he stole the money. But why should Naren scold him and send him away? You are all monks and do not realize the afflictions of householders. Take this servant back." When told that this might annoy Swami Vivekananda, she said with firmness: "Take him back; I am asking you to do so."

When Swami Premananda returned to the Belur Math with the servant, Swami Vivekananda said, "See what Baburam has done; he has brought back that fellow." But when he heard what the Mother had said, the Swami did not utter another word and took him back.

Holy Mother highly disapproved of carelessness and waste. Once, after sweeping the courtyard at Jayrambati, someone threw the broom aside carelessly. She reprimanded the person, saying that the broom could have been treated a little more gently. Everything should be shown proper respect. On another occasion, at the Udbodhan, she expressed her displeasure because an empty basket was thrown away by one of the inmates. She said to the monks that, being world-renouncers, they might not care for a trivial thing like a basket, but nevertheless it could have been preserved for some other useful purpose. One day she gave a disciple a special dish of food that she had prepared. The quantity was too great. He ate what he could and was about to throw away the rest when the Mother asked him to give it to a poor neighbour. Afterwards she said to the disciple, "We should give everyone his due. What is not edible for man, give to a cow; what is not edible for a cow, give to a dog; what is not edible for a dog, throw into a lake for fish to eat. But never waste." . . .

Holy Mother urged the monks to shun idleness, and she herself was intensely active both in Calcutta and at Jayrambati. Her life in both places generally followed the same pattern. She always got up at three in the morning, as was her habit during the Dakshineswar days, and did not retire before eleven o'clock at night. . . . At Jayrambati, where she was mistress of the house, she busied herself with various household activities and at the same time talked to her intimate attendants. When she was in good health she also took part in the more strenuous household duties, like scouring utensils, carrying water from the tank, or husking paddy. The Mother herself made the arrangements for the daily worship, such as gathering flowers, at which she was sometimes assisted by her nieces or devotees. After the worship she went into the kitchen and relieved the cook, who would then go out for her refreshment or to attend to any other personal needs. She herself cooked most of the food to be offered to the Master in the shrine. . . . In earlier days Holy Mother with her own hands served all the devotees their meals, and she herself ate only after they had finished eating. Sometimes she worked in the kitchen in the evening in order to relieve the cook from overwork. . . .

One evening an attendant was reading a letter from a disciple to Holy Mother. It was full of eulogy and adoration. After listening to it she remarked, "Often I say to myself, I am but the daughter of Ram Mukherjee. Many of my contemporaries are still alive at Jayrambati. In what respect do I differ from them? Devotees come from unknown places and prostrate themselves before me. I am told that some of them are judges and some lawyers. Why should they come to me in this way?"

The answer to her query was given by herself. She once said: "People call me the Divine Mother. I think, maybe they are right. How otherwise can one explain the strange things that have happened in my life?. . . If I say to myself that a certain thing should happen, the wish is always fulfilled."

There existed an extraordinary relationship between Sri Ramakrishna and Holy Mother. She often spoke of herself as his handmaid and instrument, as one of the many seekers who found refuge at his feet. When a devotee asked her advice she said, "I do not know anything. I repeat only what I have heard from the Master. Read *The Gospel of Sri Ramakrishna* and you will know all you need." To another who asked her blessing she said, "The Master will bless you."

How often she asked her disciples to pray for her so that she might not have a trace of vanity! She repeatedly asked the devotees to cling to Sri Ramakrishna in order to avoid the pitfalls of life. One day a disciple, asked about his welfare, said that through her blessing he was well. "You all make the same mistake," she rebuked him. "Why do you bring me into everything? Can't you speak of the Master? Don't you see that every-thing happens by his will?" Regarding the Master she stated, "He is the Supreme God and the Supreme Goddess. He is the essence of all mantras and the embodiment of all deities." She carried Sri Ramakrishna's picture everywhere and worshiped it daily, seeing in it his living presence. Often she remarked that one should not make a distinction between the physical body and its shadow in a picture. She talked intimately with the Master and fed him in the picture. And yet she did not conceal the fact that she and the Master were identical and that there was no difference between them except in outer form.

Sri Ramakrishna, too, knew Holy Mother's nature. He spoke of her as the bestower of wisdom, as his own *Shakti.* Once, seeing Latu meditating in the Panchavati, he said to him, "You fool, the deity whom you are contemplating is working herself to death by scouring pots and pans." Here are a few other statements of his about her: "The Mother who is in the temple is the same as the mother who dwells in the *nahabat* [the small music tower where Holy Mother lived at the Dakshineswar temple]." "If she is displeased with a person, it is beyond even my power to protect him." "If she is angry she can destroy everything." "If anyone gives me an offering, I send it to the nahabat; otherwise, how will the giver attain liberation?" As the culmination of his spiritual practices, the Master formally worshiped Holy Mother as the Divine Mother of the universe.

Holy Mother has been described by such epithets as the Divine Mother, the Mother of the universe, Prakriti, Shakti or Power, Mahashakti or the Great Power, and Mahamaya or the Great Deluder. These epithets are not sentimental expressions but have a noetic meaning. . . . Like modern science, Hinduism describes Shakti or Energy as the creator of physical objects and the source of the universe. But according to science this inert and nonintelligent energy is a self-creating, self-preserving, and self-dissolving category. It does not need extraneous help to project phenomena.

According to Hinduism, Shakti is the potency of Brahman and inseparable from it, like fire and its power to burn. The potency is unable to function by itself. Brahman, which is existence, consciousness, and bliss, by its mere presence impregnates Shakti, as it were. Thus names and forms are evolved. The why and wherefore of the infinite Brahman's becoming the manifold creation, or the One's becoming the many, or the Absolute's appearing as the relative, is a profound mystery which cannot be solved by the human mind. After projecting the universe, Shakti casts a spell on the creatures in order to perpetuate the creation. Hence she is called Mahamaya, the Great Deluder. The Creative Energy contains in her womb the seeds of creation and nourishes the creatures after giving birth to them. Finally, at the end of a cosmic cycle, she withdraws the universe into herself.

All women, in a sense, function as the Divine Energy. But her fullest manifestation is seen through the body and mind of a woman of unblemished character. Holy Mother was such a woman. Hence she is regarded as the Supreme Goddess or Great Power, a special manifestation of the Divine Energy. Once a devotee said to her that after her no one would worship the minor goddesses of the Hindu religion. She replied, "Why, they too are parts of me." Conscious of her divine nature, she kindled the sparks of spirituality in her disciples, accepted their worship, and gave them assurance of liberation.

Swami Vivekananda's Message to the Ordinary Person

by Marie Louise Burke

SWAMI VIVEKANANDA WOULD perhaps object to the title of this article, for to him no person was ordinary. Each was a unique manifestation of God, and each was perfect in his or her own expression of divinity. Indeed, in his eyes nothing in this universe, living or nonliving, was ordinary; so let me quickly define what I mean by this term in the present context.

By "ordinary person" I mean the man or woman who is neither sunk in a thoroughly material existence nor consciously aspires to a life of the spirit. He (and, of course, she) is well-meaning; he attempts to live a good life, and to the extent that he succeeds in this endeavor, is more or less content. He may raise a family, pursue a profession, work on the land, in an office, in a factory. He (or she) may be among the rich, talented, and famous or may be poor, ungifted, and unknown. But in one condition or the other, his desires are legion: he desires love, wealth, power, health, esteem, fame, and the many pleasures that this world affords. If fortunate, he enjoys a good percentage of those pleasures; if unfortunate, he is deprived of most of them. In either case, as many as are his desires, so many are his fears; for fear is the soft underbelly of desire. He fears failure, abandonment, loss of esteem, poverty, disease, and, above all, he fears death. His attitudes toward and reactions to the external world are governed by these desires and fears—sometimes to a neurotic and destructive degree, more often to a degree that is considered normal— "only human."

This ordinary person is thoroughly imbued with a concept of his (or her) limitations in the face of an inconceivably vast and, by and large, unpredictable universe. When he thinks about it, he finds himself to be a tiny bit of living matter, fragile, perishable, prey to hostile or, at best, mindless forces beyond his most sophisticated control. Though he benefits from the genius of his species, as well as from whatever genius and intellectual brilliance he himself may have, he is nonetheless innately and fundamentally ignorant and limited. He does not know the purpose of his life, nor the purpose of existence as a whole; he does not know the future—even a minute ahead—and his powers of reasoning, though generally adequate for the pursuits of his daily life, are circular and analytic. In the long run his reason cannot discover or prove the existence of anything lying beyond the level of the premises from which it started.

This limited body and mind constitute, as far as the ordinary person is concerned, his entire being, and, while he knows their relative insignificance, he finds them all-important. No love, no attachment is greater than his attachment to this unit of body-mind; no fear is greater than the fear that it may either self-destruct or be destroyed, as indeed it will—one thing or the other.

Now, to this person, this ordinary person, Swami Vivekananda had a revolutionary message. It was not a message basically different from that which he gave to those monastics and nonmonastics who were consciously seeking God or aspiring wholeheartedly to reach a supersensuous level of perception and existence. It was not a watered-down version of a lofty philosophy; it *was* lofty. It was not a cushioned couch on which one could relax, secure in the knowledge that all was well in heaven and on earth. On the contrary, it blew the ordinary man sky-high, and if he listened, it changed him forever. Since Swami Vivekananda gave his life to pour that message with the full force of his tremendous personality into the souls of ordinary men and women, infusing it into the very marrow of their bones, they were bound to listen. Sooner or later, that message, which will resound for centuries around the world, will be heard by everyone, everywhere.

And what was that message? From start to finish it was simple: You are not the body, you are not the mind; you are the infinite, eternal, ever-pure, ever-perfect Spirit. In his first public speech in the West, in which he alarmed the Christian clergy and electrified an audience of "ordinary" people, his cry was thunderous: "Hear ye, Children of Immortal Bliss, . . . you are souls immortal, spirits free, blest and eternal; ye are not matter, ye are not bodies; matter is your servant, not you the servant of matter."[1] And in his last class-lecture in London three years later he cried, "This is the one prayer, to remember our true nature, the God who is always within us, thinking of it always as infinite, almighty, ever-good, ever-beneficent, selfless, bereft of limitation."[2] And again, now in California: "Vanish nature from me, vanish [these] gods; vanish worship; . . . vanish superstitions, for I know myself. I am the Infinite. . . . How can there be death for me, or birth? Whom shall I fear? I am the One. Fill the mind [with this] day and night!"[3] From the beginning of his mission to its end, this is what Swami Vivekananda taught to one and all alike, insisting that the purity and strength of that Upanishadic teaching never be compromised, never diluted, never adjusted for the sake of expedience or human weakness.

On the other hand, this was not a message doomed from the outset by its very loftiness. It was not a doctrine of renunciation or self-abnegation impossible for the majority of people to follow. It was practical—a message meant to alter the ordinary person's concept of himself and of others and thereby eventually and inevitably mold his conduct in the world. "It is the greatest of all lies," he cried in London, "that we are mere men; we are the God of the universe. In worshiping God we have been always worshiping our own hidden Self."[4] "Let the world resound with this ideal, and let superstitions vanish. Tell it to men who are weak and persist in telling it. You are the Pure One; awake and arise, O mighty one, this sleep does not become you. . . . Tell that to mankind and show them their power. Then we shall learn how to apply it in our daily lives."[5]

In the wake of his great Master, Sri Ramakrishna, Swamiji left each to his own way and own path. "We must not lose sight of this doctrine," he warned in his last lecture in California, "'Better die in your own path than attempt the path of another.' . . . Wait and grow, and you attain everything; otherwise there will be [great spiritual danger]."[6] And by the same token, the path of another should never be subject to criticism or intolerance. Each had his own way and own speed of growth, and each way was valid. But throughout, underlying and directing the growth of the individual, ran the great, unshakable, unaltering concept that man— every man and every woman—is here and now divine Spirit. Just as throughout a long railway journey, the tracks, though they run straight or windingly, uphold the train to the journey's end, so Swami Vivekananda's message of man's divinity underlay and guided the traveler on the road of life.

This, then, was his basic message to one and all, East and West: we are not finite bodies and minds; we are infinite Spirit. Perhaps he taught this great truth more explicitly in the West, where the dualism of Semitic religion (which of course includes Christianity) had held sway for thousands of years and the individual had been considered sinful by nature and dependent entirely upon the grace of God for redemption.

In India, on the contrary, even dualistic religions hold that the soul is eternal and essentially pure. Therefore in India, while Swamiji forcefully reminded the Hindus of their own incomparably great religion and their responsibility of nurturing it, of living up to it in all areas of life, and of giving it to the world, he did not have to explain over and over the basic facts of spirituality. "All Hindus believe," he said in Lahore, "that man is not only a gross material body, not only that within this [body] there is the inner body, the mind, but . . . that there is something beyond even this fine body, which is the Atman of man, which has neither beginning nor end, which knows not what death is. . . . There may be differences as to the relation between the soul and God. . . . [But] it does not matter what our interpretation is, so long as we hold on to the one basic belief that the soul is infinite. . . . [And] we all hold in India that the soul is by its nature pure and perfect, infinite in power and blessed."[7]

Swamiji grieved to see India swamping the greatness of her religion with layer upon layer of local superstitions and cultural accretions; yet he knew that the greatness of the Upanishadic religion was still living in every village, shining in every eye, ineradicable, waiting only to be called forth. And call it forth he did. "Be strong once more," he cried in Calcutta; "drink deep of this fountain of yore; that is the only condition of life in India!"[8]

In his motherland, Swamiji's lectures were rousing calls to a sleeping giant, in the West they were bombshells, not meant to awaken an ancient culture, but to turn a relatively young one upside down, revolutionizing it. Swamiji was well aware of the effect of his words in America and England. He wanted to stir those pivotal countries to the very bottom of their souls. He wanted to change the current of their thought or, rather, to introduce into that current a strong, dynamic element of spirituality that would transform it.

Why? One of the dicta of the Bhagavad Gita is that the wise should not disturb the beliefs of the dull-witted. If the West had survived, indeed prospered, for almost two millennia on the idea that human beings were sinners in immanent peril of eternal damnation, and if, added to this or superseding it, it was now thriving on the more recent idea that the human being was a complicated chunk of matter that somehow could think—then why should a Swami Vivekananda come along and hurl thunderbolts into this tranquil pool of perhaps slowly evolving ideas?

The obvious answer is that the West was not (and is not) a sunlit pool, blissfully nurturing an embryonic spirituality. At the end of the nineteenth century (as we now well know), the West was pregnant with both accomplishment and disaster. Scientific technology was about to explode into unimaginable achievements and equally unimaginable and diverse means of destruction. Today both the good and the evil that the human hand and human brain are capable of have been augmented and extended beyond all belief—and this is just the beginning. If ever there was a time in the history of mankind for spiritual knowledge to awaken, for human beings to become morally and spiritually equal to their own material powers, it is now—in the present age, this unthinkably glorious and unthinkably perilous age. And on cue, Swami Vivekananda has appeared like a great guiding star.

He went straight to the mark, striking at the core of the peril, which is that the ordinary Western person has no conception of the Spirit as the fundamental reality of his being. He thinks, and he has always thought that he is a finite being. There is terrible fear in this concept. It is, in fact, a concept intolerable to the human spirit. We cannot accept it; we continuously fight against it, which is precisely why we have been inventing, since we first purposefully chipped a stone, extensions of our hands and brains that today threaten to destroy us. Civilization—its religion, its art, its science—is, indeed, nothing but the human being's attempt to conquer his limitations; it is man's reach for freedom.

But tragically, we—we in the West, at least—persistently reach in the wrong direction and only dig ourselves deeper into the pit of finitude. The soul cries continually for the infinite, and we translate that cry into a need to conquer and possess our external world.

Human desire is rooted in man's stretch toward the unlimited; fear, frustration, violence are all spawned by the inevitable failure of that attempt in the relative world. Indeed man's sense of limitation and his wrongly directed struggle to break his bonds lie at the root of all his miseries; they concoct the core of relative existence itself; but deep-rooted though that fault is, we can no longer afford the luxury of wallowing in it. Even Lord Shiva, when he took on the body of a pig, was loathe to give it up;* but today, like it or not, we have to turn our concepts and our lives

---

* In April of 1900, Swami Vivekananda related the following story to his San Francisco audience: "There is a Hindu legend that the Lord was once incarnated on earth as a pig. He had a pig mate and in course of time several little pigs were born to Him. He was very happy with His family, living in the mire, squealing with joy, forgetting His divine glory and lordship. The gods became exceedingly concerned and came to the earth to beg Him to give up the pig body and return to heaven. But the Lord would have none of that; He drove them away. He said He was very happy and did not want to be disturbed. Seeing no other course, the gods destroyed the pig body of the Lord. At once He regained His divine majesty and was astonished that He could have found any joy in being a pig." [*Complete Works of Swami Vivekananda*, 8: 127-28.]—Ed.

around and seek the unlimited where it actually exists—in the Spirit within ourselves. And from that radiant center light will spread to all aspects of our lives.

There is, indeed, no other solution to individual or world problems. No amount of political or social or economic manipulation, violent or peaceful, will make the least dent in world thought, for those labyrinthine activities take place on a level that is simply an effect of subtle causes lying deep in human existence. The problems themselves are effects of our basic ignorance and can be remedied only by an influx of spiritual knowledge. There is no other way. Man—all men and women—must learn that he is Spirit.

One question may arise here: what good will it do to have an intellectual knowledge of spiritual truths? Did not Swami Vivekananda himself say again and again that religion lies in realization? The practice of religion consists of lifting our consciousness by one means or another into states of existence beyond the realms of sense perception and reason and in experiencing those states as realities. But the ordinary man, as defined in this article, is not about to devote himself to spiritual practice.

So what have we been talking about? It will not do simply to say over and over "I am Spirit" and continue to think and to act in the mode of "I am a finite body with a finite mind." True, an intellectual grasp of spiritual concepts will not be of much good all at once, but truth, as Swamiji said, is like a corrosive that will eat its way into the hardest of stone. Recollection of our true nature will mold our actions and thoughts around itself, it will transform our lives: bushels of nonsense will drop from our minds, innumerable fantasies and hang-ups, which we did not even know we had, will disappear; we will not cherish and protect our self-image so fiercely; we will not grow so angry at slights or so despairing over failures; we will gain faith in ourselves, and "faith in ourselves," Swamiji said, "will do everything."[9]

Convinced even intellectually of our own infinitude and the infinitude of others (for there can be but one Infinite Being), fear will drop from us, and with fear selfishness will drop—and vice versa, for, as Swamiji said, "Only to selfishness comes fear. He who has nothing to desire for himself, whom does he fear, and what can frighten him? What fear has death for him? What fear has evil for him? . . . Who can injure us, the omnipresent?"[10] With the disappearance of fear from our conscious and unconscious minds how many quirks of human thought and action will not also disappear! This is a matter for psychiatrists to determine, but it seems axiomatic that much of our irrational, self-destructive, and harmful behavior is based on hidden fears, usually groundless in themselves, but exerting great power in our lives. And as our thoughts and acts grow pure, free from fear and its progeny of demons, our perceptions will grow correspondingly pure, and in turn will transform our lives.

Eventually, we will actually experience a spiritual reality that had been only a concept. Moreover, we—the ordinary people—will not be alone. "The hour comes," Swamiji said in San Francisco, "when great men shall arise and . . . make vivid and powerful the true religion, the worship of the Spirit by the Spirit."[11] We will have plenty of inspiration and examples around us, plenty of holy company and help. And as time goes on, ordinary men and women will know themselves to be as extraordinary as Swami Vivekananda always knew them to be.

But the thing he wanted is that we begin and that we begin from where we are now, wherever that may be. "Hear day and night," he said, "that you are the Soul. Repeat it to yourselves day and night till it enters into your very veins, till it tingles in every drop of blood, till it is in your flesh and bone. Let the whole body be full of that one ideal, 'I am the birthless, the deathless, the blissful, the omniscient, the omnipotent, ever-glorious Soul.' Think on it day and night; think on it till it becomes part and parcel of your life. Meditate upon it, and out of that will come work. 'Out of the fullness of the heart the mouth speaketh,' and out of the fullness of the heart the hand worketh also. Action will come. Fill yourselves with the idea; whatever you do, think well on it. All your actions will be magnified, transformed, deified by the very power of the thought."[12]

And that, I think, was the essence of Swami Vivekananda's message and instruction to everyone in the world.

---

1. *Complete Works of Swami Vivekananda*, (1963), 1: 11. (Hereafter cited as *CW*, followed by the vol. and pg. nos.)
2. *CW*, 2: 357.
3. *CW*, 1: 501.
4. *CW*, 2: 279.
5. *CW*, 2: 304.
6. *CW*, 1: 473.
7. *CW*, 3: 374-75.
8. *CW*, 3: 347.
9. *CW*, 2: 301.
10. *CW*, 2: 357-58.
11. *CW*, 8: 141.
12. *CW*, 2: 302.

The Banyan Tree

by Albert Sadler

THE RAMAKRISHNA MOVEMENT is a banyan tree. This is a glimpse at the history of the tree.

The seedling grew in Kamarpukur, a wobbly little town of thatched huts and mud shrines, and an occasional flight of cranes.

The sapling grew to maturity, sending a root down at Dakshineswar on the Ganges, and another at Jayrambati, tapping into mother earth.

A rather eccentric root set itself down backstage at the Star Theatre in Calcutta; yet another on the campus of the Presidency College in Calcutta.*

The vital energy of the tree traveled down each of these roots, making them trunks—just as it drew strength from these, its diverse moorings.

The tree was rooted in India, but it was not an Indian tree. Trees have no nationality, require no passports. The state mistakenly assumes that trees do not travel.

When Swami Vivekananda arrived in Boston in 1893, he did not come as Johnny Appleseed. This Ramakrishna tree spread without the aid of puffballs or feathered spinners. It did not travel on the wind, but by a mysterious unfolding. Its aerial roots had already touched down on Beacon Hill. The Minute Men were not watching. This time it was not the British who had landed. The brahmins were about to discover Brahmanism.

The tree's roots reached into Chicago, America's breadbasket, gateway to the vast western plains. If Boston stood at our inner frontier—the frontier of conscience—Chicago stood at the frontier of our *rajasic* future, and our *tamasic* present: land of porkbellies and rail junctions, of the red and the blue networks, and the yellow tabloids. The tree of Vedanta drew from all this—new England, new Sweden, new Germany, new Poland—and gave to all this. Gave the gift of universality, rooted yet landless. Vivekananda in Boston drew upon the withered promise of Brook Farm and Walden, and, in Chicago and New York and San Francisco, anticipated Sandburg and Kerouac, and Henry George. "I love the Yankee land," Vivekananda said. "I like to see new things. I do not

---

* The Star Theatre was the playhouse of Girish Ghosh, the great Bengali dramatist. An intimate disciple of Sri Ramakrishna, Girish in his earlier days had lived a rakish life. Swami Vivekananda was a student at Presidency College.—Ed.

care . . . to loaf about old ruins. . . . I have too much vigor in my blood for that."

The tree had reached across the oceans, joining unknown nations together.

The main trunk today is at Belur.

But this is no spindly single-trunked aspen or elm. It is a tree which is at once a forest, rooted everywhere, but unbound—an arboreal canopy of universal freedom.

❋

The Mother Goddess

by Anne Lowenkopf

WE CATCH THE Godhead much as we catch light. The very structures that enable us to experience both limit how much of each we can experience. Since we catch God with our human hearts and intellect and will, since we reach out to the Godhead because of our human need and desire, it is not surprising that what we catch—our visions of God—have both points of similarity and points of difference.

We experience anything—everything—through ourselves. It is all we have to experience with. And so, not surprisingly because we humans are gendered life forms, often our experience of the Godhead has gender.

God the Father is familiar to those of us who have grown up in the Judeo-Christian tradition; round the globe and in the past various peoples have perceived and worshiped father gods and other male deities in love and terror, hope and dread.

Though no statistic count that I know of exists, abundant evidence makes it safe to estimate that we humans have "caught" goddesses as often as gods. Some of these goddesses like the Navaho's Spider Woman and the ancient Greek's Athena have specific functions: you would not go to Athena for aid in childbirth nor to Spider Woman for strength in warding off enemies.

But some of us have caught a Mother Goddess who is all-encompassing, beyond role: "I am all alone in the world here. Who else is there besides me? See these goddesses who are but my own powers entering into my own self!" a flat announcement of monotheism from the Great Goddess herself in the famous Sanskrit hymn *Devi Mahatmyam, Glory of the Divine Mother*. Again and again the Devi (Goddess) of the *Devi Mahatmyam* is described as the one without another: ultimately no duality of any kind exists, no division between matter and spirit, no division between created and creator. The Great Goddess contains within herself not only all other deities but existence itself. Her children and all things reside within her, are of her substance, and she indwells inside them. The shortest distance to the Mother is within yourself.

This vision of the Mother is exciting attention today when for the first time in history so many young adults live alone, outside family and organized peer groups. As the constrictions of paternalism break down and are replaced by the bewilderments of choice and lack of structure, the concept of a Mother deity who all alone creates and sustains begins to feel right; young people are feeling they can understand such a deity and such a deity can understand them. A nexus of empathy radiates support, comfort, and understanding in a two-way flow.

This concept of the Mother first attracted me as a young woman who was rebelling against the notion of being born in the need of redemption for the actions of others. I still remember the thrill of excitement at my discovery of a Goddess who did not punish the created for what went wrong in her creation, who took the heat for evil and death and yet was untouched by both.

Empathy for a deity who exists alone and copes alone grows stronger as more and more young people have been raised by single parents, and more are coping with the difficulties of being a single parent. The Devi of the *Devi Mahatmyam* could and did act as a warrior queen even though she was *the* monotheistic deity. Its hymns are part of an exciting story in which the Goddess is approached by gods who are being harassed by bandits and neighbors, and she agrees to help them fight off their enemies. No question of damnation and eternal punishment here but of will against will, skill against skill, with the Devi, as one who plays chess with herself, taking all the parts. The layering of abstract philosophy and dramatic personification is molded into the story itself. Its monotheistic concepts are unwavering even while the battles and their equipment are described with all the ferocious glee which you would expect from a poet of raiding peoples. And the Goddess, though described as young and beautiful and caring, was savage and intent when she threw herself into battle.

An American brought up in the climate of Victorian notions of maternal behavior asked a contemporary devotee of the Devi how he could be drawn to such a fierce deity and was told, "Ah, but you need a strong mother who will go to battle for you when you are in trouble." Single parents who find themselves battling for survival in their work worlds, battling traffic to get home at the end of the day, battling to feed their kids and educate their kids and keep their house reasonably sane resonate to the concept that one can be both and at the same time nourisher and warrior.

The *Mahatmyam* (sometimes called the *Chandi*), first recorded in writing around 600 A.D., is by no means the oldest of hymns. But the concept of the Great Mother is ancient indeed. Anthropologists believe a vision of a Mother Goddess to have emerged in neolithic times as early as 7000 B.C. and that her worship extended in a vast area, at the very least a great arc stretching from parts of Africa northward to Lithuania and westward to Crete and Greece. Some make a case that pushes the range of her worship into Italy and Spain and as far west as the British Isles and Ireland.

Stone carvings and pottery figures can resist time, but ideas do not fossilize. So there is much debate among academics as to exactly what beliefs inspired those stone and pottery figures of female deities. Did the neolithic people worship a supremely monotheistic Goddess like that extolled in the *Mahatmyam*, or a God the Mother who holds the whole world in her hands, or was she a specialized deity in charge of childbirth and the abundance of the foods that sustain human life? Did the artifacts of female deities our archaeologists have found all belong to one related Goddess worship, as all the forms of Christianity today are related and can be traced back to a single source, or did those artifacts belong to separate and unrelated visions that were caught by mystics in different tribes? Academicians argue the point, and will continue to, because the evidence is scanty and mute.

Are the visions those mystics "caught" real? Is there an actual Mother Goddess, or any deity in human form and personality? Asking whether the Mother Goddess is real is very much like asking whether red is "real." We have discovered that red is a particular vibration of light and what we call light is waves made up of particles, and that our experience of them is their impact on our sensory apparatus together with the subsequent processing of the coded messages of those impacts by our central nervous system. We are not seeing particles and waves as such, we see red. But that experience—red—works for us; it helps structure our behavior; we react to it emotionally.

We cannot truly know whether my experience is the same as your experience of what I call red. But whatever we experience is similar enough so that once we agree on terminology—*red*, for example—if I ask for something of that color what you bring back is more likely than not going to be acceptable to me. The same seems to be true of mystical experience. Details differ from culture to culture, and they shift from age to age as peoples' own customs and understanding shift. But within the details a central core of experience is startlingly similar.

I can ask a Buddhist, an American Indian, a Jew, a Christian, a Muslim to bring me back an experience of God, and what they bring back meets my needs. Look at Gladys A. Reichard's description of the Navaho's Changing Woman: "She is the mystery of reproduction of life springing from nothing, of the last hope of the world, a riddle perpetually solved and perennially springing up anew. . . ." How similar to this description from the *Devi Mahatmyam*: "You are the origin of all the worlds! . . . You are incomprehensible even to Vishnu, Shiva, and others! You are the resort of all! This entire world is composed of an infinitesimal portion of yourself! You are verily the supreme primordial Prakriti (nature, creator) untransformed." China Galland in her book *Longing for Darkness* tells of turning her back on her Catholic origins to search for the Tibetan Buddhist black Mother Goddess Tara only to find herself as part of that search walking through the fields of Poland in pilgrimage to the Black Madonna.

Every mystic who has experienced the Godhead, personally, intensely, unmistakably, assures us that the experience is real and open to anyone who truly reaches for it. Ramakrishna, that man of God who was the inspiration for the Ramakrishna Order of monastics, replied when asked if he had seen God, "As clearly as I see you now."

What Ramakrishna saw so clearly was often a goddess, the Great Goddess, the Mother of the universe. He called her by more than a dozen names as if to demonstrate that the particulars of dogma and tradition were of little importance compared with the vision itself. (Ramakrishna made this same point in other ways, practicing the disciplines of many different religions and catching God with each of them.)

Catching sight of the Goddess may not come easily. For years Ramakrishna cried after her—a child wailing for his mother. And when he first caught her it was as a mother who gave him comfort, affection, attention, guidance. Later he discovered that "his" Mother was indeed that monotheistic deity who creates the universe and holds it within her being, and yet resides within living beings and objects.

The Devi of the *Devi Mahatmyam* came to us in Sanskrit that was written by Aryan peoples, who worshiped masculine deities. They had poured into India from the north, over the mountains, conquering, and eventually living off, the dark peoples who grew crops there. The Devi belonged not to the invaders but to the growers of crops.[1]

Mystics from each of these two traditions report they have glimpsed

---

1. Narendra Nath Bhattacharyya, *History of Sakta Religion* (New Delhi: Munshiram Manoharlal Publishers Pvt. Ltd., 1973), pp. 21; 26.

behind the veil of their deities' human forms and personalities, a formless impersonal Godhead. Aryan mystics called that Godhead Brahman. Another name is Satchidananda, which is a linking up of three Sanskrit words meaning Existence-Knowledge-Bliss that describes as nearly as possible their understanding of Brahman. And similarly some followers of the Devi have encountered behind the Mother's form and personality, a formless, impersonal Godhead they named Shakti.

Descriptions of Shakti and Brahman are exactly the same—except in one particular. Brahman is eternal and unchanging while Shakti is eternal and always changing. The two actually are one, Ramakrishna said, "like fire and its power to burn." According to East Indian cosmology Shakti's creative force spews out and develops this universe, which after an "age" draws back into itself to rest in the blissful, unchanging being of Brahman, only to spew out again through Shakti's restless power. This model is not so different from the theoretical model, proposed by some contemporary physicists, which depicts the universe exploding from a tiny and incomprehensibly dense core of existence to expand farther and farther until finally, drawn by gravitational pull, it falls back upon itself into a tiny and incomprehensibly dense core of existence, which will once again explode and expand.

And come to that, descriptions of Shakti/Brahman are uncannily similar to contemporary physicists' descriptions of the force field which creates and comprises all existence.

I find it comforting to learn that science, which I absorbed along with my mother's milk, and the mystics I go to for help in coping with myself and my world are, at core, in agreement. Nevertheless force fields, waves, and particles, though interesting, are abstractions. But the color red, however ultimately unreal, hits my perceptual and emotional self with mood-changing, behavior-altering impact. Similarly I find strength and comfort in catching glimpses of a Mother with a human face and responses reminiscent of my own human passions.

Some of the visions we humans catch in mystical experience may not be the ultimate reality of the Godhead, whether we experience a Mother Goddess or a God the Father or some other deity. Perhaps we lack the physiological equipment to experience that ultimate reality. Certainly catching any mystical experience however anthropomorphized or astigmatic takes time and effort and desire enough to convert to laser-like focus of will.

Ramakrishna, who had caught God by using the disciplines of all the various religious traditions available to him, spoke in his conversations interchangeably of Shakti and Brahman, Shiva and Durga.

Brahman is without change; Shakti, the creative energy, is ever changing. Both are one: in Ramakrishna's phrase, fire and its power to burn, or as we put it, two sides of the same coin. Ramakrishna knew from his own experience that all the different forms of God were different perspectives of the one unchanging, ever-changing, formless Godhead.

But Ramakrishna spoke most frequently of Mother, because this was the perspective that he most cherished. And he had no more doubts about the reality of that perspective than you and I have of the reality of the color red.

Ramakrishna's experience and the experiences of other mystics assure us that many of the perspectives of the Godhead open up to a Mother Goddess who functions in the lives of her devotees as protector and companion and mentor. What is important for us today is that the ability to "catch" the Great Goddess for ourselves in our own vision is open to us if we want to reach for it.

❋

Glossary

Bold face type in the text indicates the word also appears as a glossary entry.

Advaita   The nondualistic school of Vedanta philosophy that affirms the oneness of the individual soul, God, and the universe.

Aranyakas   That section of the **Vedas** which gives a spiritual interpretation to the ritualistic portion of the Vedas. It is also called the "forest treatises" because it was originally intended for ascetics who lived in the forests.

ashrama or **ashram**   A center of spiritual study or meditation. A retreat, hermitage, or monastery.

Ashtavakra   The sage who authored the **Ashtavakra Samhita**.

Ashtavakra Samhita   A classic text on **Advaita** Vedanta.

Atman   The divine Spirit in man, the Self which is one with **Brahman**, the all-pervading divine existence, the Ground of the universe.

Avadhuta Gita   A classic text on **Advaita** Vedanta.

avatar   An incarnation of God.

avidya   Ignorance, individual or cosmic, which hides the nature of the supreme Reality from our view.

Badarayana   Author of the **Brahma Sutras**. Little is known of him, though tradition identifies him with Vyasa, the author of the Mahabharata, who lived in India somewhere between 500 and 200 B.C.

Bhagavad Gita   Literally the "Song of God," the Gita is one of the most revered scriptures of Hinduism, and consists of 700 verses.

bhakti   Love of God.

bhakti yoga   Union with God through the path of loving devotion.

bhasya   A commentary.

Brahman   The absolute Reality, the Unity of all that exists, the formless, attributeless Godhead.

Brahma Sutras   Also known as the Vedanta Sutras. A treatise by **Badarayana** on Vedanta philosophy which interprets the **Upanishads**, and discusses the knowledge of Brahman.

buddhi   Intelligence or discriminating faculty which classifies sense impressions.

chakra   One of the six centers of consciousness located along the spinal column.

Chandi   Also known as the *Devi Mahatmyam*. The *Chandi* is a sacred Hindu scripture which praises the Divine Mother of the universe, identifying her as the ultimate Reality.

devi   Lit., "goddess." The word can refer to any female deity in Hinduism.

dharma   Righteousness, truth, or religious duty.

dhruva (or dhruba) smriti   The state of constant recollectedness of God.

dhyana   Meditation or prolonged concentration.

Durga   An aspect of the Divine Mother of the universe, the consort of **Shiva**. Durga is generally represented with ten arms, seated on a lion. She is the protectress of the universe, destroying the demons of ignorance and giving the blessings of divine love and knowledge.

guna   Lit., "quality." In Hindu philosophy there are three gunas which constitute **prakriti**, or nature: **sattva**, **rajas**, and **tamas**. Tamas is characterized by dullness, stupidity, inertia; rajas by activity, restlessness, and passion; sattva by calmness, purity, and wisdom. These three qualities are found in varying proportions in the external world and in all created beings.

guru   Spiritual teacher.

Ishta   The spiritual aspirant's chosen ideal of God.

Ishvara   The personal aspect of God; God with attributes.

Janaka   A famous king who was both a knower of **Brahman** as well as the ruler of his kingdom, Videha.

japa   Repetition of the Lord's name, usually one's own **mantra**.

jnana   Knowledge of the ultimate Reality, attained through the process of reason and discrimination between the real and the unreal.

jnana yoga   Path of union with the ultimate Reality through spiritual knowledge and discrimination between the real and the unreal.

jnani   One who follows the path of knowledge by discriminating between the eternal and the transitory.

Kali   One of the aspects of the Divine Mother of the universe. Kali was **Ramakrishna's** Chosen Ideal, and he worshiped her image at the Dakshineswar temple for many years. Kali is usually shown standing on the chest of her consort, **Shiva**. Around her waist she wears a garland of human arms, and around her neck a garland of human heads. She has four arms: the lower left hand holds a human head, her upper hand grips a saber. With one right hand she offers boons to her children, and with the other she makes the sign that dispels fear. She deals out death as she creates and preserves. Kali destroys ignorance, preserves world order, and gives blessings and liberation to those who earnestly seek it. While Shiva represents the Absolute, Kali represents the dynamic, or relative aspect of the Supreme Reality.

karma   Action, both physical and mental, and the effects of action.

karma yoga   Path of union with God through selfless activity.

karpanya   The feeling of helplessness; self-surrender.

Lokacharya, Pillai   Twelfth-century **Vaishnava** philosopher and writer who held that God's grace is spontaneous; it was to be sought not only through **bhakti**, devotion, but also through total self-surrender.

Madhva   The twelfth-century exponent of dualistic Vedanta. He wrote commentaries on the **Brahma Sutras**, the **Upanishads**, and the **Bhagavad Gita**.

Mahamaya   The Mother of the universe, the divine will. Mahamaya veils our vision of **Brahman**, the absolute Reality. Yet through her grace, she rends this veil, allowing us to realize the identity of the **Atman** with Brahman.

mahavakya   Literally, "great saying." A Vedantic formula that declares the oneness of the individual soul with **Brahman**.

manana   The process of reasoning in which one reflects on the spiritual teacher's words and meditates upon their meaning.

mantra   The sacred name of God given by the guru to the disciple. Repetition of the mantra is **japa**.

marga   Path; jnana marga, for example, is the path of spiritual knowledge, and bhakti marga is the path of devotion.

maya   Maya is the power of **Brahman**, the creative aspect of God. It is also the cosmic illusion that creates ignorance and veils the vision of Brahman. Due to the power of maya, Brahman, the one Reality, is perceived as the manifold universe.

nididhyasana   Deep meditation on the truth of **Brahman**.

nirvikalpa samadhi   Lit., "changeless samadhi." The highest state of realization in which the spiritual aspirant attains oneness with the Absolute.

Om   The most sacred syllable of Hinduism; the sound-symbol of **Brahman**.

prakriti   Primordial nature; the material principle of the world which, in association with **Purusha**, creates the universe. Prakriti is one of the two ultimate realities of Sankhya philosophy.

prana   In the physical body, prana is the vital breath that sustains life and manifests as thought, bodily function, and physical action. In the cosmos, prana is the sum total of all primal energy that manifests as motion, gravitation, magnetism, etc.

prarthana   Prayer.

pratyahara   Withdrawal of the mind from the objects of the senses.

pravrajika   Title of women who have taken final vows of renunciation, or **sannyas**. (The corresponding word for men is **swami**.) The term generally means a woman ascetic.

puja   Ritualistic worship.

Purusha   One of the two ultimate realities of Sankhya philosophy. The divine Self, the absolute Reality, pure Consciousness.

raja yoga   Literally the "royal yoga," raja yoga is the path of meditation. It is the spiritual path by which one attains union with the Absolute through control of internal and external forces.

rajas   The **guna** which expresses itself as restlessness, activity, and passion.

Ramakrishna, Sri (1836-1886)   A God-man of India who is considered by many to be an incarnation of God. His message stressed the essential unity of all religions, the innate divinity of humanity, and the realization of God as the goal of life.

Ramanuja   The eleventh-century saint-philosopher who propagated the school of qualified nondualism, **Vishishtadvaita**. Ramanuja wrote commentaries on the **Brahma Sutras** and the **Bhagavad Gita**, along with other original treatises which advocated his philosophy of devotion to God as the highest ideal of human life.

Ramprasad   Eighteenth-century Bengali mystic and poet. He composed devotional songs to **Kali** which **Ramakrishna** loved to sing.

rishi   A seer of spiritual truth. Usually the term refers to the ancient Hindu seers to whom the **Vedas** were revealed.

sadhana   Spiritual discipline.

samadhi   The superconscious state in which one experiences one's identity with the ultimate Reality.

samskara   Tendencies inherited from previous births which form a person's propensities in this life.

sannyas   Final monastic vows in which the spiritual aspirant completely renounces everything for the sake of realization of the ultimate Reality.

Sarada Devi, Sri (1853-1920)   **Sri Ramakrishna's** wife, also known as Holy Mother. Both Ramakrishna and Sarada Devi lived completely celibate lives; both were ideal monastics and ideal householders. Sarada Devi was the embodiment of spiritual motherhood; her life was devoted to loving service and self-sacrifice. She is seen by many as an incarnation of the Divine Mother.

Satchidananda   Existence (sat), Knowledge (chit), and Bliss (ananda) absolute; **Brahman**, the absolute Reality.

sattva   The **guna** which expresses itself as calmness, purity, and wisdom.

Shakti   God as the Mother of the universe. Shakti is the power of **Brahman**, the personification of primal energy.

Shankara or Shankaracharya   The great Vedanta philosopher who lived in the eighth century A.D., and revived **Advaita** Vedanta in India after a thousand years of Buddhist influence. Though he lived only thirty-two years, he organized a monastic system that is still in existence today. His enormous literary contribution includes commentaries on the **Brahma Sutras**, the principal **Upanishads**, and the **Bhagavad Gita**. He also wrote his own philosophical works such as the *Vivekacudamani* (*Crest-Jewel of Discrimination*) and the *Upadeshasahasri*. In addition, Shankara composed hymns, prayers, and various minor works on Vedanta philosophy.

Shiva   God in his aspect of destroyer of the universe. He is the third person in the Hindu trinity, the other two being Brahma, the creator, and **Vishnu**, the preserver. In his personal aspect, Shiva is the ideal yogi, the embodiment of renunciation, absorbed in eternal meditation in the Himalayas. He is known for his compassion: those who find refuge nowhere else—even snakes and demons—find shelter in Shiva. To save the world Shiva drank the poison which surfaced during the creation of the world. Since it stayed in his throat, he is called the "blue-throated one." Shiva is also the Absolute, the Supreme Reality. He is the transcendent aspect of God, while **Kali**, or **Shakti** represents the relative, dynamic aspect.

shraddha   Firm faith guided by reason.

sravana   Hearing or listening to the highest spiritual truth.

Sri   An honorific prefix used before the name of a deity, holy person, or book. It is also the Hindu equivalent of "Mr."

Suresvara   A philosopher-sage of India who was a direct disciple of **Shankara**. He wrote treatises on **Advaita** Vedanta in such books as *Naishkarmya Siddhi*, *Manosollasa*, and *Varttika*.

swami   Lit., "Lord." Title of monks who have taken final vows of renunciation, **sannyas**.

Swamiji   In the tradition of the Ramakrishna Order, Swamiji refers to **Swami Vivekananda**. It is also a respectful way of addressing any swami.

tamas   The **guna** which expresses itself as dullness, stupidity, and inertia.

Tantra   The religious philosophy in which the Divine Mother of the universe, or **Shakti**, is worshiped as the ultimate Reality.

Tantras   The scriptures which are identified with the worship of the Divine Mother.

tantric   Pertaining to **Tantra**; a follower of Tantra.

turiya   Lit., "the fourth." The superconscious state which is beyond the three ordinary states of consciousness: waking, dreaming, and dreamless sleep. It is the state of unitary consciousness, pure bliss. According to **Shankara**, this is not a state; it is the **Atman**.

Upanishads   The sacred scriptures which appear at the end of the **Vedas** and constitute their philosophical portion. The Upanishads form the philosophical basis of Vedanta.

upasana   Meditation; literally "sitting near." Meditation is "sitting near" God.

Vaishnava   Lit., a follower of Vishnu. An adherent of Vaishnavism—a dualistic branch of Hinduism. Vaishnavas follow the path of devotion to Vishnu, for the most part in his **avatars** such as Rama, Krishna, and Chaitanya.

Vallabha   A philosopher-saint of sixteenth-century India who wrote commentaries on the **Brahma Sutras** and the *Bhagavatam*.

vartika   A verse-commentary.

Vedanta Desika   A thirteenth-century philosopher and writer; one of **Ramanuja**'s greatest successors. Vedanta Desika, or Desika, was a voluminous writer, both in Sanskrit and Tamil. Desika stressed, in contrast to **Pillai Lokacharya**, that both grace and self-effort are necessary in spiritual life. The self-effort is necessary to achieve the Lord's grace.

Vedas   Lit., "Veda" means knowledge or wisdom. The Vedas are the sacred and most ancient scriptures of the Hindus. Orthodox Hindus believe that the Vedas are the result of direct divine revelation; they are considered the final authority in all spiritual matters. There are four Vedas: the Rik, Yajur, Sama, and Atharva. Each Veda consists of a ritual or "work" portion, and the philosophical or "knowledge" portion, known as the **Upanishads**. The ritual portion consists of the Brahmanas—texts which discuss the significance of different sacrificial rites—and the Samhitas—a collection of mantras or hymns, addressed to specific deities such as Indra or Varuna. Also included in the ritual portion are the **Aranyakas** which give a spiritual interpretation to the rituals.

vidya   Knowledge leading to the ultimate Reality.

Vishishtadvaita   The philosophy of qualified nondualism, founded by **Ramanuja**. Vishishtadvaita states that the individual soul and insentient matter are distinct from **Brahman**, but Brahman is the basis of their existence and reality.

Vishnu   The second aspect of the Hindu trinity, God in his aspect as the preserver of the universe. Vishnu is frequently shown with four arms, and holds the discus, mace, conchshell, and lotus. According to the doctrine of the **avatar**, Vishnu incarnates as a human being in every age for the good of the world.

Vivekananda, Swami (1863-1902)   The most prominent disciple of Ramakrishna, also known as **Swamiji**. Swami Vivekananda came to America in 1893 as the Hindu representative at the Parliament of Religions. After his triumphal success at the Parliament, he held classes and lectures throughout the United States and Europe, thus initiating the Vedanta movement in the West. In India, Swamiji organized the Ramakrishna Math and Ramakrishna Mission.

yajna   Sacrifice, sacrificial ceremony; in Vedic times it meant "sacrificing things for the sake of the Deity."

Yajnavalkya   A saint mentioned in the Brhadaranyaka Upanishad.

yoga   Lit., "yoke"—the act of yoking or joining together. Yoga is union of the individual soul with the ultimate Reality. It is also the method by which this union is achieved. There are four yogas: **bhakti yoga**, the path of devotion; **jnana yoga**, the path of knowledge and discrimination; **karma yoga**, the path of detached work, and **raja yoga**, the path of meditation.

Notes on the Contributors

Swami Adiswarananda has been the head of the Ramakrishna-Vivekananda Center of New York since 1973. Before coming to the United States in 1968, he was joint editor of *Prabuddha Bharata*, an English-language journal of the Ramakrishna Order of India. Swami Adiswarananda has contributed chapters to books on religion and philosophy, and has also written many articles in various journals.

Swami Aseshananda was for many years the personal secretary of Swami Saradananda, an intimate disciple of Ramakrishna who later became the Secretary of the Ramakrishna Order. Since 1955 Swami Aseshananda has been the head of the Vedanta Society of Portland, Oregon. Coming to America in 1947, Swami Aseshananda was the assistant minister of the Ramakrishna-Vivekananda Center of New York, and of the Boston and Southern California Vedanta Societies. Swami Aseshananda is the author of *Glimpses of a Great Soul: A Portrait of Swami Saradananda*. "Meditation According to the Upanishads" is a revision of an article of the same name which appeared in the May-June issue of *Vedanta and the West* and the book *Vedanta for Modern Man*.

Swami Ashokananda was the head of the Vedanta Society of Northern California from 1932 until his death in 1969. From 1926 until 1930, he was the editor of the *Prabuddha Bharata*. His books include *Avadhuta Gita of Dattatreya*; *Meditation, Ecstasy and Illumination*; *When the Many Become One*; *Spiritualizing Everyday Life/Worship of the Spirit by the Spirit*; *Swami Vivekananda in San Francisco*; and *Man's Journey to His Destiny*.

"The Starting Point " is an excerpt from "A Review and a Forecast" which originally appeared in the July, 1930, issue of *Prabuddha Bharata*.

"True Worship" originally appeared in the "Notes and Comments" section of the November, 1930 *Prabuddha Bharata*, under the heading "Worship and Its Best Form."

The language in these articles has been slightly modified in a few places for the sake of readability and comprehension of a Western audience. We would like to thank Advaita Ashrama in Calcutta for their permission to make these changes, and to reprint these articles.

Swami Atmarupananda is an American monk of the Ramakrishna Order, living in the Vedanta Society's Ramakrishna Monastery in San Diego, California. He was assistant to the editor of *Prabuddha Bharata* from 1977 to 1981, and has written many articles for Vedanta journals, some of which have been translated into European and Asian languages.

Swami Bhajanananda was the editor of *Prabuddha Bharata* from 1979 through 1986, and has contributed many articles to various Vedanta journals. Swami Bhajanananda is an Assistant-Secretary and Trustee of the Ramakrishna Order.

Pravrajika Bhavaprana is an American nun of the Vedanta Society of Southern California in Santa Barbara, and has contributed articles to various Vedanta journals.

Rabbi Asher Block was ordained as a rabbi by the Jewish Theological Seminary, receiving an M.H.L. and later also an honorary D.D. degree. He has a B.A. from Yeshiva University and a Master's in philosophy from Columbia University. In addition to a long creative career in the rabbinate, he has edited several journals, and authored articles of religious interest for publications both in the United States and abroad.

Pravrajika Brahmaprana is an American nun of the Vedanta Society of Southern California, in Santa Barbara. In addition to writing articles for various Vedanta journals, she also edited *With the Swamis in America and India* by Swami Atulananda, and *The Vivekacudamani of Sri Sankaracarya*, translated by Swami Turiyananda.

Marie Louise Burke—also known as Sister Gargi—is the author of the six-volume series of books on Swami Vivekananda entitled *Swami Vivekananda in the West: New Discoveries*. She is also the author of *Vedantic Tales*, and has frequently contributed articles to Vedanta journals. "Swami Vivekananda's Message to the Ordinary Person" is a slightly revised version of an article that originally appeared in the 1988 *Souvenir* of the Ramakrishna Mission in New Delhi, and later appeared in the January, 1990 *Bulletin* of the Ramakrishna Mission Institute of Culture.

Francis X. Clooney, S.J., a Jesuit priest, is Associate Professor of Theology at Boston College. Father Clooney is the author of *Theology After Vedanta:*

An Experiment in Comparative Theology, and *Thinking Ritually: Rediscovering the Purva Mimamsa of Jaimini.* He has written many articles for various publications, both in the United States and India.

U-Shaka Craig is an intern psychologist practicing in Alameda, California. This article was drawn from Ann Myren's interview with Dr. Craig.

George Fitts, now Swami Krishnananda, is an American monk of the Ramakrishna Order. He lives in the Hollywood branch of the Vedanta Society of Southern California. "These Shackles Must Be Broken" appeared in the original *Vedanta for the Western World* under the title "Thoughts."

Gerald Heard was an author and lecturer, and his articles frequently appeared in Vedanta books and journals. He founded a religious college in Trabuco Canyon, California, which was given to the Vedanta Society of Southern California in 1949 and became the Ramakrishna Monastery. "Dryness and Dark Night" appeared in *Vedanta for the Western World.*

Aldous Huxley attained international fame as the author of *Point Counter Point*; *Brave New World*; *Ends and Means*; *Grey Eminence*; and *The Perennial Philosophy*; along with other works. He contributed numerous articles for Vedanta publications over a period of many years. "Idolatry" and "The Minimum Working Hypothesis" appeared in *Vedanta for the Western World.* The latter article subsequently appeared as part of Sebastian's notebook in *Time Must Have a Stop.*

Christopher Isherwood attained international fame as the author of *The Berlin Stories*, from which the movie *Cabaret* was made. He also wrote *Ramakrishna and His Disciples*; *A Meeting By the River*; *Kathleen and Frank*; *Prater Violet*; *Where Joy Resides*; among many other works. He edited *Vedanta for the Western World*; *Vedanta for Modern Man*; and, with Swami Prabhavananda, translated *The Song of God: Bhagavad-Gita*; *How to Know God: The Yoga Aphorisms of Patanjali*; and *Shankara's Crest-Jewel of Discrimination.* He wrote extensively on Vedanta for over thirty years, and maintained an active interest in Vedanta until his death in 1986. "The Gita and War" and this book's introduction are taken from *Vedanta for the Western World.*

Pico Iyer is an author, an essayist for *Time* magazine, and a contributing editor at *Condé Nast Traveler*. Before beginning his work at *Time*, Pico Iyer taught English literature for two years at Harvard University. His books include *Video Night in Katmandu*; *The Lady and the Monk: Four Seasons in Kyoto*; and *Falling off the Map: Some Lonely Places of the World*.

Father Thomas Keating is a Cistercian priest, monk, and abbot. He has authored many books including *Open Mind, Open Heart*; *The Mystery of Christ*; *Finding Grace at the Center*; and *Invitation to Love*. The founder of the Centering Prayer Movement and Contemplative Outreach, Father Keating currently lives at St. Benedict's Monastery in Snowmass, Colorado.

Swami Lokeswarananda is the head of the Ramakrishna Mission Institute of Culture in Calcutta, India. Swami Lokeswarananda is the author of *Practical Spirituality* and *The Way to God: As Taught by Sri Ramakrishna*. He has translated and written commentaries on the Isa, Kena, Katha, Mundaka, and other Upanishads, and has also written several books in Bengali. Swami Lokeswarananda has contributed many articles, both in Bengali and English, to various journals.

Anne Lowenkopf is the author of *American Indian Religions; The Hasidim: Mystical Adventures and Ecstatics*, and several other nonfiction books. She teaches writing in Santa Barbara, California.

Swami Nikhilananda, a disciple of Sri Sarada Devi, founded the Ramakrishna-Vivekananda Center of New York in 1933, and remained its head until his death in 1973. Swami Nikhilananda translated the Upanishads, the Bhagavad Gita and other scriptures, and also wrote biographies of Sri Ramakrishna, Sri Sarada Devi, and Swami Vivekananda. The author of *Hinduism: Its Meaning for the Liberation of the Spirit*, and *Man in Search of Immortality*, Swami Nikhilananda also compiled *Vivekananda: The Yogas and Other Works*. His greatest literary contribution was his translation from the original Bengali into English of *The Gospel of Sri Ramakrishna*.

"Sarada Devi: the Holy Mother" is an excerpt from the *Vedanta and the West* article, "Some Glimpses of Holy Mother" which appeared in the September-October, 1962 edition of *Vedanta and the West*.

Swami Prabhavananda was the founder and head of the Vedanta Society of Southern California from 1930 until his death in 1976. He was the author of *The Sermon on the Mount according to Vedanta*; *The Spiritual Heritage of India*; *The Eternal Companion*; and *Religion in Practice*. In addition, he translated the Bhagavad-Gita; the Upanishads; *Shankara's Crest-Jewel of Discrimination*; and *How to Know God: The Yoga Aphorisms of Patanjali*. He also contributed many articles to Vedanta journals.

"The Avatar" originally appeared in the January-February, 1955 issue of *Vedanta and the West* under the title "The Concept of the Avatar." "Grace and Self-Effort" was taken from *Vedanta for Modern Man*; "The Problem of Evil" and "Control of the Subconscious Mind" appeared in the original *Vedanta for the Western World*.

Albert Sadler is currently Professor of Religion at Sarah Lawrence College, New York. He received both his M.A. and Ph.D. from the Union Theological Seminary at Columbia University, and has taught in America and abroad. An author, editor, and publisher, Dr. Sadler has written numerous articles on various spiritual and scholarly topics.

Swami Satprakashananda was the founder and head of the Vedanta Society of St. Louis from 1938 until his death in 1979. Before coming to the United States, Swami Satprakashananda was the associate editor of *Prabuddha Bharata* for three years. Swami Satprakashananda authored many books, including *Hinduism and Christianity*; *The Universe, God, and God-Realization*; *Methods of Knowledge: According to Advaita Vedanta*; *Sri Ramakrishna's Life and Message in the Present Age*; *Meditation: Its Process, Practice, and Culmination*; *Swami Vivekananda's Contribution to the Present Age*; and *The Goal and the Way*.

"Divine Love" originally appeared in the book *Vedanta for Modern Man*. "A Meditation: God Dwells in the Depth of Your Heart" originally appeared as a chapter entitled "He Dwells in the Depth of the Heart" in Swami Satprakashananda's book *Meditation: Its Process, Practice, and Culmination*.

Richard Schiffman is the author of *Sri Ramakrishna: A Prophet for the New Age*, and *Mother of All*. He lived and studied in India for five years, and is the former editor of *Matrusri Journal*.

Swami Shraddhananda came to the United States in 1957 as assistant minister of the Vedanta Society of Northern California. Since 1970 he has been the head of the Vedanta Society of Sacramento. While in India, Swami Shraddhananda was the editor for five years of *Udbodhan*, the Bengali-language journal of the Ramakrishna Order. He has written several books in Bengali, and one in English entitled *The Story of an Epoch*. Swami Shraddhananda has also written numerous articles, both in English and Bengali, for various journals.

Huston Smith is a leading figure in the study of comparative religions. For fifteen years he was Professor of Philosophy at the Massachusetts Institute of Technology; his other major appointments were at Washington University in St. Louis, Syracuse University, and the University of California, Berkeley. His seven books include *The World's Religions* (formerly *The Religions of Man*), *Forgotten Truth*, and *Beyond the Post-Modern Mind*.

Swami Swahananda is the head of the Vedanta Society of Southern California. A former editor of *Vedanta Kesari*, Swami Swahananda has written many articles and several books. *The Chandogya Upanishad*; *Hindu Symbology*; *Meditation and Other Spiritual Disciplines*; and *Monasteries in South India* are among his publications. "Peace" is an excerpt from the article "Working for Peace," which was published in the January, 1990 edition of *Vedanta Kesari*.

"Symbols in Hindu Spirituality" originally appeared under the title "Notes on Religious Symbols" in the July-August, 1959 issue of *Vedanta and the West*.

Swami Tyagananda, an author of many articles in Vedanta journals, is the editor of *Vedanta Kesari*, an English-language journal of the Ramakrishna Order. He lives in the Ramakrishna Math, Madras, India.

Pravrajika Varadaprana is an American nun of the Vedanta Society of Southern California, in Santa Barbara, and has contributed articles for various Vedanta journals.

Brahmachari Veda Chaitanya is an American novice of the Ramakrishna

Order living at the Vedanta Society of Southern California's Ramakrishna Monastery in Trabuco Canyon. He is the author of *Jiva Gosvamin's Tattvasandarbha* (written under his premonastic name of Dr. Stuart Elkman). Veda Chaitanya was one of the editors of *Go Forward: Letters of Swami Premeshananda*, and has also written articles for various Vedanta journals.

Swami Vedarupananda is an American monk of the Ramakrishna Order living at the Vedanta Society of Southern California's Vivekananda House in South Pasadena.

Swami Viprananda is an American monk of the Ramakrishna Order living at the Vedanta Society of Southern California's Ramakrishna Monastery in Trabuco Canyon. From 1978 to 1982 Swami Viprananda was on the editorial staff of the Institute of Culture of Calcutta, and assisted in editing the sixth volume of *The Cultural Heritage of India*. He is also one of the editors of *Go Forward: Letters of Swami Premeshananda*.

Swami Vivekananda was Sri Ramakrishna's foremost disciple who brought Vedanta to the West in 1893 when he represented Hinduism at the World's Parliament of Religions. "Real Religion" is a selection from "God, Soul, and Religion," along with an excerpt from "What Is Religion?" which appears in Volume I of *The Complete Works of Swami Vivekananda*. Additional paragraph breaks were added to the original text for the reader's convenience.

Pravrajika Vrajaprana, the editor of this book, is an American nun of the Vedanta Society of Southern California in Santa Barbara. Along with writing various articles for Vedanta publications, she has also edited *The Way to God: As Taught by Sri Ramakrishna* by Swami Lokeswarananda, and is the author of *My Faithful Goodwin*.

Index

brahmachari, 36
brahmacharini, 36
Brahman, 13, 14, 16, 20, 25,
43, 60, 100-01, 104, 191
impersonal, 27
Prajapati, 241
Shakti as, 273
symbols of, 100
within-the-creature, 14
Brahmananda, Swami
("Maharaj"), 30, 31, 35, 194
quoted, 173, 220, 222, 223
Brahmaprana, Pravrajika, 285
essay, "Contentment in a
Discontented World," 219
brahmin caste, 246
thread of, 246
widowhood in, 254-55
Brihadaranyaka Upanishad, 73, 144
See also Upanishads
Buddha, 15, 62, 240
Buddhism
establishment of, 242
mantras in, 187
Buddhists, 136
Burke, Marie Louise (Sister Gargi),
285
essay, "Swami Vivekananda's
Message to the Ordinary
Person," 259

C

caste system, 97
Chandogya Upanishad,
quoted, 64, 66, 90, 182
See also Upanishads
Chakra(s)
as centers of consciousness, 158-
59
Chandi, 269
defined, 268
Chicago, Illinois,
The 1893 World Parliament of
Religions in, 32, 122, 138, 266
Chosen Ideal, 101, 104,
163, 180, 190

God revealed as, 180
Kali as Chosen Ideal of
Ramakrishna, 244
Christ, 15, 20, 27
quoted, 143, 169, 170, 175, 193,
240, 249
Christian,
advaitic experience in, 143
fundamentalism in, 33
and Sufi mystics, 20
Christianity, 51, 139 *passim*
dominant characteristic of, 126
Christians, 136
classic proofs for God's existence,
112
Clement of Alexandria,
definition of prayer, 196
Clooney, Francis X., S.J., 285
essay, "Reading Vedanta at the
End of the Twentieth Cen-
tury," 144
Consciousness, 65
defined, 158
three states of, 171
See also universal Consciousness
Craig, U-Shaka, 286
essay, "A Psychologist Looks at
Vedanta," 233

D

Dakshineswar, 25, 26, 28, 29, 31,
255, 266
Kali, temple of, 247
Darwin, Charles (1809-1882), 115
engine of progress, 115
desires,
difference from attachment, 209
reduction of, 162-63
detachment,
as a spiritual practice, 209
Devi Mahatmyam, 268, 269, 271
See also Chandi
devotion,
Hindu psychology of, classified, 176